'I'll be Ten Minutes!'

Phil Baker

PHIL BAKER

© Phil Baker 2025

The rights of Phil Baker to be identified as the author of this work have been asserted by him in accordance with the Copyright, Designs and Patents Act of 1988.

All rights reserved; no part of this publication may be reproduced, stored in a retrieval system, or transmitted in any form or by any means, electronic, mechanical, photocopying, recording or otherwise without the prior written consent of the publisher or a licence permitting copying in the UK issued by the Copyright Licensing Agency Ltd. www.cla.co.uk

ISBN 978-1-78792-107-8

Book design and lay out by Phil Baker.
Developmental Editor: John Winstanley (www.develedits.com)
Other acknowledgements: Lux Holden (www.develcreatives.co.uk)

Production management by Into Print
www.intoprint.net
+44 (0)1604 832149

Acknowledgements

The author wishes to express his gratitude to the following for supporting the publication of this book:

Mr Philip Crook
Nigel Keating
Angela Stancliffe
Baz Parky
Claudia Fracalanza
Jim Graves
Tuija Takala
Tanya Edgar
Natasha Julian
Joe Kenan
Terence Birnie
John Miller
Jordan Willis
Timothy Mason
Elliot Tutt

Phil Baker

Contents

Acknowledgements... iii
Foreword... vi

1   Setting the Scene 1
2   The Beginning... 4
3   Girls and Strange Happenings 23
4   Never fall head over heels, for a Fairy!.. 49
5   Life after Marriage, Cement & its consequences........................ 65
6   More Music & Women.. 79
7   Brighton, Hove (Actually) & Pharmaceuticals............................ 88
8   Addicts, Alcoholics, Bikes and a Police Informer 100
9   The Bodyguard and the Nuclear Dump..................................... 113
10   The Knife attack, The 'Postman' and other fraudsters 125
11   Up North, Courts, Birth, Hernia and more scraps!.................... 133
12   Music, Agents, Rats and Door Fitting.. 140
13   Births, Depression and Challenges 146
14   Tribute Bands and Community Centres 160
15   PULSE – Echoes of Floyd 167
16   Stardrivemusic and Event Management 186
17   Chorley FM 202
18   Beyond The Dark Side beckons and then it got even darker 214
19   The Aftermath of BTDS and Rex Roman.................................. 225
20   Uriah Heep Legends 236
21   Songs to the World and a bit of Bakering.................................. 248
22   Playing God and playing a High Priestess................................. 259
23   Climbing a Mountain with Corky.. 270
24   And Finally.. 282

Index 294

Foreword

From 13:00hrs on the 26th March 2020, the UK is legally in lockdown due to the Coronavirus that is spreading across the globe. I (like most of the rest of England) am stranded at home and have decided to use this enforced incarceration, to go back to the draft of this book.

Prior to this I've been very busy, working around the UK for various companies as an electrical technician/event site manager and around the world as a session musician too.

I moved back to Liverpool in 2016 before my father passed away the same year, so I could be closer to my mum as my sister Lynn relocated to London in 2015. I'm worried about Sis as she's working at **The National Hospital** (for Neurology and Neurosurgery) which is slap bang in the middle of all this chaos. According to the news, this lockdown will last for a few months. All work in the entertainment industry has stopped overnight as the government has classed it as a 'non-essential' business. I face a backlog of work to do in theatres, such as Portable Appliance Testing (PAT), rigging safety checks and other equipment inspections. We are expected to abide by the 'Stay Home, Protect the NHS, Save Lives' slogan otherwise we will be punished with fines! Hence, it's a good time to try and get what you are now reading, closer to finishing.

This book is not just about what I have done in the music industry as it recounts what I've done with the rest of my life too. One of the reasons I've written it, is because so many people I've known and worked with have said '…you really should write a book!' As I'm typing away, I'm finding it difficult to decide which events I should include and what to leave out. I've tried to capture as many funny tales as I can because I want to make people laugh and have a chuckle as the world is in need of cheering up right now.

Included are events that have taken my life down certain routes both good and bad. Some, I would never have thought I would have chosen at the time. On reflection, I feel that, for the big moments, your life is mapped out for you, and you don't have a choice. You think you do, but I believe there are multiple levels that people are travelling along in this life. Yeah, a bit heavy! I bet that'll get you thinking, but I'm not going to tell you exactly what that means, or where in the book, those eureka moments are, you'll have to wait.

There's always a lot of shit going on in this world that we don't understand and, like most of the existential questions that humankind has wrestled with since we could communicate, we may never do until we die. If there isn't anything after we shift our mortal coil, then it won't matter anyway. We'll be either worm fodder in a decomposing box somewhere for insects to chew on or ashes to the skies from a chimney stack. The physical trace will be recycled and any messages from our souls may never reach us, and no one (like now) will be any the wiser. I like to think that there is something after we pass away, whatever it is.

There are also certain events which may be vague, but this is to either; protect who is involved or to not incriminate myself in something I have seen or been dragged into, either by choice, or necessity. I'm not trying to point fingers at people either. Some of the names will be real, others will not. The former, I've either asked for permission or they have passed away. I've taken a guess that (in the latter case) it won't make any difference – unless relatives are impacted and, if so, I apologise now and ask you to let me know so I can amend and provide an update in a second edition.

There are other names I've changed or left out completely due to circumstances at the time which will be obvious. I've tried not to use surnames because, in this day and age, if I put one in, who has done something wrong to me, it will alert the eccentrics. Such people will be on the web trying to find out who they were and, most probably, give that person a hard time or, they will give me the same grief for naming them!

As I'm writing, I sent a message out on Facebook the other day for any photos that friends of mine have from years ago and that has brought more stories/tales/events I'd forgotten about. Thank you! I've then had to add a lot of these in years I thought were finished in my initial drafts.

I wasn't going to add any photos but, after a few discussions, there'll be many if I have space. I hope you enjoy them as much as I had by their inclusion.

There will be events that I've missed, that someone I know will remind me about after the book is published.

I will be happy if you tell me so I can add them to future editions…. assuming I get enough money from the sale of the first one and I feel there is a demand out there…. that, my friends, is up to you!

Phil Baker August 2025

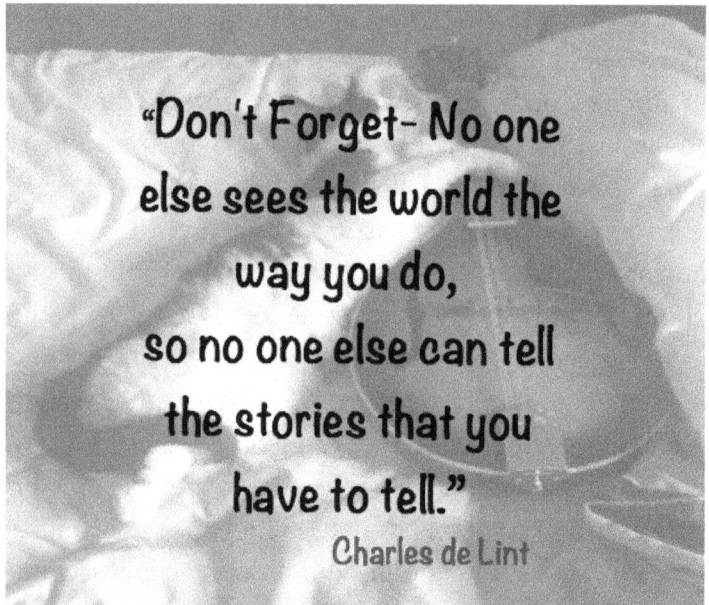

Dedicated to my Family and anyone who has crossed my path through the years and/or sadly passed away. But, for now, these include in date order: my dog **Tysie**, my **Dad**, **Dave Harris**, my cat **Gypsy**, **Lee Kerslake**, **Ken Hensley**, **John Lawton**, **Big Jim** and my **Mum**, who passed away July 2025. R.I.P. and I miss you all.

CHAPTER ONE

Setting the Scene

6th March 2015. It is 11.45am inside the **U.S. Consulate, Belfast**. I'm staring through a bullet proof glass screen, at a middle-aged lady. She is looking at all the paperwork that I had handed in half an hour before, to another middle-aged lady at a different bullet proof screen. Both are equally sound proofed with no audio assistance for the hard of hearing. This means I have to recount what happened to me some twenty-odd years before, at a vocal range audible to all the other U.S.A. Visa applicants in the room. So much for confidentiality and free entertainment for all and sundry!

'We cannot issue a temporary visa to you due to the nature of your criminal convictions.' My heart sinks, as I start thinking about the repercussions of what she has just said.

'However,' she adds, and I sense a glimmer of hope, 'we will be sending a recommendation to the **Department of Homeland Security** that they issue a Waiver of Ineligibility so that we can grant you a visa.'

'Thank you,' I say, she smiles and adds, 'are you still with the ex-girlfriend who attacked your new girlfriend with a bread knife and who told all these lies to the police?'

I feel like saying, 'are you bloody mad or something? Are you actually listening to me!'

But, what I say, compliantly, is: 'no, I am not, and I'll get this other form to you by the end of the week.'

It is a form that I thought I'd already handed in, but was informed by the first woman, who I had to explain my circumstances to, so publicly, that the information I'd paid for from ACRO (Association of Chief Police Criminal Records Office), "WAS THE WRONG FUCKING ONE!!!!!!!"

'Thank you very much.' I say, as I turn to leave, while chewing through my lower lip. My head is pounding with the commercial dilemma: I'm not sure if I will arrive in time for the *Rock Opera (More details in chapter 22)* in **New York** next month and (worse still), what the consequences will be if I don't get there at all!

On top of this, I have the family concern of: do I tell my Mum and Dad (who are outstanding British citizens) that I have a criminal record from something that happened twenty years ago? All this came about because of something I admitted to in a police interview. I was desperate to get out of the station, following the embellishments of my ex's circumstances. This (ironically) was to get her off charges, when I had her arrested for attacking my new girlfriend with a knife in my own home! Confused? Welcome to my life and read on!

I leave the building, picking up my phone from the security guard who tries to have a chat with me about whether I'm a Blue or a Red. I am talking to him but I'm away with my imagination, thinking about the consequences of this impending decision that I have no control over. I walk to the bus stop, catch one to the Europa Bus Terminal. I have a bite to eat in a café, take a coach to the airport and wait for the plane. All the while, I'm milling over everything that has happened to me in my life and how the paths that I have taken over the years, that have brought me to standing in the US Embassy a few hours before, hoping that they will grant me a Temporary Visa.

Later that day, when I'm back at home, I phone ACRO, only to be told that,

'Yes, you applied for the wrong one and the right one will cost £80 for the premium two day service!'

I'm now up to nearly £300, including flights to Belfast, to obtain a visa for a show that I'm not being paid for at present (it's a long-term project). Furthermore, I can't expect my Finnish friends (who wrote the Rock Opera) to have to pay for something that's not their fault. They're paying for the flights/hotels etc and, at this moment in time, I'm thinking about how the hell I can pay them back the £520 for the flight that we had to get in January due to rising prices. Even though I hadn't applied for the visa at the time, I didn't realise that I would have to try and find out information about my ex-wife who I split up with 27 years before, including her date of birth! Who can remember the date of birth of someone who only married you because you'd make a good father to her daughter but only told you after you got married! As you can appreciate, it wasn't a surprise that we split up nine months after taking our vows. More of that later. But it was that day in 2015, when I decided to start writing a book about my life. I'll be going off track now and then, something that you'll see I do quite a lot. I'm known for doing this in both my professional and personal life. A good friend described my stories as,

'Going on a car journey with Phil from Birkenhead to London. Starting on the M53 to the M6 and then veering off onto the M4 via the M5, divert north on the M25, back up the M40 and then onto the M42 before arriving back on the M6 and then south onto the M1.' Well described Peter.

CHAPTER TWO

The Beginning

The best place to start I suppose! I was born in **Liverpool Woman's Hospital** 4th August 1960. My Mum told me there was a thunderstorm while I was being born. It was the worst she has ever known even to this day! She was staring at it through the skylight as I arrived. She thought to herself,

'My God what am I bringing into this world!' And has told me this, many times since.

'You'll make a mark on the world,' she said to me at some stage too. I'm still waiting or maybe I have without realising it.

My Mum had been prescribed the **Thalidomide** tablets for morning sickness while she was pregnant with me. For anyone who is unfamiliar with the story of these tablets, those who did take these tablets, had children born with deformities such as, short arms, or short legs or none at all. The pharmaceutical company who manufactured them had to pay compensation to many.

Either my dad threw the pills in the bin, or my Mum never collected them from the chemist. But, if my Mum had taken them, my whole life would have been a completely different story. The drug is still used for other medical conditions surprisingly, but apparently there are warnings on the packet if taken while pregnant or conceiving. Why in the world would a drug like that still be allowed to be used even if it does help cure cancer!

My first memory was when I was about three years old. I crashed my tricycle into the cooker and took a big chunk of enamel off it. My parents had only bought the cooker a few weeks before. Around the same time, I was smashed in the throat by a swing in the park. Thankfully, I don't remember that. But I do remember being stung by a bee and some wasps and when I ploughed my bike into a bush of nettles during a ride at my cousin's house! I think I started life in a way that I was meant to carry on as I have never done anything by halves. Memories involving the **NHS**, include a three week stay in **Alder Hey Children's Hospital** getting my sinuses flushed out when I was about six years old. I also had to go to The Ear, Nose and Throat Department at **Liverpool Hospital** and get my nose cauterised when I was about nine. I had terrible nosebleeds from the slightest flick to my nose. I had a child's version of varicose veins in my nose and, once bleeding, it wouldn't stop for hours. The cure was to shove hot wooden splints up the nasal passages! To say it was uncomfortable is an understatement even with some anaesthetic on cotton wool being put up there first.

I had a good upbringing and home life. At the time, my dad had a newsagent's shop, and we lived above it until I was fourteen. **Bakers Newsagents**, 166 **County Road**, Liverpool, L4 5PH.

The telephone number was 525-2814. The phone was posh for those days; a big old black one that had a rotary dialling ring. The circumference was a bit smaller than a Compact Disc

(CD) and you had to turn the numbers round in a clockwise direction until you hit the metal stopper, and the dial would go back to the starting

point. I guess this is where the meaning of dialling a number originated. I've included a picture of one as it may jog a few memories. The letters were used when you had to dial the telephone exchange and get connected to someone else's number, would you believe! So, if I wanted to call a number in the Liverpool area like, **Anfield**, that number could be ANF XXXX. Telephone numbers were a lot shorter then when fewer homes had telephones in them – hence many people had to use public telephone boxes which were on street corners.

There was no push buttons and speed dialling then. I used to dial a fictitious number, and talk on the phone, "Loddle Doddle, Loddle, Loddle Doddle, Ha Ha Ha". My mum loves telling people about this even now and I'm in my mid-sixties! I've just started going down the wrong slip road off the M53, I'll come back enroute.

I remember watching the moon landing on TV, making a spaceship from one of the massive empty cigarette boxes that the cigs used to be delivered in for my dad's shop. Hiding behind the couch when ***Doctor Who*** was on, you know the usual things kids do.

Outside the home, on the streets of Liverpool in the late 1960's and early 1970's was a little different to inside the flat. There were gangs in most streets around Walton – just like anywhere else in the bigger towns and cities of England. I remember the main gang, from Delamore Street, called themselves the **Deli Mob**. Thinking that name up must have taken a lot of brain power, just like **The Sparrow Hall Gang** and, can you guess where they used to hang out? Yes, no surprise – **Sparrow Hall Park**. I'm not going to dwell on all the things that happened on the streets, but one memory springs to mind which, at the time, scared the living shit out of me and my two friends.

It was a midweek evening, and **Everton FC** had just played **Carlisle United** at **Goodison Park**. Un-beknown to us, an Everton fan had his testicles or Gentleman's Balloons (which I think is a fantastic description) cut off by two Carlisle United fans in the subway at **Rice Lane**. This was across the road from where I sang in a choir. I had just finished playing football in the park with my two mates and we were walking home. As we turned into **Bedford Road,** all we could see at the bottom of the road was about 200 football hooligans brandishing baseball bats and knives – you get the idea.

"GET EM!!!" they shout.

If you have never been in this situation at twelve years old, it's very hard to describe the emotion. I suppose the only words for this are: "SHIT WE ARE GOING TO DIE!" For the next fifteen minutes we were chased all over the place, not knowing why we were being hunted by a pack behaving like starving animals who have just spotted prey. Finally, we ran into a side street with no exit;

"WE <u>ARE</u> ABOUT TO DIE!"

All we could do was hammer on a front door of the nearest house and hope for the best. This beautiful young girl opened the door.

"Please let us in missus, there's a mob chasing us and we don't know why!" I say panting as the beasts arrive at the same house. The skinhead, brandishing a baseball bat at the front of the herd, came to a skidding stop. His jaw dropped as the girl shouted,

'What do you think you are doing chasing these poor lads, they're scousers, leave them alone.'

Unbelievable, she was actually the girlfriend of that skinhead. Of all the houses in that area, we knocked on the door of the **Cock of the Kop's** girlfriend! I don't think they would have asked if the three of us were those they were chasing or not, before beating us to a pulp. The fact that there was <u>three</u> of us? Enough said.

After they had explained what had happened in the subway, we stood there watching them all walk past, tooled up. Whether they ever got the Carlisle lads, I never found out. That's how my life seems to have gone over the years and if we hadn't knocked on the right door, I may not have been here and doing what I do now. I am a big believer in fate, and, on that day, it had a reason for keeping me alive. Furthermore, that was most probably the same event when I started believing that we all have a set path we walk down.

Anyway, back at home, I had; a very small set of drums when I was four or five, a **Bontempi** organ at eight (remember them?) and at ten, my first guitar! The latter would remain my main instrument for the next 55 years.

My parents bought that first one from **Hessy's Music Centre**. Hessy's as it was affectionately known, was one of the main music shops in the city centre (62 **Stanley Street**), but it's not there anymore. **The Beatles** bought their instruments from there too (according to a blue plaque that is fixed to a wall close to the site). If you got a guitar from them back then (the shop that is and not that moderately successful band!), you were offered three, free, lessons. My tutor gave lessons to three budding guitarists at a time on his own and out of sight in the basement of the shop. He was a strange guy, but, let me make it clear, he did not molest me or anyone else and I did learn all the basic chords I needed. However, looking back (as a parent) on lots of similar situations to the environment of those lessons, I wouldn't have left my kids alone with anyone no matter if any were free or not!

From eight, I sang in the choir at **Walton on the Hill**, (Church of England) a five-minute walk away from home. There, I learnt a lot about reading music and vocal training from our Choirmaster. His favourite friend was a slipper, that was so shiny, from being used on our bottoms, you could see your face in it. In most English schools of the sixties and seventies there was always a slipper or a cane somewhere to keep pupils or choristers in check. That's the way **corporal punishment** was in those days. On the other hand, Mr Whiteside was a fantastic Choirmaster and Organist and, to be honest, we were probably little shits most of the time who deserved a whack every now and then. The clergy were great people, and their favourite place was the **Black Bull Public House** next to the church. They seemed to spend more time at the bar than the altar! Based on their example, perhaps, that's why I took up drinking at such an early age.

I was a member of the local youth club, which was around the corner from the house of that beautiful young girl who saved us from the football hooligans. Somehow, I obtained a bottle of sherry when I was about eleven. I drunk it all on my own, in the toilets of the youth club. Then I threw up outside, while the Youth Club phoned my parents. To say they weren't happy, is like having to ask if the Pope is Catholic. At least it's better than what my mate Graham did a few years later when we were bell ringers at the church (or Campanologists to give the correct terminology). He trimmed a few strands off the hemp ropes that connected to the bells, thinking he could smoke it and get high. When this didn't work, he started drying nettles out and made spliffs with the nettles, but didn't smoke them himself at first. If he had, then when he started selling joints at school, he would not have had to wonder why everyone was being sick. At least I was only sick once with the sherry incident. I think I was grounded for at least a fortnight. Graham, well he got expelled from school for a few months, if I remember rightly.

I don't think anyone found out, that during breaks at bell ringing practice, Graham and I used to sneak into the vestry and have a quick swig of the wine. That was the only reason I was there after jacking in the choir. However, I must thank the Church Choir for my first appearance on television. I've vague memories of singing and doing some acting (if you can call it that!) at the church in seasonal religious plays (Easter and The Nativity etc). But what is very clear, is singing when the **BBC** broadcasted from our Church. This was for one of their Sunday recordings of the *Songs of Praise* show.

Apart from the choir, my first time on stage singing in public, was when my parents, sister and I, stayed in a caravan in **Wales** and I got up in the social club of the site and sang with the resident band. I reckon I was around eleven or twelve. I sang *Take me Home, Country Roads*, (by **John Denver**), well I sang the chorus's harmonies with the singers. Before that, my singing was limited to my grandma's bathroom on Sundays (good reverb in there). I sang hymns and carols in the bathroom and to be honest, that's all I knew. I did have vinyl 45's by The Beatles and **Rolling Stones** but I hadn't actually found Rock music yet, which was what really kick started my desire to sing non-religious tunes.

Back then, I was also fascinated with riding a horse. There was a girl who used to come onto the caravan site (where the social club was where I sang *Country Roads*) a few days a week and charge people for having a trot on her horse. I say horse, it was probably a pony and, if not, it was a fucking big pony. My mum reckoned it was a horse and was agreeable for me to get on it. So, once I'd climbed into the saddle, this girl says, 'just give her a little tap with your feet and off you go.'

I think I did it a bit too hard, and off the horse gallops with me shouting 'HELP!' and holding on as best I could. If someone had filmed it, I would have made a lot of money on the TV funnies of people doing daft things or being surprised by animals or other situations. I was a very lucky lad because, the horse bolted under the lower branches of a tree, which I ducked to avoid. Rather like that accident with the swing, a knock to the throat could have been disastrous for my vocal cords (others may disagree and say it might have improved them!). Sorry I reversed up a roundabout off the M6 that time.

I started teaching myself the guitar. I chose to have a few lessons with a classical tutor until, one particular day that changed my outlook on music forever. I was twelve years old; it was a Saturday in the summer of 1972. I was doing three weddings that day singing in the choir. There was a long break in between the second and last one, so I went for a walk. I could hear music coming from the youth club. As I got closer it was a band rehearsing. I peered through a window, and they were playing **Railroad** by **Status Quo**. WOW! It changed my total outlook on playing guitar. 'That's it, that's how I want to play,' I said to myself, and it all went downhill from there.

I can't remember the name of the band, but they let me come in, sit down and listen to them the next time I went to watch. In the early 1970s the whole look of a band was about the size of their amps, and speaker cabinets. Furthermore, if you had two pedals, normally a fuzz and a wah-wah, (as that's the type of sound effect they made), that was top dollar then, as they use to say. It all looked amazing and I'm not sure if it was just the music that did it for me back then. These days, guitar amps, pedals and everything else that comes with the guitar are additions that are really cheap compared to what it would have cost back in the '70s.

Today, you can buy a combo amp (i.e. the amplifier and speaker are housed in one cabinet) that's no bigger than my toaster and it will produce more volume than a 100-watt home music stereo. You could use it on stage and have your guitar coming back through the monitors on stage so you can hear it ok.

For Xmas that year, I got a **Kay** electric guitar, small amp, strap and lead. My parents bought them all from Hessy's, but I didn't need the three free lessons this time, thank God! It was about £20, which was the average week's wage for women over eighteen back then.

The proper Wah Wah Pedal and the cheap Kay one.

I did paper rounds for my dad, and I may have said I'd help towards it. Not sure if I did, but I bought a Kay wah-wah and a fuzz pedal a few months later. The only problem with my wah-wah, was that you had to flip a switch with your finger to turn it on. Not ideal if you were in the middle of a song. For any of you unfamiliar to such pedals the more expensive ones of the day (**Cry Baby** GCB 95 etc) had a switch under the pedal itself and all you had to do was push down on the pedal with your foot to switch it on. But at the time, I was still in my element with my bright, red, wah-wah pedal, despite having to bend over to switch it on in the middle of a solo!

Kay Guitars – now there's a blast from the past! These were the cheapest guitars you could buy and to be honest, there wasn't loads of choice in the early 1970s. Early entry guitars like **Stagg** had not had an impact in England and **Encore** came later. If you couldn't afford a **Gretsch, Gibson, Fender** etc, then Kay was the economy guitar to learn on. I don't want to get technical but, for any guitarists out there, the action on the 12th fret was about 10mm, so you can imagine trying to play some form of a solo, was near impossible. You could play chords at the nut end of the guitar neck and barring chords further up took a while to learn but that's what you did. It certainly built the strength up in my left hand. I learnt how to bring the action down though, and, with a little bit of tweaking, it wasn't that bad a guitar as a first electric. Let's put it this way, I was lucky, thanks to my parents. Some kids wouldn't have got anything like that and for that I owe them a huge 'thank you.' Learning an instrument is strange sometimes. I could play for weeks and never progress, get pissed off, put the guitar down for a couple of days, pick it back up and learn some new technique straight away. Not sure about anyone else, but that's how it was for me.

So, back to the story. I had packed the choir in; became some form of a Campanologist; started growing my hair long and my mate at **Liverpool Collegiate School (Gary Lornie)**, had introduced me to **Uriah Heep** and many other rock bands of the time. I was going into the rebellious stage of being a teenager and I left home for a day! But I was persuaded by Gary's Mum to go back after turning up at their house in **Crosby** with a bag of clothes, complaining that my parents wanted me to get my haircut! Those days you were defined by what you wore, and the choices were very specific.

A **Skinhead** (or **Bonehead**) had a buzz cut or shaven head, dressed in slim fitting shirts, **Doc Martens** or steel toe cap boots, 'parallels' or straight length pants and followed Football. **Freaks** or **Troggs**, had long hair, wore trench coats, flared trousers and followed music. I was a Freak although I did go down the football route for a bit but not for long.

From 1971, Gary and I went to the same school, and he had already started going to concerts. His parents were a bit more relaxed due to living in a hippy commune not long before I first met him. His Dad was a clever guy (Computer Programmer from what I remember) so please don't think I'm knocking hippy communes. I would like to say though that, on reflection, I wouldn't have changed my parents for the world. My parents worked so hard to make sure that my sister and I had a good upbringing, and, for that, I will never be able to thank them enough. My Dad was president of the **National Federation of Retail Newsagents** for a year and Vice President for a year too. A very well-respected man in the retail business. He had a fantastic, dry and sarcastic sense of humour which I think has rubbed off on me. One example of this was when one of the paperboys got his haircut and, as it grew back, two strands of hair spiked upwards and were longer than the others. My Dad called him 'Aerial' from then on and that name stuck with him and amongst his mates too. In the second year of Grammar School, I joined the **Collegiate Cadet Force** (not to be confused with the Combined Cadet Force at Liverpool College in the 2000's.) I suppose this was a bit strange, as I was growing my hair, and we were in army uniform for the meetings. But Liverpool Collegiate had its own rifle range in the basement, which was one of the reasons I joined. We went out to **Altcar Rifle Range**, had a few weekends on army manoeuvres and spent some time with the regular army. The army lads let us have go at driving their **Scorpion Tanks** which, at the time, were the top dollar fighting machine. It didn't last, I think because I was told I would have to get my haircut if I wanted to stay in the force, and that wasn't going to happen due to my love of music.

Anyway, going back to Gary and another guy called **Pete Scott** or '**Scotty**' who still lives in **Liverpool**, they introduced me to **Liverpool Stadium** (a 3,700-capacity boxing arena on St Paul's Square, Bixeth Street). For concerts the Stadium only used half of the arena and held around 1500. I suppose the nucleus of friends apart from these two was everyone down at the Stadium and The **Moonstone** (later renamed Mylo's) in St John's precinct. These included: Duv (**Keith Duvall**), Tree (**Phil Williams** who now lives in **New Zealand** and is a friend on Facebook), **Steve Finnigan** (aka **Finny**, who I reckon had or maybe still has the hardest bones in the world) and **Graham Gardiner**. Of all of these fine nicknames, I always thought Tree's was best as we called him '**Willo**' for short, then **Willow Tree** and then just 'Tree'. Once I moved to **West Derby**, Graham and I were most probably the closest out of everyone, only for the fact that he lived about a minute's walk from my house. We both spent more time at weekends with Gary, Pete and Finny. Graham and I used to hit the pub through the week too. Duv, was at school with us and we used to pass a fair bit of time in the park through the week and he was one of the guys who was with me when we got chased by that football mob. He did go to the Stadium, but not as much as the rest of us. Tree was a seven days a week mate. I'm sure I will be corrected in the reviews, Ha! Ha! (if I get any).

I am now going off at a service station, but it needs to be said, two things;

Liverpool Stadium and that scene at that time.

To anyone who never went to the Stadium back then, it is very difficult to describe the atmosphere and the craic. To the famous musicians of the time, this venue was renowned to be one of the best places to play in the world. I saw **Hawkwind, AC/DC, Robin Trower, Thin Lizzy, Camel, Gong, Ted Nugent**, to name but a few. We used to keep a tally of all the gigs we went to around Liverpool including the Stadium and the most I did was in 1974, 104 concerts. It was so cheap then usually 50p and we all felt that 75pence was extortionate for a ticket! **The Empire, The Royal Court, De Montford Hall** were all great venues, but Liverpool Stadium just had something special. It was a shame it was stopped having concerts in 1978 and closed in 1985 and was demolished in 1987, not out of choice. There's even a Facebook Group called **Liverpool Stadium Daze** which I'm a member of and we meet every now and then in Liverpool City Centre, reminiscing about our time there. Liverpool Stadium was a temple, if you will, as we would religiously go down on a Saturday and sit outside on the steps all afternoon. It was better if there were girls with you of course, but it was our safe haven. With all the shit going on with Boneheads fighting Troggs in those days, the Stadium was our refuge.

I mentioned Finny, but didn't explain why he had the hardest bones in the world. Well, we were all going to a party off **Muirhead Avenue**, one Saturday night. We called in at the local offy (off-licence) for cider and beer and there was a couple of Skinheads outside the shop. One thing led to another, and this guy hit Finny square on the jaw. I thought 'Shit here we go!' To my amazement, Finny just stood there with the Skinhead curled up on the floor holding his hand. Finny laughed and off we went on our way all casual like. However, I did have a problem later on with them. The Skinheads got in through the back door of the house where the party was, and I got beaten with a metal pipe. That's just the way it was in those days.

On another occasion, I was attacked at a bus stop one Saturday night by a load of Skinheads whose leader thought swinging a baseball bat at my head was fun. After blocking the swings with my arms, he was about to take another when the number 12 bus arrived and I jumped on, to the sound of the bat smashing into the door of the bus. Fate again, as if that bus hadn't turned up at that particular time, I would have been in hospital, or worse as there were a dozen of them and I was on my own. My arms were bruised for days and luckily my trench coat had taken a lot of the power out of the onslaught, or I would have had two broken arms.

The other time the number 12 bus saved me was one Friday night, after I watched one of my mates (who ended up inside for manslaughter a few years later) take on five guys who had attacked him and he won. Unbeknown to me one of the attackers recognised me and knew I lived in **West Derby Village**. They got on a bus and got off two stops before mine and waited until my bus came along. I saw them get on and there was no way of getting off the bus without going through them.

'We're going to have some fun now,' they sneered.

The bus doors opened, one of them grabbed my hair, and I smashed him in the face. We all tumbled off the bus and the other four started kicking the shit out of me while I had the other guy in a head lock. Every time they hit me, I hit him in the face, a fair exchange. Finally, I took a boot to my head, and I collapsed on the floor and heard the bus driving towards me. I couldn't see as my eyes had swollen up, but I knew I was in the gutter of the road and the bus was about to drive off over me.

'I'm about to die' I thought.

As it was, the driver had seen one of the thugs get a knife out as I landed on the floor. The buses in those days had a front end that extended about a metre from the front tyre arch. So, the driver drove his bus over the top of me to protect me. The thugs ran off and I ended up in **St Paul's Eye Hospital** that night. Again, fate was on my side as my coat had been slashed and that could have been worse. Whoever that bus driver was, I owe you a massive 'Thank you'.

After this latest incident, which happened to other people across the city too, a guy called **Spud** saw me in the Moonstone the following night with my eyes swollen so badly, they resembled fist size blueberries. There was a band on at Liverpool Empire on the following night. Loads of skinheads went. Coincidentally, I believe 'a call was made'. We were told to stay out of the city centre that night. As the gig finished, a load of Hells Angels turned up and beat the shit out of some of the audience, so we were told. We didn't have any problems with skinheads after that, it all just seemed to stop. Thanks, Spud.

I'm leaving the services now.

I bought **Uriah Heep Live,** after borrowing Gary's copy of the LP for a while.

We had a record player at home called a **Black Box**, which was the first stereo player of sorts. It came with two speakers one on each side of the wooden boxed turntable. I found that if I turned the knob to the left speaker, it had the effect of removing the bass, leaving the full treble sound and I could listen to **Mick Box** playing power chords and lead guitar. Then, turning the dial to the right speaker, I could listen to **Ken Hensley** playing slide guitar, when he wasn't playing keyboards of course. I have actually played guitar for Ken in Uriah Heep Legends but that comes later.

By now, the classical style guitar was thrown to one side, and I started learning rock music. This did not go down well with my parents: long hair, concerts, rock music, you get the picture. I'd started smoking cigarettes, I never liked smoking joints and still don't. The odd occasional drag just to be sociable, might have occurred over the years, but it has never appealed to me. I did discover drinking beer though (the sherry incident didn't put me off) and I used to go to the local pubs before the concerts. When there were no concerts, we all went to The Moonstone. This was another temple, if you will, like The Stadium. Local bands played there every Friday and Saturday night. That's where the drug of playing live, and wanting to write my own material, hit me, more than anywhere else. Yes, I was already playing in bands but to stand maybe a metre away from a local band in a small place like that, well it was just a catalytic high. There are a lot of bands who play the small venues now and some are okay, some are great, but the local bands in the 1970's had some kudos and a lot more charisma. They used to get paid for gigging and didn't have to worry about working through the week. Back then pubs and clubs appreciated what the bands were bringing to their establishments. How things have changed today! Pay for play now is just bollocks and I was hoping after the Virus lockdown, things might have changed but it hasn't.

There were some great local bands who played at bigger venues in Liverpool and toured further afield too. Some of these include : **Export** (their bass player was going to be my best man later on, for a wedding which never actually happened), **Rock School** (a version of this band supported **Rod Stewart** on one of his tours in the late seventies), **Montana**, **Supercharge** and **Strife** (the bass player, by pure chance, was the engineer at the studio **DMTM**, a band I was in, recorded our single there, see chapter 4). As with the Stadium, there is a Facebook Moonstone page too.

After the fire in St John's Precinct in the late 1970's, the Moonstone was refurbished and called Mylo's after **John Mylett.** He and his girlfriend sadly died in a motorbike accident in Spain while on holiday. A great drummer and the two of them were so in love. That's the thing, you never know when death will occur, and I reckon they needed to go together, as

I don't think either of them would have recovered if one of them had died and left the other behind, so sad.

I used to play Tennis at **The Bohemian's Tennis Club** in my teens. Apparently, I had the hardest forehand in the club. I actually knocked a guy out in one of the league matches: ball hit him straight between the eyes, the wind had caught it sideways, and he didn't get out of the way in time. I thought I'd bloody killed him until he got up a minute or so later, with a big indent between his eyes where his glasses had got squashed between his forehead and the ball. I only mention the Tennis Club, because **Pete Best** (Ex drummer of The Beatles) used to drink there, and I chatted to him about music. He told me the full story of how they got rid of him which is not for me to tell. I did ask him if he was bitter, but he informed me that he had a good life (he had a Rolls Royce sat in the club car park, FFS) and if he needed some extra cash, he just phoned the papers, and they'd pay him a load of money for a story. This is the 1970s we're talking about. Sorry, I was off onto the M4 that time.

The most memorable gig I remember at the Moonstone, was a guy from **Bury** who came on as a three piece and played **Jimi Hendrix** better than Hendrix. Honestly, I am not fibbing. I sat there for the first song, absolutely gobsmacked at how this guy was playing. He'd been helped onto the stage, and I thought he was a bit pissed until the end of the first song. He turned to the amp and fumbled about for his pint of Guiness on top of the amp (not a good place to keep it really), held it with both hands, while drinking it, and then gave it to his roadie who put it back on top of the amp.

HE WAS BLIND! Wow this guy played so well and he couldn't see. Absolutely amazing. I spoke to one of the crew after the gig and he told me that he was actually a concert pianist, but they couldn't find a guitarist who played better than him, so formed a trio, doing Hendrix instead. I later discovered that this guitarist's name was **Tony Crabtree,** and he passed away a few years ago. The fact remains that, after watching Tony, I started playing guitar in my bedroom in the dark to learn to play without looking at the strings so I could sing. Something, that has helped me so much over the years.

The next time Tony played at The Moonstone it was like a mini **Woodstock**. Everyone was on the floor wearing flowers in head bands, little else and smoking dope etc., you get the picture. There are a few writeups about the Moonstone on the web, described as (wait for it), '....some sort of Heavy Metal, Hippie venue.' That description was close but way off the mark too. Before **Eric's** and after the **Cave**, it was most probably one of the most important and influential venues to anyone who was into rock music in Liverpool at the time.

Me in Dale Street 1974.

The Moonstone.

Liverpool Stadium.

The Stadium with me & Sue.

Liverpool Stadium me bottom right.

Me aged 7 years old.

Thanks to Sue, Yvette and everyone from Liverpool Stadium Daze Facebook group for these pics.

Aunt Twacky's Bazaar

I used to go to a café in **Matthew Street** (yes, THE Matthew Street) above a shop called **Aunt Twacky's Bazaar** on Saturday afternoons, performing songs in front of everyone else, including other musicians. I think it's a pub now. That's where I first started performing my own music. I suppose I wrote my first song about thirteen years old entitled *Memories*, all about losing the love of my life, which hadn't actually happened yet, but maybe I was psychic. Those days of getting on a small stage in front of a small number of people was good training. I've played in front of 5000 people and playing to 30 or 40 people stood right in front of you is a lot more nerve racking even today.

After we'd moved to the house in West Derby, I performed *Memories* to **Anfield Music Agency**. The sister of a guy who lived next door was the chaperone for all the **Miss World's**, and I sang *Memories* in front of Miss World in his house. He knew the guy who ran the agency and so I went there and played *Memories* and *The Leaves* (all about nuclear war).

I was told, 'come back with something more commercial,' and that was that. That deflated me a bit as you always think your first song is the greatest tune ever. I've played the original recordings of it to various people to this day, and most think it's a really good song. Ironically, I did some solo gigs in the northwest social clubs in the late 1990s for Anfield but that's as far as it went.

I did perform a piece of music a few years earlier. I'd written an organ piece when I was eleven years old. It was a very simple version based on the awesome organ piece, Widor's Toccata in F. I wrote all the music out. It took me weeks. I suppose, I was composing something out of another tune, oh hang on, a lot of musicians do that today don't they! I took it into my music teacher at school just to show him the notation, but he then asked me to perform it in front of all the class on the piano. This resulted in having the piss taken out of me afterwards and called **Liberace**. I bet some of those pupils most probably later in life, ended up in a similar pack of Skinheads that chased me and my two mates. On reflection, the music teacher should not have got me to do this, as the worst thing to do in a class, is to show that someone is a smart arse! But I think it did help in a way, being able to play in front of an audience under any conditions is good training. At the time it put me off a little, but music was my life, or so I thought.

By third year, 1973, I was taking music as a specialised subject, only six pupils in the class. Four guys, who thought having double class music on a Wednesday was an easy lesson, and **William Johnson** or Billy as everyone knew him and myself. Billy and I used to do all the homework for the other four, in exchange for cigarettes etc you get the idea. Ten years later and I'm watching **Top of the Pops** and who should be fronting **Frankie Goes to Hollywood** but Billy aka **Holly Johnson**. Right place at the right time I suppose. I felt sorry for Billy at school. Even then, he knew he was gay and used to get picked on a fair old bit. He gave the bully of the 4th year a right hiding in a fit of rage. The bully's surname was **Cassidy**. His first name was David but not who you think it is, and he deserved everything he got. Good on you Billy or should I say Holly. I've never met him since. Different music circles I suppose and, despite having a fan club in **Finland**, I am not famous. Everything seemed to be heading the right way in life, especially with the music side. Then came GIRLS!

Chapter Three

Girls and Strange Happenings

I have never had a straightforward relationship with a member of the opposite sex. It wasn't that I was having doubts about my sexuality, it was just that I never had a 'normal' relationship, full stop! Even, when I went to the youth club, and we went on a day out. Everyone was messing about, and I got a stiletto heal stuck in my arm by one of the girls (who I actually fancied). It was an accident, or maybe it was a term of endearment? Either way, I never found out and I still have a small scar from the metal heel tip.

Perhaps my failure in relationships, was due to the curse invoked on me by my first official girlfriend, after I finished with her on Valentine's Day in 1975. I had gone to the Liverpool Empire to see **Black Sabbath** the previous year and met Jayne at the concert. She was eighteen, I was fourteen and we used to go to lots of gigs together. Things got really serious between us (which was fine) until one day she said that she wanted me to leave school when I was sixteen, get a job and have five kids together! There was no way I was doing that, so I finished with her. Things went very dark, very quickly to the point when she tried to end her own life! Her mother was screaming to my mother on the phone, saying it was my fault. I think it's the only time I've heard my Mum get angry on the phone and told her to sort her daughter out! Not sure if that was a good or bad thing, however, as you'll read later on, Jayne was on pills as she was a neurotic but turned out fine. But, looking back now, she was always a bit strange, and I guess young love is blind. My doubts about her started when we did a Ouija board one night at her house with her sister. It spelt out 'LEAVE US ALONE' and then all the candles blew out! Never again! More to do with spirits later and I'm not talking about

Whiskey, Gin or Vodka!

After me, Jayne started going out with a guy called Sean. He was Irish, hard as nails and his dad ran a pub on the Liverpool Dock Road. Sean and I were great friends until he met her. At a concert one night, she leapt at me like a shrieking banshee and said, 'I curse you from this day until the day you die that you will never stay in a relationship,' or something to that effect. Sean then punched me in the face and told me to leave her alone! What?! Jayne and I did get together again about two years later (? yeah, I know!), but only for a few months. It was a lust thing and I'm a gluten for punishment, or, maybe, I was hoping that she would revoke the curse! Unfortunately, she didn't, as far as the rest of my life has proved. I had a few girlfriends after Jayne as you do when you're that age, I wasn't a bad looking lad, so I was always going to meet someone now and then. Maybe, with the way I was then, that hasn't helped in my personal life. On reflection, if I hadn't worn my heart on my sleeve and maybe been a bit of a bastard to the opposite sex, then things might have been different. But then if I was like that, I wouldn't be me now.

The first example of 'The Curse of Jayne', was when I was just turning seventeen and met a young nurse called Janet, who worked at **Clatterbridge Hospital** and who I really liked. By then I'd left school and I was working at **Evans Medical Ltd** (which eventually became part of Glaxo), even though my music teacher had wanted me to stay on and go to the **Royal School of Music** (something that, in hindsight, I should have done). I met Janet at a social event at Glaxo, her mum worked in the canteen. Things were okay, I used to get the train over to the Hospital for the weekend, stay in her room, play the piano to her in the students digs and we'd go walking in the fields nearby. All was good, until she borrowed some money off me to go on holiday to Greece. She came back off holiday, showed me a few photos of a couple of German guys she had met over there. Her words were.

'Oh, I slept with them, I hope you don't mind. You still want to go out with me don't you?'

I sat there, mouth wide open, not believing what I was hearing. I got up and left. It took me six months to get the £70 back she'd borrowed.

Oddly though, it came via her mum all in coins. For ages, my pockets were weighed down by a couple of bags of mostly coppers and the odd bit of silver. If it was to do with the curse, then the bar staff at the local pub loved me for it!

More about relationships later as I move onto the *Strange Happenings*. There have been some things that have taken place around me that fit under this heading, and I can still recall two of them vividly to this day. The first when I was about nine or ten years old. We still lived above the shop, and I had a large bedroom at the back on the top floor of the flat above the shop. My bed was on the side of the room that ran parallel to the gable end part of it. The window was on the same wall, so moonlight used to spread across the bottom of my bed from left to right. In bed one night, I was looking down the length of the bed to the wall at the other end of the room. A keyhole appeared on the wall as a beam of light came through it and shone straight onto my head. I thought I was dreaming, no, I thought maybe that the light coming in from the bedroom window might have been shining across the right angle, no, this was real. If it had only happened for one night I would say that I had been dreaming, however, this continued most nights for weeks, possibly months. I couldn't wait to get to bed each night, eager for the keyhole to appear, it was so soothing. Later in my teens I told a couple of people who were into **Buddhism,** and they told me that I was honoured, as this was the keyhole to life itself. To this day, I still do not know what that was, but I'd be quite happy to sit there and let it happen again. It was so peaceful.

The second, *Strange Happening*, was when I was fifteen years old. I was writing a lot of songs then. Some love songs (I wonder why) and some about other experiences. One set of lyrics I wrote, which are now the 3rd track of my album **Songs to the World** (2013), are based on the following event. It was a normal evening. I went to bed about 11pm and I hadn't been drinking, and I wasn't on any drugs. We had now moved to a proper house in West Derby Village and my bedroom was next to my Mum and Dad's. I went to sleep and had this very vivid dream. I'm walking through a thick forest and came to a clearing with a big old house in it. Thunder, lightning, heavy rain etc – you get the picture. I came to a window and a guy who looked very ancient, started telling me off,

'What do you think you are doing? You know what you should be doing!'

I had no idea what he was talking about, and it all seemed like a dream but very, very real, until the vision turned into reality. The image disappeared and the bed started shaking violently and rattled on the floor. I was pinned to the bed, it felt like the bottom end was lifting up so that my feet were above my head. I don't know how long this went on for until it suddenly stopped. I heard my Mum knocking on my bedroom door asking if I was okay and what was the cause of all the noise. I shouted I was all right but still had my eyes shut. To say I was scared is an understatement. My Mum went back to bed, and it took me a few minutes to open my eyes, wondering what I would find in my room. When I did, very, very slowly, I peered down my bed to the long mirror attached to my wardrobe on the opposite wall. There was nothing out of the ordinary other than what happened to my watch and the clock. My watch (one of the new digital types at the time), was flashing a date and a time that was not correct. I really wish I'd written down what was on that display screen, but I pressed a button, and it went back to normal, so I'll never know. The bedside alarm clock had stopped ticking. I'd had that clock for years and it had never stopped. After a few years I gave up wearing watches as they always used to either stop or go wrong in one way or another. I used to send other alarm clocks funny for a while too. My Dad gave me a watch later in my teens that he had used for 20 years. I had it two days and it stopped and never worked again. The watch repairer was baffled as he couldn't find anything wrong with it. For a long time after that, I used to be able to put my finger close to other people's noses and watch the static jump across and give them a shock. There are not many people I have ever told these events to, maybe because some might think I'm a bit weird or that I'm talking a load of bollocks.

But these were my experiences, and I would be interested if anyone else has had similar ones.

Back off the motorway, to around 1973/74. I used to practice guitar every day in my bedroom and even built my own speaker, which eventually caught fire at a rehearsal with a band a couple of years later! The man who lived above the shop next door used to listen to me practising and came round one day asking if I'd be interested in playing guitar for a band he knew. 'Wow!' I thought, first band at the age of fourteen! I said yes and we did two gigs. One at the youth club, and the other was at the infamous Remand Home on **Menlove Avenue** in south Liverpool playing to the inmates, which was a bit daunting at first but turned out really well. The man next door to my dad's shop worked there and got us the gig. I still have the letter from **Liverpool City Council** thanking us for doing it and how much the lads enjoyed us. We played some Uriah Heep numbers, all of *Dark Side of the Moon* and a couple of numbers by the **Mahavishnu Orchestra** which was an achievement considering I'd only been playing electric guitar for two years. Unfortunately, the other two band members, who were older than me, were just about to go to university and the band split up. I was gutted. With frequenting the Moonstone, I knew a lot of musicians who used to drink there. Yes, most of us were underage drinkers, but that's the way it was then, if you looked old enough then you got served, no questions asked, or ID sought! I didn't have to wait long for something else, now that the music bug had bitten me.

There was a band called **Fat Elsie,** yes you read it right. If there's a name for a band you would never use – it's that. They were looking for a guitarist to share parts with the other guitarist who thought he was **Marc Bolan**, a poor imitation unfortunately, especially fronting a band called Fat Elsie. I have two recollections, first, was playing at a night club in Liverpool. I knew the girl behind the bar, and she gave me half a bottle of Pernod for free, which I stupidly drunk, before I got on stage. It's the worst gig I have ever played, and I never got pissed again before a gig except once, no, actually, twice. I'll explain those later. There were '…mitigating circumstances your Honour.'

My second recollection was while rehearsing with the band. I bought, correction, obtained, from my dad's shop, a copy of **Practical Electronics** magazine to build my own guitar stack. The guy who lived above the shop next door, built the cabinet for me, but I wired it up with a speaker, or, to give it its proper name, the driver, from **Tandy** (remember them?). I had a 100-watt **Sound City** PA amplifier, donated by the guy next door too. I wasn't very good with electronics in my teens, proving this by nearly sending myself across the room when I touched the speaker outputs on the back of the amp. Although, in hindsight, I think what happened next may have been caused by the outputs being faulty as the chassis shouldn't have been live and I think the driver wasn't big enough to cope with the amp. We were rehearsing and I turned around to see the grill of the speaker cabinet on fire! Only thing nearby was a pint of milk (I used to drink milk all the time, still do), so that was the end of that. It did last for about five gigs over a couple of years, including the ones at the youth club and the Remand Home. That would have been interesting if it had gone up in flames there, I might have been kept in there for arson! One of the lessons I learnt at that time was don't try and put a fire out with milk as it makes a bloody mess and stinks too. After that, I bought a 4 x 12inch speaker cabinet the standard guitar player's dream.

Anyway, I went off down the motorway the wrong way again, sorry. As you can imagine Fat Elsie didn't last long. It's a shame as the keyboard player was awesome, in fact the rest of the band were great, err, except for the Marc Bolan look alike. A legend in his own mind. It was good experience though including 'Don't get pissed before the Gig' rule.

I'd bought an **Arbiter Flying V** for playing in Fat Elsie. The guitar looked good but that was about it. Flying Vs are not the most user-friendly guitars. While playing in bands outside of school, in school itself, I performed in **Pirates of Penzance**. Also, a few of us in our exam year (1976) got together and did a concert on the stage of Liverpool Collegiate. I can't remember all the songs, but Pete Scott reminded me of it and mentioned us playing a Quo number in the set. Anyway, after Fat Elsie, I was still writing songs, bought an **Aria NK700** (which I regret ever selling now). It cost £500 on Hire Purchase guaranteed by my dad. That was bought from **Rushworth & Drapers**, (Church Street, Liverpool), which I used to frequent a lot, and I used to love to stare at all the guitars and equipment. I've been looking on eBay lately at buying another NK700, but, as they are so collectable, they are too expensive for me.

While all of this was going on, I got the results of my **O-Levels**. I was very good at Chemistry, and I should have stayed on to do **A-Level** music. But, because I was an arrogant teenager, who wanted to get a job and leave home, I applied for a few positions and got two interviews: one at **I.C.I.** in **Runcorn** and the other at Evans Medical in Speke. Both jobs were working in the laboratories, and I got offered both posts. My grandpa (Mum's Dad) was the one who persuaded me to take the Evans position, as he knew the company. Another reason I chose it was that I would not have been able to go to The Stadium and Moonstone as often and see all my friends. Again, it's strange where fate takes you, because if I had taken the I.C.I. job, I would have had to leave home, move to Runcorn (it was a long way to go on a bus to work in those days). Also, certain events over the next few years would never have happened and, I most probably wouldn't be sat here now, writing this book. After writing that last sentence, on reflection, I could still be sat here writing this book but, I would have come to the same place via a completely different route. I feel that if I'd taken the I.C.I. route, I may have ended up in the music industry, but certain catalysts would not have been there that triggered various events through my life that made me who I am today. Most probably I would have settled down with 2.4 kids, a job for life and forgotten all about music….. maybe…..? I'll never know will I. And, later on, I moulded other people's lives that possibly, if I hadn't been there, they may have never gone into professions that they did. I'm not blowing my own trumpet, well I am a bit, but they have told me and thanked me many times: that's how I know.

Mushroom mayhem

Other memories of that time include Graham, myself, and another lad called Stephen, eating Magic Mushrooms while listening to *Awaken* by **Yes**. Then going off down to the Catholic Cathedral aka '**Paddy's Wigwam**' while this song is still playing in our heads. Sat on the outside altar, watching the vast floor breathe as it talked to us and rats ran in and out of the cracks of the face that had appeared on the ground.

Don't piss anyone off with a gun

Going out on New Year's Eve once with Tree, Graham and a guy called Dave, to a real dodgy club, down a back street in Liverpool where two guys threatened us with a gun inside. We were kicked out, Graham had his faced smashed with a bottle and loads of people were fighting outside, as if someone had flipped a switch. The police turned up, only to find that the two guys in the club with the gun were coppers too. A very strange night that I wrote into a song (**Only at Night**), which is the first track on my first album.

Forget the kitchen sink

Graham and I loved the **Lake District**. We decided to go there camping on the train. Apart from the tents, we had everything bar the kitchen sink. It was fucking ridiculous. You'd think that being in the **Cubs** for a while, we might have learnt something. Obviously not, as we had too many pots, pans and I even took an acoustic guitar. We got the train to **Ulverston** and went to the pub, big mistake. Came out pissed, got picked up by the police who could see the state we were in and politely dropped us off on the moors. It was pitch black and we stopped walking in no particular direction when I had a sudden feeling we had to stop and set up camp. When we woke in the morning, there was a very large drop about 100yrds away from where we had pitched. For some reason, despite my inebriated state, I just knew we shouldn't wander any further. We walked back to Ulverston to get the train. By now most of the pots and pans had been launched into the bushes. We were heading for **Coniston,** you could camp at the top of the **Old Man,** free of charge and without anyone's permission back then. The Old Man is a very large hill or fell, but it's bloody steep. We get to Coniston, have a beer and then go up the Old Man to camp. We are halfway up, and we see a tent in a field. Graham says, 'Ok this will do'. I'm not too sure as we were told you could only camp at the top. While hiking, I noticed lots of signs about 'Sheep Dog Trials', didn't give it a thought. There were three guys in a tent who said we could stop in the same field, so we set camp and headed off down to the nearest pub. We all get pissed, leave and stagger back to our tents and fall sound sleep. I wake up in the morning to the sound of dogs barking and sheep bleating. I pop my head out to find that the other tent has gone, and we are in the field that the local farmers are holding the actual sheep dog trials in. In the immortal words of **Blackadder**, it rhymes with clucking bell! A farmer appeared outside the tent with his hand out, 'that will be a pound', he says. We pack up very quickly and leave. 'Now that's why there are sign's everywhere of Sheep Dog Trials', I think.

It is Saturday and we walked back down the Old Man and to find somewhere to camp which was a proper site. We set up and went to the pub again and came out around 10pm after we scored some **Artane** (Now actually used for Parkinsons Disease). We are now on the beach bit of Coniston Lake. I'm talking to an imaginary guy who walked out of the lake and is sat down next to me. It is a perfect summer evening with clear skies, stars and an open fire. Graham is attempting to hide in a bush and all he ever said to me afterwards, was something about seeing a naked lady. I was playing the guitar as well and a few people had come to the lake from the pub to take in the atmosphere. So, imagine the sight of us two; one strumming and talking to someone who wasn't there and the other hiding very badly in the bushes performing (to anyone else, not on the same drug), some crude form of voyeurism.

We returned to Coniston a few years later, in a van owned by a guy called Dave. Dave who was a lot older than us, I think had a drink and drugs problem and was banned from driving at the time, so I drove. It was legal for me to drive as I'd passed my test the year before, but I'd never driven a van before, which had a Guinness beermat as a tax disc replacement. Ten people in a transit van who had all taken Artane, was a driving experience as I was clean and sober while everyone else is acting like a box of frogs. I waited to take anything until we had got to the camp site in Coniston. I wish they had waited too. In a nutshell, Dave, who had drunk two bottles of sherry as well, nearly got us killed when he tried to grab the steering wheel on the motorway. He also got us kicked out of the pub in Coniston for annoying everyone in it, asking if they'd seen a six-foot white rabbit he was looking for.

We drove back to the campsite, where I took my tablet. Dave disappeared, then popped up behind a wall and shook a few tents that fell down and made a lot of people very angry. He didn't shake them very hard, so they couldn't have put them up right is how he justified it. Dave didn't have a wicked bone in his body, only a full-time drink and drug problem. But someone called the local policeman who arrived on a motor bike. He told us to follow him in our van to the Coniston Lake car park. As I drove, I started to feel the effects of the Artane. We parked up in front of a wall in the car park and were told to stay there for the night. We weren't charged or cautioned and off the Copper went. A bit different in those days or maybe he didn't want the paperwork or ask why there were ten people in the back of the van.

In the night, Tree and I sit with Dave in the front seats trying to keep him from doing anything wild. Dave was completely off his trolley and after a while said he wanted a piss. We did too, so we let him out thinking that we will keep an eye on him, only for the wall in front of us to start moving towards the van. I'm thinking the handbrake is off, but the van isn't moving. This went on for a while. Next thing, Dave disappeared. We looked for him for a bit but gave up. We woke in the morning to find he was still missing. We were worried, but he turned up after about six hours from when he went for a piss. He had barbed wire cuts all over his hands and arms, two broken ribs, a broken wrist, no shoes and his feet were completely caked in mud, and he was muttering something about sheep! As far as I know to this day, he still doesn't know where he went and I'm not sure what he was trying to do with those woolly animals. The rest of the weekend was pretty quiet compared to that night, oh, except for me having to drive the van in the morning and still having flashbacks from the Artane. I saw medieval peasants standing in the fields looking onto the road with pitch forks and sticks shouting at me,

'We'll get ya!'

I have my head out the window and I am shaking a fist shouting,

'You won't fucking get me.' I think it shocked everyone else in the van when I did it.

I got on to the M5 then- sorry. It is 1977, I'm still working in the Labs at Evans/Glaxo and playing guitar but not in a band! I'd rehearsed some songs with one of the guys in the labs who played bass, but nothing came of it. I was wondering what to do next, when another guy, who worked in the offices of Glaxo, came in to see me in the lab. There'd been a small poster put up in the corridor about a music project, but I hadn't given it that much thought. Focused on playing in the same type of band narrows your outlook sometimes. I believe someone had mentioned to him that I played and wrote songs, hence he came to meet me. Peter (that's all I will refer to him as), at that stage in my life, helped me into something fantastic. Six years later he would become the bane of my life. Peter's opening comment to me was,

'I'm involved in a project, a musical for the **International Year of the Child**. We need musicians, would you be interested?'

'Yes, I would,' says I. It was based on the true story from the 13th Century. A German lad called Nicholas, of around fifteen years of age, has a vision from God to get a load of kids and take them over the Alps to Genoa in Italy. From there he was to take them onto Jerusalem to stop the Holy Wars. According to traditional accounts, up to 30,000 children followed him. Most died enroute or were put into slavery. It's a very sad story. Nicholas was one of only two children, who came back. The show was an adaptation of the original play written by **Paul Thompson** for schools to perform, and, based on the true story and the play, was transformed into a musical by **Keith Milner** (Director) and **Brendan McCormack** (Musical Director and renowned as John Lennon's favourite guitarist). I wrote some of the extra songs for the show. The musical was the project, and it needed a band to play the songs. Furthermore, they wanted someone to come to the front and narrate some of the scenes. But this had to be done in a musical style of delivery before the scenes were played out. The band would have to perform all the other incidental music and songs that made up the whole show. I had only ever played Puck in *A Midsummer Night's Dream* at junior school and took a minor part as you know in Pirates of Penzance. All a long time ago and a world away from what I was being asked to do at that moment. So, during *The Year of the Child*, I was on a ninety-degree learning curve. It was fantastic standing in front of the audience as a type of minstrel watching their faces while telling a story through melody, not just words and playing the guitar at the same time. Something, which I suppose helped me later in other musical ventures. Anyway, a band was formed through various auditions, all of us being around our late teens, but we did have Brendan who kicked our arses and made us a great band. He brought in a session guitarist to help us out who had played on an **Eric Clapton and George Harrison** albums. This guy was amazing and very humble too. No big I am, considering he was one of the only session players that got their name put on albums as an acknowledgement of their input.

I had a long chat with Brendan one day about his life as a session player. He was also an incredible guitarist. I didn't take that route, and why you'll see in a bit. Brendan taught me more about music in those twelve months, than anyone else has and I am indebted to him. He passed away March 2009 and, unfortunately, I never got a chance to talk or meet him again after the musical. I did a few session gigs for him that he couldn't do due to work commitments elsewhere. One was at a club in Liverpool on New Year's Eve in 1977. It was the first time I played live, reading guitar tabs, and I was (in a word or three), 'Shitting a Brick', but it went really well, even the rest of the band ended up jamming with me to some Quo, Rolling Stones and other numbers. I got paid £25 for that gig, which was the Musicians' Union rate for a three-hour recording session in those days and, it included a union break in the middle. Having never had experience of this, I was amazed when the rest of the band simply finished a song, put on their coats and said 'right, break time,' and left the stage. Didn't matter if everyone was dancing! How things have changed.

Rehearsals for the musical lasted for about six months. They were all done at **I.M. Marsh College** in **Aigburth** which is now part of **John Moores University**. It was a sports campus but had a Drama department in the 1970's. I have some great memories of that space at that time. I remember arriving there a few hours early, playing the grand piano on most Saturday afternoons, before the rehearsals. Me on my own, with **Elton John, Barry Manilow** and **Carpenters** songs to keep me company – wow! It was so relaxing, and the acoustics resonated the sound, it was my special time. Although rock music was my passion, I used to listen to a lot of other styles of music in my early teens, which I must thank my Mum for, and this has stayed with me all my life.

To fill the parts of children in *Year of the Child*, the local schools were asked if their infants and other under sixteens would be interested in auditioning for it. Keith Milner and his team did an amazing job. Liverpool was twinned with **Cologne** and, apparently, Nicholas in the 13th century lived near Cologne. So, it was only right to invite some of the children of Cologne to be involved in the musical. As showtime got closer, and given the wide spread of ages, varying experiences and languages, the rehearsals (I can only describe, tactfully,) were a little manic at times.

Later that year, I was willingly (would you believe it) attached to a cross, 20ft off the floor in the **Anglican Cathedral** in Liverpool, naked (except for a nappy/loin cloth). The role meant hanging by my fingers to two very large nails, with a small plinth of wood supporting my heels. Health and Safety would have a fit and closed us down these days if you did that! This was only a small part of the show. As I mentioned earlier, I played guitar and sang, but a lot of the children in the show thought I looked a little like **Jesus** and so I was voted to be Jesus in this particular scene. I'm not a religious person, but to be in a position like that, it made me think about religion. During this part of the show, **Jim Webb**, did the laser show for the musical and had lasers firing off all over the place when I was on the cross. He also looked after sound, lighting and played some bass in the band too. He made the first holograms in the UK. He's got a spectacular portfolio (G.L Services and author of Laser Safe PC) and you'll find him on the web, no pun intended! The musical was performed for two nights in October of 1977 and attracted write ups in the **Liverpool Echo**, radio interviews etc and, for a seventeen-year-old, it was an incredible experience.

In addition to this musical, I was asked to write the music for a version of the play *The Crucible*. This was being performed at a college that one of the girls in the People's Crusade went to. I produced part of the show myself and I loved it. In fact, carrying on with musicals was another avenue I could have gone down.

Around this time, I was invited to the house of the drummer (**Aidey**) in the People's Crusade band. He was an amazing guy. His dad was an artist and had an oil painting of a Supernova, covering the whole of one wall in the living room, with a Mexican Bullseye Puffer Fish (dead of course) as the main lamp shade in the centre of the room! Sitting there, with this dried out body of a fish sort of staring at you with a light bulb inside it was an incredible sight. I assume it was varnished or something like that as I haven't thought about it since but, how the bloody hell, do you make a lampshade out of a fish! Aidey had these sayings he'd made up, for example a Pub was called 'A House of Merry Fluid' and the fish and chip shop was, 'The Extinct Aqueous Beastie and Vegetable Shop.' He also invented two words, **Bragilic** and **Parhagency**, which didn't mean anything at all. You will not find them in a dictionary. If they appear in a dictionary after this book is published, then I claim copyright or whatever you have to claim for a new word.

If we were in a pub and a guy we were talking to was boring us, Aidey would say,

'Yes, but is it Bragilic? I sense a touch of Parhagency.'

Not to let on that he didn't have a bloody clue what we were talking about, he'd just walk off. Problem solved. Aidey's best statement was,

'We will leave the house of merry fluid and walk the pathways of the world (the pavement) and we shall enter the extinct aqueous beastie and vegetable shop and say to the proprietor of the establishment, please could we sample a morsel of your extinct aqueous beastie and vegetables fried in a deep and crispy nature.'

We did this once. We got thrown out!

My other memory with Aidey, was sat in his house on a Sunday afternoon with another couple of members of the band and, yes, it was one of those rare times I'd had a tote. The four of us decided to make cartoon balloons out of thick paper, write on them with black markers; '*20 John Player Special please*' and '*How Much?*' and '*That's a bit expensive*' you get the idea. We then went up to the local off licence and didn't say a word; used the balloons, pulling each one out of our coats in order, while Aidey and I were at the counter. The other two guys were walking around the shop with the balloons and, if someone engaged in conversation, out would pop something like '*Why did the chicken cross the road?*' The girls behind the counter thought we were a bit strange at first, as did some of the other customers, but we had them laughing in the end. Great fun.

Aidey was such a funny guy and a great friend at the time. It was so sad to find out that he'd passed away in his mid-twenties. He'd got into **Heroin** and overdosed. I don't think his dad helped. His father used to grow his own **Cannabis** plants in the garden. His son wasn't off to a good start really, was he? Very sad on reflection. He was also a fantastic drummer, and I'll always remember him. Rest in peace mate.

The real Blood Donor (non) sketch!

I'm taking an A road off the M5. Something completely un-related happened this year. I was at **Old Swan Technical College**, doing an **Ordinary National Certificate** in Science on a day release. The Blood Clinic set up one of these days. I'm fine with injections but taking blood out of me is something completely different. But it was my first time, and I wanted to give blood as I thought it was something I should do; to make that; 'little bit of an effort and do a positive thing,' as **The Spinners** said in a short promotional TV film. Anyway, I'm sat there with my mate, after we had given blood and we're having a cup of tea and a biscuit. Suddenly I felt strange and said, 'I need to lie down'. I stretched on a spare couch and WHAM! I started shaking as if I was having a fit. When I came round, there were a few nurses, males mostly, thankfully, who apparently, I'd punched while I was having an uncontrolled moment. My mate told me that I was throwing my arms about all over the place, and it needed five staff to hold me down. The Chief Nurse, an elderly lady, said to me,

'We advise you not to give blood **again**!'

They came to Glaxo about six months later and she spotted me and said,

'Don't ask him for blood he hits people!'

I've never given blood since, except for samples, and I have never had a fit before or after that. Apparently, some bodies just don't like giving blood.

Back on the M5. So, after this amazing show, it was a bit of a let-down, to go back to work and back to reality. So, it was fantastic to be told we were going to perform the show in Cologne in 1978 and to be asked if I would be interested in busking in **Bold Street** to raise money for the trip. 'YES! YES! YES!' We got a licence from Liverpool City Council to perform on three Saturday afternoons.

Lufthansa Airways gave us the flights for free for the whole cast. We had to pay for our train tickets on **British Rail**, (surprise, surprise) but they did give us first class for the price of second class (nice one). We had to carry the guitars, drums etc on the train and the tube. That was an experience! We had to fly from **Heathrow**, hence, the reason why we ended up on the tube with all the equipment. Keith Milner got a load of kids in Cologne to be part of the show, and we all stayed at the homes of parents of the children involved. We were there for two weeks. My memories of the shows in Cologne include interviews with **BBC World Service**; photos in the local papers; being ask for our autographs which was something I'd never had to do before and something that didn't happen with the shows in Liverpool. To top it all, I had my first ever **McDonald's** over there. My main memory was, you were asked if you wanted gherkins! I don't think that happens these days.

Locals in foreign bars and the Dawn of blind love!

On the downside, I made the mistake of playing pool in a bar with a guy who made it known to me that he had a pistol in his coat. This was because I was complaining about him making the rules up as he went along. All the usual things that happen to an eighteen-year-old! Halfway through the game, he got the pistol from the bar tender making sure that Aidey and I saw him do it. I said to Aidey,

'I'm gonna beat this guy, just be ready with the pool cue if he goes for the inside of his coat.'

I'm not sure why I said that, but we finished the game, I potted the black, waited to see what would happen. Well, unlike those classic Western movie saloon bar moments, when the gunslingers size up to each other with an **Ennio Morricone** soundtrack, he just walked over to the bar tender, handed the pistol back and left. We thought it was a good idea to leave too. Bit of a stupid thing to do, beat a guy at pool in a foreign country, whose got a piece in his coat! Ah well, I'm still here.

The other memory I have of that time is, Aidey shaking a Salt & Shake crisp packet in British Rail first class. On the way back from the buffet cart, the bag burst showering all the gentlemen in bowler hats, with crisps.

The shows went really well, and we made the agonising trip back, the same route we had taken, with all the equipment. It's funny how certain events in your life control other factors and this takes me to the next chaotic relationship in my life.

A Blind Date with a Guitarist

While I was busking with other members of the cast, raising money to get to Cologne, un-beknown to me, there was a young lady who came down every week to watch me play and sing, her name was Dawn. I'm in work a few weeks later and one of my colleagues called Kathy says to me,

'Would you like to go on a blind date?'

Apparently, she knew Dawn and that Dawn had mentioned to her that there was this guy busking in Bold Street that she liked, and she said she knew it was me. We met up and that was the start of a four-year relationship. Regrettably, there was a lot of jealousy, on Dawn's side due to my music. She did not like other women watching me sing and play. This wore me down. Don't shout, I even turned down an audition for a Rock Musical in London that Brendan had set up, because she didn't want me to go. Love is blind, but I think I was just a foolish git. However, in my defence, looking back now, I was quite arrogant and feel that if I had become famous, I'd be dead now either with alcohol or worse, I might have ended up like Aidey!

Dawn and I did everything together seven days a week, apart from living together. This is not a good thing for young people, we all need space. We had bought a house in the Lake District to move into once I had a job transfer to Glaxo in Ulverston. She'd already sorted a transfer with her job working in the **Civil Service**. It all fell apart eventually. Don't get me wrong, we had some great times together, but ironically what brought us together in the first place, me playing guitar and singing, was the thing that was pissing her off, because she didn't want anyone else to hear it! She even helped to pay to do my first recordings in **Amazon Studios** (**Kirkby**), which I still have the master tapes from. Anyway, as a means to an end or one of Blackadder's 'cunning plans', I let one of the guys in our crowd, who'd always fancied her but was a bit of a pratt, go on a date with her. I was hoping that she'd see that I was a much better bloke than him. But she felt a bit awkward about going on a date while I was sat in the pub, so she said to me,

'Why don't you take the bar maid out for a drink, you've always liked her.'

We both (wrongly) thought it was a good idea. However, both couples ended up in the same club (The Cave in Matthew Street for anyone who remembers it). I think, this was 1981/82 and a friend of Dawn's, who she worked with, called Pauline who rode a **Suzuki Katana** motorbike, fancied me and told Dawn that I'd taken the bar maid home for you know what! Dawn saw me leave but didn't see what happened afterwards. After the bar maid and I left The Cave and, realising that nothing was going to come from this, I went home, and the bar maid went off to see some of her mates elsewhere. Dawn and I had a heart to heart two days later and she confessed that she went back to her date's house and virtually raped him (oh yeah, he obliged!) because she thought I was doing the same thing! Well, that was the end of that. Dawn married him and, as far as I know, they are still together and live around the corner from my Mum! My sister has spoken to her a few years ago but I've never bumped into her. After this I went off the rails for six months, I completely lost the plot. Pissed every night, taking loans out to cover money I needed to fuel the drink and spend on meals with people who I thought were friends but were just there for the ride. It's very hard to go from spending seven days a week with someone, for four years, to nothing at all. **The Maharaja** in **Renshaw Street** made a lot of money out of me for a while. Most probably why they are still there, I visited them last year and they are still a great restaurant.

Riding with the Hells Angels.....while riding my!

At this time, I bought my first motorbike (**Triumph Bonneville T140V**), got involved with the local Hells Angels although never joined them and started DJ'ing at their club (**Night Riders**) in the middle of the city centre. It was a very strange time in many ways. At one stage I had to rebuild the engine as the main bearings needed replacing, a common fault with old Triumphs unfortunately. Dave (the guy with the transit) taught me how to strip and rebuild an engine. That's how I got to start learning to work on motorbikes.

My Grandpa had shown me about cars when I was younger, as he was still taking them apart in his seventies and I used to sort out the usual maintenance. But stripping engines was a first and after that I don't think I took a car or motorbike to a garage for 30 years. While the Triumph was off the road, I purchased a **Robin Reliant**. What I didn't know was that the head gasket had gone. I only needed the thing for a few weeks. I was seeing a girl in **Preston** for about the same amount of time. I'd fill the Robin up with water, drive up the A59 and two thirds of the way there, there'd be smoke in the car. Only way to know the car was overheating. I had to pull over, fill the water back up, spend the evening in Preston and drive home having to stop intermittently on the way back to fill the radiator. One evening on the way home I'd forgotten to fill my water container, so tried to get as close to home as possible. I overtook this truck, smoke billowing out of the windows due to the oil overheating. I pulled over a few miles down and the truck stops behind me with the driver running out with a fire extinguisher! Luckily, he had water with him, and I got home safely. I never went back to Preston after that and got rid of the Robin Reliant. I couldn't really take her out in that car could I, FFS! I don't even know how that engine kept going. Eventually, a guy bought it and drove it to **Frodsham** which was 30 miles away. He phoned our house to complain it had broken down, but he was told it was 'sold as seen' and if there was a problem with the engine it was nothing to do with me.

I liked riding over to the **Wirral** on a Saturday night with the Angels. **Lol Wolfe** (what a great name) had bought a customised Hearse, we filled it full of beer and rode our bikes behind it, over to **Birkenhead** for a party. The ticket collectors in the Mersey tunnel just let us through without paying. It was like something from a film. The Hearse had this red glow coming out of the windows from the interior and there must have been about 30 or 40 bikes following it.

On another occasion, I was taking one of the Angels, Mark, in a hired van down to Wales to pick up a bike he'd bought only to get there and get shot at. He must have pissed someone off. We drove back with nothing, and no explanation and I never got paid for the van either. I think he was trying to keep it quiet so not to lose face.

I recall riding to the Lake District with the Angels and having to go back to the **Salutation Hotel** in **Ambleside** to pick one of the guys up as he had a flat tyre. I had full beer cans strapped around my waist on bungee cords, which was the only way to carry them. I came around a bend, my headlight goes off and I have to guess. I guessed wrong and I slide up a grass bank cans flying everywhere. I lifted the bike back up, fixed the headlight back on the bike and picked him up. I didn't get hurt as I had huge **Ape Hangers** (handlebars) on the bike, and the bike and the bars kept me off the road itself. Bit of a sad one but ended up funny.

There was a guy in the Night Riders club when I was DJ'ing there. An ex-Northern Ireland squaddie who had been court marshalled for something he hadn't done, but he never got over it. All he was trying to do was to protect the person from a sniper and accidentally knocked them to the floor. They hit their head on the kerb and died. Pissed up in the club, he was trying to have a pop at the Sergeant of Arms (Bruce) who was huge. I'd seen this guy take on five big blokes and take them all out. I pull this guy away, he starts on me, we fall to the floor, I have my arm around his neck, and he takes a full bite into my arm. I lose it and he ends up getting kicked out. We all then go back to Colin's house (who was the brother of Mark who I took to Wales) and he makes us all Mushroom tea. As the mushrooms take effect, I turn to the guys and say,

'Does anyone want a bite of my arm because everyone else has?'

That triggers laughter that lasted for about four hours while we're trying to watch The **Cannonball Run**, a film I love but will always give me memories of something completely different.

Getting into sticky situations and the return of the curse of Jayne

Coasting on the M4 now. Firstly, I nearly got the sack from Glaxo as I was getting home at 3am, going to work and then out DJ'ing again at Night Riders six nights a week. I don't suffer from hangovers, which doesn't help. It was just lack of sleep. What didn't help, was a young lady, would pick me up after the club and give me a lift home via **Newsham Park** in her car, enough said! I've never been able to look at a **VW Polo** the same! To this day, I don't know how that all started, but it stopped after she told me her boyfriend, that I knew nothing about, had come home after working away!!!! It must have taken him a long time to get home, because the affair lasted for about three months!

At one stage, I was that skint, I had to walk the seven miles to work one day. I would say that was one of the worst years of my life. Not <u>the</u> worst, that's later on. Between the start of the Musical and splitting up with Dawn, I'd moved from the labs in Glaxo to Quality Control, working in a small office in the warehouse. It was in this job that I nearly got the sack, being found fast asleep on the bench in my workshop.

Do you have a licence to drive that Forklift?

There were some funny moments too, I nearly smashed up a forklift! I needed a pallet down from one of the racks, it was a Saturday and only a few people were in. The guy who was supposed to get it for me was busy, so he told me to get it down myself. I'd done it before but not with this particular forklift which was twice as quick as all the others, and it set off like a rocket. The guys saw me shooting past the top of the racking, hearing a loud bang as I went straight into a steel staircase. No one was injured but all the battery packs, that had jumped out of their locations, had to be pushed back into place on the forklift, using another forklift. I learnt another valuable lesson that day.

Syrup is stronger than you think

I used to take the samples of syrup being delivered off the tankers as they pumped the 20,000lts into the tanks a fair way into the building.

Talking to the driver, one day, he forgot to open the valve that lets the air in as the liquids pumped out. The brand new £10,000 stainless steel tank on the back of the wagon imploded. He tried to suck back what is left in the pipes and thought it was clear. He took the hose off as I readied myself to take the after-filling sample, and WHAM! About 300lts of warm to hot syrup came out of this pipe, straight into my chest knocking me over. I lay there on the floor with all this syrup everywhere. It took ages to get it all off me. These days you could get compensation for that. The syrup was always quite hot 40/50 degrees centigrade so that it would pump better, just in case you're wondering.

Back on track now. Going back to my near job loss, I would not have got out of that situation if it wasn't for a certain lady called Angel (not her real name) who I met at a party in Birkenhead. I will be indebted to her for the rest of my life. We met, I moved out of my parents' house (who at the time had just about had enough of me) and into her flat in **New Brighton** and she sorted my life out. I was on my final warning at Glaxo.

After Angel and I had become an item, returning from many of the rallies we went to she would fall asleep on the back of the bike while we rode up the motorway. Both of us rode bikes but normally we would only take one bike to long distance rallies. Most of the time, I would ride back home from rallies sustained by some external help. She couldn't fall off with the tent, panniers and sleeping bags keeping us tight on the bike. Any bikers will know what I mean. It was a privilege that my partner trusted me enough to fall asleep behind me. I always knew she'd fallen asleep when her helmet landed on my back.

Another memory of Angel and I is riding down to **Bristol** for me to take my Part 1 bike test after I'd been pulled up for not having a full licence. My aim was to get my test before I was taken to court. I rode the XJ750 **Yamaha** I now have, down some of the way and she took over riding before we arrived there. I take the test, and the test instructor knows exactly what's going on and gets me to take the test on the 125cc and then on the 750cc – all around the cones too. I pass both! Angel rides the bike back all the way.

I took my part 2 motorcycle test in **Bootle**, Liverpool. I borrow Chris and Tina's (friends from the Admiral) 125cc to take the test. I go round a few corners and the examiner flags me down and says to me, 'Okay, what bike do you have at home?' I say a 750cc Yam, he replies,

'You're chucking that round like a toy. Piss off, you've passed!'

During my time on the Wirral, I rode with **Snatchgrabbers MCC**. This is the bike club I hung out with on the Wirral after I'd moved in with Angel. Out on the open road one fine day, riding to **Worlds End** in Denbighshire Wales we all came hurtling around a bend to be confronted by 200 sheep in the road. Well, the first rider ended up in hospital and I was so fortunate not to end up the same way. This was thanks to the instructor I had when I took my part 1 bike test. He showed me how to brake at speed around a bend and so as I cranked over on a bend flat out, I survived without falling off.

Six months after moving in with Angel, I had a new job at Glaxo, as an assistant inventory controller in the planning department and a full motorbike licence and as I mentioned a newer motorbike (Yamaha XJ750 Seca). In short, all was good, except for the curse! I will not go into details of why we split up because of what she did for me, but let's just say the curse of Jayne had struck again. I suppose what didn't help was my job, doing fourteen-hour days, and I'm not surprised we split up. I should have worked at the relationship a bit more too. Here I go again! Another good thing that came out of our relationship was Angel introduced me to BBC Radio 4 which I still listen to, to this day.

Off down the M53 now -

Miff and Tunnelled visions!

Miff is an enigma and an amazing guy. I used to meet Miff (**John Smith** as is his name) at the Wirral end of the **Kingsway Mersey Tunnel** once a week, to go for a beer. Just after the tunnel had opened, I see him come out of the tunnel exit and get pulled by the Tunnel Police. Miff told me later:

Policeman declares, 'Congratulations, you're the first person to do 100mph through that tunnel.'

Miff, 'do I get a **Crackerjack** pencil?'

Policeman, 'No, you get booked!'

Every time he got pulled up by the Police, they wouldn't believe his name was John Smith. I have so many tales of his adventures. Let's just say that he is another character in the rich tapestry of my memory that may get revealed in another book!

The other story involving tunnels starts with Sue, a good friend, who had married an American Air force Pilot stationed at **Upper Heyford** near **Banbury.** The ceremony was in Birkenhead, but they needed someone to drive a hired van to Banbury with all of Sue's belongings. I volunteered as it was a Sunday, and I had time to make the journey both ways. However, it was in the winter of 1983. That day happened to be one of the worst for snowfall that year. So, after saying goodbye to Angel with a, 'don't worry I'll be back by late evening,' I set off to pick up the other two for the 300-mile round trip. Today it would take about four hours, may be a little more with a break or two, but nothing like the ten hours just to get to Banbury. Well, sometimes the M40 can take that long these days!

Along 90 odd miles of the way, we had to follow a snow plough which we picked up in Stoke! Once we got to Upper Heyford, we discovered that a **C.N.D.** protester had stolen a snow plough and blocked most of the roads around the air base. It took another two hours to collect the groom's stuff and take everything to their matrimonial home on the outskirts of Banbury. Angel didn't have a phone in the flat and none of us had her parents' number to get a message to her. She was looking at a news bulletin on the TV and a van was smashed up in an **RTA** on the M6. It was the same colour as ours and Angel was assuming the worst. After finally unloading the van at about 10pm, I said goodbye to the newlyweds and began my trek home on the A423 -which back then was a much smaller and less used road up towards **Daventry** (22 miles away). I thought it was very strange that I didn't see any one until it dawned on me that I was driving through a tunnel of snow. You could only just about see the tops of the trees. So, I get to the end of this white tube, only to find that the road is blocked by police.

'Where have you come from sir?' the officer asks me.

'Banbury,' I say.

'BANBURY!' he shouts, 'this road's been closed for the last two hours.'

They hadn't thought about the housing estates on the outskirts of Banbury. No fool would even want to attempt to drive through all this, except me! I eventually got back to Angel's flat at 4am, to be welcomed by a slap across the face and a:

'I THOUGHT YOU WERE DEAD!!!' With a 'so relieved you're safe' hug.

Looks can be deceiving

Second recollection was when I was riding my bike from New Brighton over to Liverpool for a job interview. It is a beautiful day, and I only had my suit on rather than leathers which was stupid if I'd fallen off but that's how I was riding at the time. There's a road that runs down to the Mersey Tunnel I mentioned earlier. There's a long sweeping bend at the bottom of the road before it comes to the toll for the tunnel. I pull up at the traffic lights at the top of the hill. This young guy pulls up next to me on a **GT380 Suzuki** with his girlfriend on the back, both are wearing all the flash riding gear. He's stood upright as his bike seat sits level with the handlebars and has a top speed of 100mph. I'm riding my Yamaha XJ750 Seca, it sits lower in the frame and has a top speed of 127mph, but he's not taking that into account. He looks across and down at me with my suit on, assumes I'm an amateur, smiles and says to his girlfriend,

'Watch this!'

I know exactly what he's going to do. He didn't get a chance! I shot off down the hill, rising out of the seat for the bend. My wide kipper tie is stretched straight in the wind (all **Biggles** like), I fly round the left hander (I won't say how fast) and down to the toll. I pull my glove off with my teeth, scoup a 20p coin from my pocket and throw it into the toll collection bucket and cruise through the tunnel and out onto the dock road. I wait at the lights, which take ages to change, and he pulls up next to me. His girlfriend is in a fit of giggles and all wriggly while the would-be boy-racer is shouting, 'shut up!' to ease his embarrassment. The lights turn amber, and I say to him,

'Looks can be deceiving mate,' as I set off on green.

I've never seen him since, but hopefully he learnt a lesson that day. It wasn't a clever thing I did, but it annoyed me and still does that people look at someone, put two and two together and make five, but I proved the point. Enough said.

I haven't got many photos of around this time due to how things were, but I've been able to find a couple from The Snatchgrabbers MCC on Facebook. Thanks guys.

The Tap Eastham Rake on the Wirral.
I'm in the centre, standing with a pint in my hand.
The pub is still there and is still a great place
for bikers. Chris, Tina and Miff are all in this photo.

I think the Admiral in Rock Ferry around 1983.
I'm in the centre and have the usual bunny ears
sticking out of the top of my head.

Chapter 4

Never fall head over heels, for a Fairy!

Once Angel and I had split up, I didn't go off the rails. I had learnt my lesson and would never go there again. I ended up renting a room off the girlfriend of the bass player from DMTM (see below) who made the electrics for torpedoes for **Marconi Underwater Systems Ltd**. What a job! His girlfriend as nice as she was (without being horrible, and no pun intended), didn't know what a sink was or what cleaning products were. It used to take me a least a full day once a month to sort out the house, because no matter how hard I tried to keep my stuff tidy and hygienic (especially in the kitchen), she never cleaned up any of her mess. It got to the point where it was easier for me to eat out, because there were no dishes or cutlery in the house you could use. There were two cats who became my alarm clock each morning, not out of choice. They slept in the airing cupboard above my bed. It was warm and they could drink out of the cold-water tank above. All true believe me. Every morning at around 6.30am, the cats would jump down and land on my head or my chest to wake me up. The cat's food was prepared and presented in the same cutlery and dishes as we ate out of. This was another reason why I used to do housework.

There was a friend, who, in different circumstances, we would have got together. She had all the classic traits of a **Barbie Doll** – tall, blonde, slim and her dad had a **Rolls Royce**, she worked but didn't have to. She used to come around a few nights a week and we'd play **Backgammon** for money. These **Lambrusco** lubricated gaming sessions with her, were the only thing that kept me sane while I lived in that house. I eventually moved into a flat in Birkenhead with a load of girls from the bike club. They were happy having a guy around (a safety/handyman, if you will), and I was happy to live somewhere with girls who gave a shit about where they lived.

Work at Glaxo was still good but tiring. Peter (who had introduced me to the musical), was now my work colleague in the planning dept. He was a union rep too, who didn't believe in personal hygiene and spent as much time off sick as he did in work. It was very difficult to sack staff then, especially union reps. When he was in work, he created more problems than any that needed solving. At any given time, we used to look after approximately twenty million pounds worth of stock. During this early time of using computers, these machines would suggest the quantities of items to order based on what had been taken out the previous day. One of our tasks was to override these based on the actual available space we could see by floor walking through the warehouse; unnecessary cost versus quantity, prior to the fully automated systems we have today. The system was called 'Just in Time'.

Peter's job was to look after packaging, but his attitude was to agree with the computer. For example, while he decided to be ill again, we received six truckloads of two litre glass bottles in one day; a quantity that would normally be delivered over a period of two months due to space! This type of slap-dash ordering was common for Peter.

I used to do fourteen-hour days four days a week (Friday was a half day) but it paid well. I was still in debt though, due to the previous episode of trashing my life before I'd met Angel. I had stopped playing music for a while when I went AWOL but now returned to the guitar again. There are a few photos of me playing at The Admiral in Rock Ferry (below), and a few others exist somewhere of me in Angel's flat and dressed up at a fancy-dress party as a caveman, don't ask.

I'd sold the Aria (what a great guitar) when I was having money troubles, and only after sorting myself out with the help of Angel, I bought a Westone Thunder Active II. Also, an **Ovation** Acoustic, which (for any guitarists), was the model that had an aluminium neck. It plays fine but, when you want to re-fret it, you realise, you can't, as the frets are part of the moulded neck! A new recording studio was set up under New Brighton Station and I re-recorded two tracks there and a new song;

*Memories, **The Leaves*** and a track I'd written a few years earlier, called ***The Missing Link.*** The latter was all about aliens and how we are not from this world. I'd wanted to record it for ages and now was my chance. There was a guy called **Wando** who we all knew. I never knew his real name (I vaguely recollect Martin but that's it). After Brendan from the *Children's Crusade,* Wando was the most talented person I knew. He had a three-piece band that used to do original stuff, similar to **Rush** with bass pedals and the like. The drummer ended up playing for a band called **Tokyo** after playing drums for DMTM.

Wando had perfect pitch, you could fart, and he'd say, 'B flat' (and he was right!). He came down to my sessions at the studio and was a great help putting some new idea's forward for the arrangements. I still have the recordings of these tracks. I re-recorded *Missing Link* in 2013 for my album *Songs to the World,* but I kept a lot of the structure we'd used some 30 years before. Last time I saw or heard of Wando was late 1980's. He was working in London, writing the scores of pop music for the song sheets you used to buy. I'm sure he was happy, but he had so much more to give to the music world. Maybe he did at some stage. I don't know if that ever happened.

The Admiral circa 1983'ish. The Gibson I borrowed.

In 1984, I joined another band on the Wirral called DMTM. Don't even ask me what it meant, something like 'Demon Mega Thrash Metal', which wasn't what we actually played. We just played good rock. On reflection, let's just say, the name was nearly as bad as the name Fat Elsie. I'm sure **Cammo** (The vocalist who formed the band) will have something to say about that but I'm sure we could have thought up a better name.

We played quite a few gigs in the northwest mainly at bike rallies and biker venues including The Admiral in Rock Ferry and **Stairways Night Club** (on Oliver Street East, Birkenhead). This is when the second time of playing pissed occurred. The band had a gig just before Christmas 1984 at The Admiral. Unfortunately, Glaxo had their Christmas party at the social club in Speke on the same day. The factory shut early on a Friday and as I had promised to sing at the party, dressed as **Boy George** (don't ask!) doing *Karma Chameleon*, the plan was to do that, then get a taxi over to the Wirral for the band. In between each show I drank half a bowl of punch!

After being picked up by the taxi, still dressed as you know who, but carrying a briefcase, the punch took effect on the 45-minute journey. By the time I arrived at The Admiral the band had a guitarist pissed out of his head, dressed as Boy George. We did the gig and apparently it went fine, but I don't remember a thing. I will say, that to this day I can't stand listening to *Karma Chameleon*. Unfortunately, but I'm sure it would be hilarious, I do not have a photo of me dressed as Boy George.

On reflection DMTM (and myself) had delusions of grandeur. We were a good pub rock band, but we were never going to make it big. Ron (who ran The Admiral at the time) stumped up £1000 for the band to record a single *Fighting for Air* and press 1000 records which apparently you can still find on YouTube in its dark depths. I still have a copy of the Vinyl. I think it's a great song. We recorded it at a studio in Cheshire that the guitarist from the **Black Abbots** owned. Now he was a character, I think he had a few personal problems, but he didn't give a shit. His line was 'Give 'em the bells of Shannon', which I believe, translates to 'give them everything you've got'. A bit like the sketch on YouTube these days but with more cowbell than the bells of Shannon!

We turned up on the Sunday morning to do the mix down and we could hear music coming out of the studio. This was odd as the place was a fully soundproofed building, the control room was inside another soundproofed room. The owner of the studio was in the control room, two empty bottles of whiskey and the music on, that loud you could hear it outside. He just got up, left us all to it, as we had an engineer (bass player from Strife) and a producer who was shit and on £100 a fucking day for sitting in there and now and then saying something. He was something to do with **Brookside** on **Channel 4** and had the same name as a famous DJ on **BBC Radio 2** in the afternoon who has since passed away. But that's as far as any similarity goes.

Around the same time, redundancies had been announced at Glaxo and Ron offered me the job of running The Admiral for a while. I'd been the DJ for the discos on a Sunday afternoon there, in what must have been the first kids' play garden in the country. I was also the unofficial "entertainment manager" for the pub. I saw this new full-time position as a way of paying off the rest of my debts with the sum offered in Glaxo's voluntary redundancy package. I grabbed it with both hands. I ran the pub for a year, and at the same time, I set up a couple of mobile disco systems and had a couple of guys working for me. All seemed good, until the fairy came into my life.

I'm onto an A road off the M4 as during this time, a few experiences while running the pub stick in my mind for completely different reasons.

Spooky goings on

All the staff and punters knew we had a ghost of some sort in the pub. I heard them tell how they had seen her/him coming up the cellar stairs before I heard footsteps on the stairs to my bedroom. I was living in the pub on my own with **Elsa** (an Alsatian), and when she took to hiding under the bed, I began to start to worry. When I walked through the bar, whiskey glasses used to shoot off the shelves and break on the floor, always breaking just at the top of the stem never anywhere else. That was not as frightening as you might think as I became accustomed to it! But it was what happened late on a Sunday afternoon that freaked me out.

I had closed up and Elsa and I were on our own. The chef always left me a meal to have after closing and I'd put the food in the kitchen microwave and was waiting for it to ping. Suddenly, a pile of plates that were washed and securely stacked at the other end of the room, flew up and smashed on the floor. There was absolutely no way they slid off or an unexpected earthquake had jerked them. I dashed to the bar and pumped the brandy optics for a glassful and downed it in one!

Whoops! Writing it off

I am not a clumsy person, but one day I dropped a gallon bottle of whiskey on the floor after tripping on the step into the bar. The wooden floor smelt great for weeks. Ron just wrote it off as breakages… a bloody gallon of whiskey!!!

Lead role in a porno movie

You read of this happening in adult magazines, but you never think it would happen to you – it's a fantasy, right? At this time, I was not seeing anyone; looking after the pub was a 24/7 occupation and left no time for a girlfriend and a 'something for the weekend, sir?' Furthermore, it was a condition of the insurance, that there always had to be someone on the premises, even when it was shut. Hence, any occasions I could get away and have some time for myself, were few and far between. However, Miff, used to stop with me at weekends sometimes, rather than riding back to Liverpool. I trusted Miff and knew, when he stayed, I could go off and do something on my own when the pub was closed to the public – back then the licensing laws restricted opening times more severely, than today.

There was an odd-looking couple who drank in the pub. He was in his mid-to-late fifties, and she was a lot younger – more of a girl than a woman, in her early twenties. I was used to people of the same age knocking about together, but, thirty years difference! Hey, what did I know, this was The Wirral and maybe things were different around here! So, as they were regulars, I engaged them with the customary 'hellos,' 'goodbyes' and general chit chat. I learnt not to ask too many questions to the customers (as you know). On a weekend that Miff stayed over, I can't recall if I mentioned this fact to them specifically, but the couple made a point of talking to me after I said I had time to go off somewhere. Later on, just as I shouted for 'last orders', they invited me back to their house for a drink.

I'm not sure what and how much I had drunk before, but soon enough, I am sat down in their living room with a large glass of wine. I noticed that one wall had curtains from the ceiling to the floor and stretched right across one side of the room. We were getting along fine, laughing and joking around when the bloke asked if I would like to watch a "sexy movie?" I was relaxed and curious, so I agreed, and the film was inserted in the video recorder. I sat there for a few minutes, thinking 'I'm sure I know that guy in the film.' I was right, it was one of the regulars from the pub, I couldn't believe it or recall exactly who though. Overcome with alcohol, I fell asleep only to be woken up by the girl, kneeling in front of me. My flies are down and she's…well, exercising her vocal cords on me!

'It's okay,' she said, 'he's in bed and doesn't mind.' So, BLOODY HELL I WENT FOR IT !!!!

Afterwards, exhausted, I discover that he wasn't in bed, he was behind the curtain in the same room as us, filming everything!

I awoke in the morning for her to take me upstairs expecting me to perform while the cleaner was hoovering the house. He had already left for work. I made my excuses and left.

I didn't see them in the pub again and was unsure what to make of what happened and shrugged it off. But, a few weeks later, I was telling what had happened to a guy in the pub who I had a lot in common with, who I trusted and, I had to tell someone. He listened intently and, when I finished, he took a long draw of his pint, put it down slowly. He paused and looked at me thoughtfully.

'Not you as well!' He declared in a relieved exhale, 'Ha! It happened to me too a few months ago!'

We both laughed loudly and wondered how many others they had gone through.

Disclaimer: anyone who recognises my look alike in a homemade porn movie circa mid 1980s – "…rumour control (those were) the facts!"

I Come from the Bog

We were at a rally in Leek, Staffordshire at a big stately home. There was an Irish guy who had ridden over from *The Bog*. He must have not been blessed with the 'luck' of his fellow countrymen. On the Friday, his bike broke down some 30 miles away from the rally camp site. He managed to hitch a lift but then pulled out a bottle of vodka and drank it all on the way, woke up the following day and couldn't remember where he'd left his bike. As if that wasn't bad enough, for an unknown reason, his tent burnt down on the Saturday. Consequently, as news of his misadventures circulated, he won the rally's 'Tale of Woe' plaque. To top all that, he ends up mislaying his trophy! He and his plaque could still be in Leek now as far as I know.

Black Russians and Unintentional Violence

People who know me, know that I'm quite a placid guy, I have a lot of patience and I've never been involved in too many fights luckily…so far! However, these were two exceptions around this time of my life. The first, I'll refer to as 'Prospect' for the Hells Angels.

At the same rally in Leek, a few of the Hells Angels were there, which was no big deal, but there was a prospect (who are the ones you have to worry about) trying to prove himself in order to join them. He kept picking on one of the most easy-going guys I knew, who would never lift a fist to anyone, no matter the provocation. I went over to the prospect several times saying, 'Come on mate. We're all having a good time. Leave him alone.' Eventually he got pissed off with me, grabbed my **Donkey Jacket** and hit me four times in the face. Each time I told him he was making a mistake. The fifth never contacted. I lost it and knocked him through two rooms.

'I told you not to hit me; next time I'll break your fuckin neck!' I calmly walked back into the bar with all my mates looking at me aghast. They'd never seen that side of me, and a lot of people never will. Looking back now, he was a big guy, but his mate, who came in behind him to see if he needed any help, blocked all the light out. I'm glad the prospect told him to piss off saying it was his problem, or it could have been a completely different story.

The second incident while I was running The Admiral. I had worked a six week stint and hadn't been out of the pub doors; bit like how it was during lockdown. Anything I needed was delivered; food, alcohol and cigs. The pub had everything I needed, as they did back then. Before the start of week seven, I decided to go out on a Saturday night. I wanted to get 'suited and booted' as they say (but not literally) and hit a night club. You know, those moments were you just need something different from what I would call my normal. I popped out Saturday afternoon, bought a suit, came back got changed, made sure all the staff in the pub were okay, Miff was stopping over again and off I went.

I had a couple of beers in one or two pubs and then went to **Atmosphere**, which was the local trendy club at the time in Birkenhead. I step up to the door.

'You can't come in mate, sorry, we're full!' ….FFS!

It was only ten o'clock. So, off I go to The Stairways nearby, which, for any of you who don't know, was one the best Rock Clubs I've ever been to. Three floors, but it only needed two doormen who were martial art experts; they didn't take any shit from anyone. These doormen deal with punters, who cause trouble, with a single punch, throwing them out onto the street with a few concealed digs as they went. In all fairness, there wasn't that much trouble in there this night. They laughed at my attire, which, fair dues, is totally out of place. I explained why I'm in smart threads, they laugh louder and, as Bikers look after their own, they take pity on me and let me in. I don't linger as these guys had a reputation (as did the owner) if you know what I mean. The owner was great, by the way, and his wife was stunning. She often worked behind the bar in the room on the third floor. This was more of a chill-out space for the jeans and leather clad revellers who needed a rest from the exhaustion of sweaty head banging sessions in the rooms below.

I climb to the top floor, and I have a drink with the owner's wife. **Black Russian** was my tipple at the time, and I knock back a few while sat at the bar minding my own business. Then three guys, who I've never seen before, swagger in and start taking the piss out of me wearing a suit. I shrug it off as fair game, light banter and ignore them; their pissed, I am too. One of them then takes it up a gear and keeps pushing the ante. I'm out for the first time in ages, enjoying good company and more than relaxed. I will say they started this first but I've no time for this, so fuck it! I decide I've had enough. After they start on me, a series of my fists land sweetly, one of the trio has a grip on my lapels and the other two warp themselves around me and push me to the exit of the third floor. We all end up falling down the stairs while I'm punching the seven bells of hell out of them as we fall to the next floor.

The doormen use their shovel sized fists to hold all four of us up on our tip toes. I tell them what happened, and the knob heads get thrown out. The thing about this whole incident is I had no recollection about it. I had woken up in the morning and couldn't move. I had bruises all over my body, as a result of bouncing down the stairs and taking patches of plaster out of the wall on the way, no doubt. It was only one of my mates, who had seen it all, who came into the pub on the Sunday to see how I was who told me. If he hadn't explained I would never have known. I guess that's the effects of far too many Black Russians mixed with adrenaline, which I didn't bother doing again, the suit that is!

Emerging from the wreckage

And finally. Today it has become more acceptable to talk more openly about traumatic events that have happen to us or ones we have been witness to. That was not something I did back then. Life was tough and anything that knocked me down made me get up, shrug it off and get on with my life. Dwelling on what upset me and being depressed were not part of my DNA. However, something so sorrowful, that I still remember to this day, affected me more than I actually realised at this time.

It started as a normal working day at the pub. It was a bright sunny morning, and I let Elsa out the back. As I sorted the bar before opening, there's a knock on the main doors. I open them and a rosy cheeked bloke, with a cheery face, is holding a jerry can.

'I've broken down on the by-pass in my wagon. One of the core plugs has gone on the engine and I've lost all my water. Can I get a top up and use the phone to get a mechanic out?'

'Not a problem mate.' I invite him inside and point towards the public phone at the far end by the toilets.

'Do you want a cup of tea?' I'm happy to have some company, take his preferences and, remembering that section of road, I add, 'oh, it might be worth phoning the Police as well, to get them to bring some cones to put out as there's no hard shoulder on that part of the by-pass, some daft git will crash into your truck otherwise.'

He nods and is soon talking to the mechanic and the Police. While I'm sorting some glasses, he thanks me for the brew and tells me he drives a flat back and is on his way to pick up a load. So, its empty, apart from the standard heavy wooden blocks or 'chocks', needed to wedge under the tyres. Most HGVs carried them back then to use when parked up for anything longer than a short stop. It is an extra precaution to the brakes. Then, as if remembering something, he takes a gulp from his mug and says,

'I'll be back in a mo, I'm just popping back to tip the cab up and chock the wheels.'

Tipping the cab, is standard practice so other drivers can see he's broken down and awaiting a repair, I carry on gathering up empty bottles. A few minutes pass and I take them outside to the bins and check on Elsa. Seconds later, there's this god almighty sound like a bomb explosion from the direction of the by-pass. I shove Elsa back inside and run out to the gap in the fence where the driver had come through. I start to run as I see the front end of a Mini rammed under the back of the wagon. 'SHIT!' Is all that races through my mind. I reach the Mini and the driver is slumped backwards in the seat with the back end of the long vehicle lodged just above the steering wheel. Tyre marks behind are short but very dark, indicating that the brakes were applied very late, and the impact has pushed the wagon forward and over the front wood chocks. The driver's door window is smashed. I reached in.

'Are you ok mate?' I say, as I place a hand on his shoulder.

His head drops forward, revealing the whole of the back of his head. It's been sliced off. It must have happened as he lurched forward, and made a downward, nodding, collision with the metal back edge of the truck. I assume he's dead and turn my attention to the wagon driver as I can't see him. He must have sensed my presence as he appears from the left-hand side of the truck. We stare at each other from opposite sides of the crumpled wreckage. His face drains white as he takes in the scene.

'I was just on my way to chock the back wheels when he hit …. Oh my good god!….what if I had done the back ones first!'

He has his hands on the top of his head, I step back, and we both take in the severity of the situation. He was one hell of a lucky man. We are both dazed and I'm thinking; 'what if I'd gone to help him and we were both at the back of his vehicle at the moment of impact!'

The Police turn up and we tell them what happened. In time, the coroner's inquest concluded that it was no one's fault. The Mini driver was only twenty-eight years old, with a wife and three kids. I thought he hadn't seen the truck, dazzled by the bright sun shining in his eyes, as the Rock Ferry by-pass could be like that on such days. However, the Autopsy revealed he'd had a heart attack immediately before he ploughed into the rear of the wagon. I cannot wipe out the image of the back of that bloodied head – a jellied mass of hair, bone and brains. Occasionally, I wonder how the lives of his partner and their kids turned out.

Those two drivers were strangers who passed through a very small fragment on the path of my life. But what a life changing event occurred for all three of us in perhaps fifteen minutes! I'm sure you are aware, so many things go on in other people's lives that you read in the papers or watch on the telly, then put it down, switch over and carry on. In this case, another statistic of an RTA! In hindsight, maybe I should have organised a fundraiser or something but, in those days, things like that didn't happen as much as they do now. I do understand the "gallows" humour that paramedics, police and first responders have to an RTA. I guess, in the 2020's it is part of training: 'How to put those images to one side and carry on' with what we know as the PTSD today. But those professionals in the 1970's and 1980's had their own coping strategies and, a dark sense of self-deprecation, bordering on the macabre, was one of them (and probably still is) and perhaps I include myself in that too.

***

Coming onto the M25 and that Fairy

I was invited to a party while I was running the pub. I was minding my own business when **Maz,** a good friend of mine, introduced me to this beautiful woman, dressed as a Fairy. Her name was **Sharron**, and she started chatting to me and that was it! She became my future wife, but with a twist. The curse had struck again. We'd been seeing each other for about seven months. She had a baby girl, **Rebecca** from another guy before I met her.

An aside: the guy next door to Sharron, had a business that made chocolate dildos. He had one in a box on a window ledge in his house (as you do!) and he told me that he had a factory in London. The fact he lived 240 miles away was a bit strange, however I think he was a drug dealer too. All a bit odd but another of a lot of tell-tale signs, I didn't heed!

Another Aside: while I was running the pub, I received a Valentines card from someone. There were a lot of clues about lances, sheaths and innuendos, and it was pretty obvious that the card was from one of the Nurses who drank at the Admiral. Two or three other cards came from those girls I had shared a flat with before I took over the pub and all were drop dead gorgeous: rode motorbikes and were single at the time of the cards. I never found out which of them sent me the cards and, again, if I had spent more time trying to solve the cases, I may have gone down a completely different route through life. I didn't and ended up meeting the Fairy.

By this time, I had left the pub and was now working as a Production Planner for Evans Medical in **Horsham** in Sussex. A management buyout by five senior managers at Glaxo had bought the Evans part of the business and I'd been asked if I would be interested in coming to work for them. I took the job and travelled down on Sunday evenings coming back to Merseyside on Fridays. I suggested to Sharron, that we got married and move down there. A new start, a new life, what could go wrong?...... Everything, that's what could go wrong!

We had the big white wedding that her mother insisted on, all the trimmings and I thought I was going to be happy. Maybe, after all the shit that had happened over the years, had brought me to a moment when

I had finally found a normal relationship. How wrong I was.

The day after the wedding, we drove down to Sussex. Soon, bought a house in a small village called **Upper Beeding** on the **South Downs**, with help from my Mum and Dad, who paid most of the deposit. I can't remember exactly, when she told me that she had only married me because I'd make a good father for her daughter, but when you are told that, what do you say? I was dumbfounded, another situation when, 'SHIT!' was an understatement. Her daughter and I had a great bond while my wife just watched TV all the time. She did, eventually, get a job at Evans Medical for a while, but only because I told her that costs in running the house were rising. One income wasn't enough, which is about the norm for everyone these days. She became a forklift truck driver working for Quality Control which amazed me, but it still didn't help, what had been said, six months before, which (as far as I knew), was still true.

It was all happening during 1987, the year of the famous hurricane which hit the south coast of England in the autumn (another omen of doom?) I woke up in the middle of the night to a house with no power. I looked out of our window to see if the neighbours were affected too, and one of those circular clothes lines in the garden, was spinning so fast that by morning it had snapped in two.

Evans Medical had millions of measles vaccines in refrigerated containers. My immediate concern was, if the electricity had gone there, we would have major problems. I headed into work and try to see how we could get power to the containers. I took four or five different routes. Not a chance. Trees down everywhere. I even drove as far as **Worthing** to go up the A24. There were boats parked on the promenade. I've never seen anything like it, or since. I eventually got to the factory flat out tired and was greeted by the Chief Engineer.

'The Measles Vaccines are okay?' He said.

He had arrived just in time and sorted a generator out for the fridges. We were all relieved.

When you've seen a forest with a band of trees about 100m wide that look like they've been flattened by a 100m wide tank that's created a tunnel, miles long, you realise just how powerful Mother Nature is. The tunnel went straight across the road I was driving down a few days after the storm on the way to Crawley. I had to stop and get out of the car. I really wish I'd taken a photo of it. I have scanned the web to try and find something similar, however if you google 'Storm of 1987' there's thousands of pictures.

As for the house, that was fine no damage, but I lost all the tropical fish as we didn't have any power for two days.

Then, one day out of the blue, Sharron declares:

'I just want you to be earning £40k a year and have a six pack!'

'What did you marry me for then?'

Oh! I remember now! So, after about nine months of "married bliss", she said to me that she had fallen in love with me now and everything was okay. What the Fuck!

'No, it's not!' I said.

After a few awkward weeks, Sharron said she wished she could go back up north, and, after a couple of days contemplating this mess, I said that the move would be best. Straight after I said it, she phoned her parents telling them that I wanted a divorce and that it was all my fault!

Looking back now, I do have fond memories of Rebecca and myself. She was a great kid. While I was trying to find out the date of birth of my ex-wife for the visa application, I actually found out where Rebecca was living (and in her late thirties early forties). I thought about contacting her just to say hello but thought better of it. Sharron most probably never told her about me, and, perhaps, she would have been too young to remember.

As a final end to all of that "fairy" business, I was told that she married a Canadian Film Director and lives in Italy. Hey, whoever you are, if you ever read this, 'I hope you earn more than £40k and have a six pack, or you're stuffed mate!' I thought at the time.

Rebecca & myself 1985.

A Forest after the Hurricane of 1987.

CHAPTER 5

Life after Marriage, Cement & its consequences

I can honestly say, even though Angel had helped me get back on track, if I hadn't gone through the ordeal with Dawn four or five years before when I went off the rails, I most probably would have gone off the same way after this. That is because, although splitting with Sharron wasn't a problem, losing Rebecca was. I have left Rebecca's name in this book because if she does recognise me from many years ago, then she has the choice if she wants to get in touch as no one knows her surname. She was just like my own daughter, and I still think of her today. Don't get me wrong, I have two wonderful grown-up kids who I love and wouldn't swap for the world, but I suppose when you're living with someone, their siblings become part of you, and you grow close to them and treat them as your own children. At the time, I was heartbroken losing Rebecca. Musically, I only picked the guitar up to play to Rebecca, and I didn't play the guitar for a while after they went back to Liverpool.

Moving on, I ended up having an affair with a wonderful lady who I'll call 'Lady'. I won't say who she is, or reveal her personal details because, certain people (who would cause upset) could put two and two together and, as far as I know, they are still alive at the moment *(March 2025)*. At the time, Lady told me if I needed to confide in anyone, she was there for me. She had a shit marriage too, and even though they'd only been married for a few years, she said she'd loved me ever since she met me. We clicked and spent many months together. But I did something really stupid, trying to keep our affair secret from friends and it all went wrong.

I was chatted up by a Scottish woman who worked with her, who suspected something. She knew I wasn't seeing or living with anyone and wanted to know why I wouldn't go home with her after a party. So, in a moment of weakness one night, I went to her home. I was thinking, I'll just sit down on the couch have a chat with her and then go home and she won't be any the wiser. This Scottish woman was very forceful, that's all I'll say! I regret that decision, because it got back to Lady and it hurt her, so much so, that she refused to see me. Not long after, talking with a common friend of ours, I discovered that she was in hospital with an Ectopic Pregnancy and, despite my request to see her, was told that she would never speak to me again. A complete error of judgement and stupidity on my part that I have regretted for the rest of my life. I hope she sorted it out with her husband. That hurt me for a long time and still comes back to haunt me even now. I still often wonder what would have happened if we had got together properly, but there I go again, fate takes us down a different route, or maybe the path that you're supposed to travel, and maybe she was pregnant because of our time together, and it wasn't supposed to be.

The public are like sheep

While all this was going on, I was having to sell the house Sharron and I had bought, to be able to give Sharron half of the money as part of the divorce settlement, (that's another turd in the tale that won't come out here). Once it sold, I bought a flat in the same village and, not long afterwards, a motorbike (**Honda CB750F2**) as I was poached for a job at a *Packaging Company* in New Kings Road, London (not far from **Putney Bridge**). I won't name them, as I don't want any lawsuits against me. The bike allowed me to commute to my new job. Even in 1987/88 the traffic up the A24/M25 and down into London was horrendous, hence, the bike allowed me to scoot through the jams and tailbacks. However, as an Account Executive for this company, I was supposed to come to work in my car to be able to go out with clients for lunch on most days.

On the bike it was fine, and, if I left home at 6.30am in the car, I'd be in work for 8am. However, if I left fifteen minutes later in the car, I wouldn't get to work until about 9.30am that's how bad the traffic was. Most of the time I had to go in the car. Driving for four hours a day if you included the drive home was always shit. I don't have a problem driving for a living, trucks, bikes, vans are not a problem but just to be sat in traffic jams – no way!

The public are like sheep. One morning I was driving down from the Robin Hood roundabout and shot down the bus lane as I was late. A Traffic Copper was in one of the side streets pulling drivers in, doing exactly what I was doing. I got flagged into the street along with another two cars behind me. The drivers in the other cars started blaming me for getting the 25 quid fine that we each had imposed on us. How stupid is that!

'Are you just sheep or something?' I said and was considering hitting them both for one of the lamest accusations I'd ever heard at the time. I'm a placid person normally and for me to think about punching anyone just because they're thick and can't think for themselves got me thinking. It's called 'road rage' and I understand why!

That job lasted six weeks and I left mainly due to what happened to one of the client's as well as the way the journey to work was affecting me mentally. The company kept pushing one of my client's orders back in the scheduling. He eventually, lost his contract with his clients, because we hadn't supplied the goods he needed in time. My client had paid for the goods up front, and I was put in the awkward position of trying to make excuses for the delay. In short, my arse hole of a boss was pushing his order back to keep the bigger fish happy by diverting supplies from smaller clients. I decided to stop lying for him, so, while the arse hole was on holiday, I handed in my notice and left.

Speeding off on a tangent and over a roundabout!

My CB750F2 Honda and I, will always remember what happened one sunny Sunday afternoon. I had just ridden to Worthing, to drop off my contract at the Solicitors for the flat I was buying. I was staying at friends in Horsham at the time as the ex-matrimonial home had been sold. I pulled up on the A24 at the **Cowfold** traffic lights. It's a dual carriageway, and I weaved my way through the stationary traffic to the front and pulled up next to a top of the range **Honda Civic CRX**. The driver was wearing shades his lady friend was in the passenger seat. As I have said earlier,

I'm not one for racing, but as we set off at the lights the guy just cut me up, so I let the bike rip! There was no traffic in front of me and only two roundabouts before I got to Horsham. I cannot tell you how fast I was going but let's just say you couldn't see anyone behind me.

The second roundabout had roadworks due to the construction of an underpass. Open road is one thing on a bike, but I always adhere to speed limits in road works and built-up areas. So, I come into the road works doing 30mph, over the roundabout and down the other side. That's when an unmarked Rover V8 Police car comes up next to me in the outside lane, with two uniformed officers inside. They gesture for me to pull over, which I do. As I am carrying out the manoeuvre, the CRX comes screaming up behind, flashing his lights and gesturing the Rover to get out of the way, only to see a little sign pop up in the back displaying: "POLICE PULL OVER."

While desperately braking hard, I caught sight of his face: it was a picture! Eventually, he pulled over and halted about 50yrds down from where I was, and both of the officers get out of their car. A female officer walked back to me, while I watch the male officer give the CRX driver a loud rebuke for the offences he's guilty of. My conversation with the female officer went a bit like this.

'Sir, do you know what speed you were doing up the dual carriageway?'

'I have to admit officer, I may have been doing around 90mph?'

'I think you were going a little faster than that as it's taken us eight miles to catch up with you, it looked like you were racing?'

'I'm really sorry Officer, I wasn't racing, it was an empty road, and I let it go, but (nodding to CRX driver) he's a nutter!'

'You came into the road works and adhered to the speed limits, so I'm just giving you a verbal warning.'

'Thank you very much, what's happening to him?'

'He's getting done for Dangerous Driving.'

I rode off after producing my documents. Apparently, they'd been sat in all the traffic at the Cowfold lights and saw everything. They passed the CRX chasing me, but he didn't even think it would be a Police car so raced it as well as chasing me.

Anyway, I'll go back to the story – October 1988

After four weeks of working in London I realise I've made a mistake. While sitting in the pub wondering what to do, my friend Shane came over and I explained my circumstances to him. He offered a solution.

'Why don't you join us at the Cement Works. You can work on cars and bikes and stuff like that, maintenance fitting is just the same but with bigger machines. You'll be self-employed and earn a damn sight more money than what you're on now?'

Three weeks later, I'd left the London job, changed my suit for overalls, and started as a subcontractor at **Blue Circle Cement** in **Shoreham**. Travel time was about three miles from where I lived, and I did it for three and a half years. It was twelve-hour days, seven days a week for most of the time. Plenty of drinking at night, followed by an Indian meal, then back in at 7am. It was the hardest work I've ever done but I was earning a shed load of money. It also toughened me up mentally and physically, for what I would go through during the next 30 years. I learnt how to deal with a lot of awkward situations and how to cope with pain when injured which happened on a number of occasions. But, working with tough guys on equal terms, enabled me to forge some great friendships

For those who do not understand the process of making cement, I'll give you a quick summary before I tell you about three of the events that occurred during this time. Chalk is in flint stone which comes from the quarry to be smashed up in huge vats by a massive steel cog. Huge vertical arms attached to the spinning cog, pulls the flint around in the vat while it is washed by water to extract the chalk. This slurry is pumped into separate vats with clay in them and the two get mixed. They are pumped up to the Press House, which in turn forces the slurry into a huge hydraulic press which squeezes the excess fluid out, to be channelled back to The Well to be recycled. What comes out of the Press House is called Cake (clay and chalk). The Cake is moved on conveyor belts to the top of a 300ft long cylindrical Kiln (imagine a 300ft chimney on its side) which is turning and at an angle. The Cake, broken by chains at the top end of the Kiln, rolls down the cylinder while being gradually heated up to 2000°C at the bottom far end. It is now referred to as Clinker and it rolls out, cools down and carried along to be dropped into grinding mills. These contain about 38 tonnes of ball bearings. Various chemicals, such as lime and polysorbates are added. The mills spin and grind the mixture into cement. A very simple process but its engineering at its heaviest. It may have changed in the last 30 years but that's how it had been made at that site since 1947 when it opened.

The Kilns we had to maintain.

That's all you need to know to understand:-

Drowning

Up to this incident, I could only imagine what it would be like to drown (perhaps you are the same?) Messing about in the public baths as you learn to swim, may have resulted in moments of panic and a few mouthfuls of water as you splash about with the rudiments of the crawl or breaststroke? Soon you master them and try to dive deeper. You push the limit of how long you can hold your breath for and, maybe, time yourself at home during a bath? But, as you push to the limit, at the very last second, you pull up and gulp in a lungful of air: hold that thought!

One day at work, one of the contractors and myself had been sent to the Press House because one of the valves, that takes the water back down to the well, had broken down. The submersible pumps in the drains were working to their maximum to pump all the water out back down the hill. Due to this, most of the grills on top of the ten-foot sumps (that you normally walked on above the drains), had been lifted off so that the pumps could be placed in them. We sent the new valve up on the crane and headed up to the control room checking with the Blue Circle guys that anywhere that needs to be roped off was, and that it was safe to walk around downstairs. I was told, 'yes, it is safe' and I went back down to collect our tools because we couldn't get them up the small ladder we had climbed up to where the valve was.

Unbeknown to me, all the safety ropes had fallen into the murky water on the concrete floor, so they could not be seen. I walked around the conveyors as we'd been instructed to do a few days before, emphasising that, if we walked under the conveyors, we'd be booted off site. I obeyed the order and took the route around the conveyor and walked off the edge of one of the sumps. I fell straight down into ice cold, dirty water, feeling a rather large submersible pump trying to pull me down the ten feet to the bottom. As it was trying to pump the water out and I could hear the noise of the pump in the water, it was all very eerie. Ironically, if I'd gone under the conveyor, I would have been okay! But, when you are earning around 600 quid a week, if you get booted off site, you lose the whole lot! So, I stuck to the rules.

I don't know how I got out, especially with the injuries I sustained. All I remember is putting my hands out above me and feeling the concrete edge of the sump. Then I tried to haul myself out, fell back in and tried again. I was wearing steel toe cap wellies that are full of water and the water is also absorbed into my tough overalls. Beneath this (luckily, perhaps?) I only had shorts on as it was summer. The next thing I remember is lying in the water on the concrete floor and feeling that my legs were sore. I got up and slowly climbed the stairs to the control room where all the guys shout out, 'Hey, Scouse fell in the water!'

They soon came to realise that not all was right. I took off my wellies and rolled up my overalls to reveal a two-inch hole on my shin and the bone was visible. I'd sliced my leg, through the thick rubber of the wellies, when I collided with one of the steel uprights that normally support the grills that you walk on. I reckon that, if I hadn't had the wellies on, I would have broken my leg and would have never got out. I think the water was so cold that it may have stopped my leg from bleeding too much. Unbeknown to me, it let a few things into my blood at the same time. Fair swap I suppose.

Anyway, the first aider was radioed, and he came in, took one look at the shin bone and fainted! WTF!! I don't think I helped moving the skin on my leg and saying, 'look you can see my bone!' I think I was in shock. I was taken to hospital, had Hydrogen Peroxide put in the hole to kill any bacteria. The doctor had to give me internal stitches while I watched after injecting anaesthetic into the bruising first, which hurt more than the stitches I can tell you. I also had a bruise on my left leg from my knee right up to my hip where I'd slid down the wall of the sump. I still have the scars to prove it. Added to this, the hospital forgot to give me antibiotics, not realising how contaminated the water was that I'd fallen into. I got diagnosed with blood poisoning from the water a couple of days later. Blood poisoning, Ah! I wouldn't wish it on my worst enemy! I woke up, had to slide out of bed and drag myself along the floor to get to the phone to call the district nurse. I was that bad, I was visited daily for the next five days to have them check-up on me. I was off work for about a month or so, and then back to it.

Burns and the Grinding Mills

In the cement process, there are hundreds of thousands of ball bearings grinding up the Clinker. As you can imagine, both the bearings and the special alloy plates (that are bolted to the inside of the mill shell), wear down over time and need replacing. Some bearings end up wedging themselves in between the plates – we refer to them as 'pebbles'. Before you can replace the plates, you have to get the wedged pebbles out. The only way to do this is to use special welding rods to burn them out. These are white hot, and you pop them out of the gap with a crowbar if they do not drop out by themselves. So, to carry out this on one occasion, myself, and a recently taken on apprentice for Blue Circle, climb inside the mill. There is not a lot of room in there (see photo below). One of the pebbles is taking ages to shift. The apprentice stands as tall as he can to allow for maximum leverage on the crowbar. I'm crouched as far away as possible, and suddenly the molten pebble shoots across to me and lands on the outside of the top of my right leg. I immediately bolt upright but, it burns through my overalls, the tracksuit bottoms underneath, down my lower leg and burns a hole out of the side of my boot. The lad's horrified. I say to him let's get the job done and then I'll go and get it checked out. That's what you did in those days. You just got on with the task in hand and worry about yourself once the equipment was back up and running.

When I got back to the workshop, I was sent to hospital. I had third degree burns, was given a Tetanus shot and I returned to work. I hope that incident didn't scar the apprentice, mentally, for life, as it did me physically!

This is a picture of one of the grinding mills with 38tons of ball bearings in. We used to climb in through a small hatch to work inside. They were approximately10ft/3metres wide but with a third of the cylinder full of ball bearings- there wasn't a lot of room!

Wind and working on Towers

There was a conveyor that went across the main road from the Cement Works to the packing plant that took the freshly made cement to get packed. The Conveyer sat on two towers, one on each side of the road. There were a few, corrugated asbestos panels on the side of the towers that had come loose in the winds. They'd possibly been like that since the hurricane eighteen months before.

Shane and I had been asked to take them down and replace them. This could be done off the steel staircase, which was inside the tower frame, but you still had to hang over the side, with no harness mind, this was the late 1980's and working practices were like that then. With my legs wrapped around the handrails and sat on top of it, I had hold of one of the panels. Shane was undoing the bolts only to find the last one was a different size of nut and we only had a handful of tools with us.

'Are you okay to keep hold of the panel and I'll just nip down and get the right socket?' He says. 'Yeah, no problem.' say I, and off he goes.

Moments later, a gust of wind blows fine fragments of dust into my eyes, I blink but I can't see. I can't rub my eyes as I'm holding onto this panel with my legs wrapped around the handrail of the staircase 40 or 50 feet up in the air. I'm totally blind and start to panic. It might have only been a matter of minutes before Shane returned, but it felt like a lifetime to me. Once we've got the panel off (yes, we couldn't leave it like that), I clung to it until it was secured. Unable to see anything, he guided me back down. I was driven to hospital with scratches to my eyeballs from the asbestos dust.

Conclusion: for the Health & Safety brigade!

Although some people in the 'H&S World' would say, 'they were all stupid and preventable accidents' and maybe, in this day and age, they are. But at that time, we were contracted to do all the jobs the unions wouldn't let the Blue Circle employees do because they were deemed 'too dangerous'. And, if you didn't want to do them, there were plenty queuing up to take your place and grab the money. The saying in the 'Contractor World' is: 'JUST DO IT'. I can expect that still lives on today in some form or other. Now, on reflection, they were a tough bunch of men, and working with them, gave me some hard life-affirming lessons that I will carry to my grave. Yes, (to quote Elvis Costello) 'accidents will happen', and there were guys who weren't as fortunate as me. Some, through no fault of their own, either died (only one on the Dunbar site) or equipment broke, and they ended up in hospital for a long time. I've seen some extremely dangerous shit, but to put it bluntly, after the family man in the car under the wagon accident, the rest was a piece of piss. Saying that, there were more funny stories than sad ones, and I could write a whole book on those few years I spent there. However, I will tell you a few, two of which, are the ultimate windups.

Windup One – Where's Neville?

Two guys (Ted and Paul) and I are on 21day, twelve-hour night shifts during the required, so called, shutdown, which was to allow for maintenance to be done. Everything on site is in duplicate so, when all the equipment from one of the Kilns is stopped for shutdown, the other Kiln keeps running so the workloads are running to schedule.

We're sat in the pub one afternoon, a few days into the first week, and our conversation turned to the careers lessons we had at school. Paul says he watched a film about a typical school lad on work experience. Each week he would go and do a different job. I said to Paul 'what was his name?' He said, 'Neville Sponge.' Ted and I burst out laughing and I say, 'so, you've got a schoolboy in an educational film called Neville Sponge? Well, it's not a typical schoolboy name on Merseyside or maybe it is around your area?' Paul saw the funny side and Ted then recalled when he worked on the oil pipelines, in the 1970's. One of the guys had been sacked but he didn't hand back his worktime in/out punch card – he gave it to one of his mates. For anyone who doesn't know what a **punch card** is, it was a card with your name on that used to get issued every week and you inserted it into a machine with a clock on the front that would stamp or punch your time onto the card when you arrived and left work. The wages clerk would check the cards every week, so they knew how much to pay you. This is where the phrase, 'Clocking in and out,' came from.

Back to the story. Because the pipeline was so long from one end to the other, the supervisors carried on paying his wage up to the end of the contract. His work mates took it in turns to keep clocking him in/out, collecting his (cash) pay packet every week and used it to subsidise their beer money!

So, (in the word of **Spandau Ballet**) 'to cut a long story short', we decide to invent the ultimate contractor on the Blue Circle site called Neville Sponge. We 'obtained' a clock card for him, a hard hat with his name on it, tools with his initials stamped on them…you know the script. We'd clock him in as we left to go home in the morning and clock him out as we arrived in the evening. Through the night, we'd leave tell-tale signs of him working on various sections that required a different skill set for each one – an adjustable spanner here an electrical screwdriver there. Only a few of us knew what was going on – which is key to such a ploy. So, most of the vast number of contractors on site (because of the shutdown), didn't have a clue and thought Neville Sponge was the ultimate contractor and could do anything. A bit like, a real-life **Bob the Builder** except Neville was as fictitious as Bob is. But, saying that, Bob is more real than Neville because there is a picture/cartoon of him!

People would come up to us and ask, 'where's Neville?' and we'd come up with some plausible reason where he was (or wasn't). Bearing in mind this went on for two weeks, and these were the same sort of idiots who read (and believed?) the **Daily Sport** headlines, like a 'Second World War Bomber plane on the moon and a London double-decker bus buried at the South Pole!' WTF! The next shut down came around and one of the contractors who had been working on the last shutdown said to me 'Is Neville Here?' I said, 'No not this time.' He took off his hat and slammed it onto the floor, shouting, "Fucking Hell! I really wanted to meet that guy." Say no more.

Windup two: Arthur Dent's Embarrassing Moment

I was told that there was a Pyjama Party going on in the local pub one night and all the contractors were going. I put on my dressing gown and slippers, I don't own pyjamas, so wore very little underneath. I took a taxi rather than freeze waiting for a bus as it was November time. When I arrived, I discovered it was fancy dress! I felt a bit of a cock but, hey, it's just a laugh. If the windup had already started, I was unaware. At the end of the night, we're set to go to the Indian in **Bramber**, that we frequented every night of the week, so that's not unusual. It is closing time, and someone says the phone is engaged. I 'volunteered' to go down first to book the tables and one of the bar staff is set up to take me there as she passes the Indian on her way home. Meanwhile, the dozen or so of our crowd left, await taxis. I enter the restaurant (still in my dressing gown and slippers) to make the reservation. The manager, Mr Noo (that was his real name) writes down the number of people on their way, while scratching his head with a perplexed expression. I explained that I was dressed up as Arthur Dent (from the **Hitchhiker's Guide to the Galaxy**), and everyone would be in fancy dress as well. I sat there for fifteen minutes, and Mr Noo is telling all the other customers that I'm not an escaped inmate from the local mental institution. Guess what…surprise, surprise…No one turned up! When the penny finally dropped, I ordered a full meal to console myself. But the joke kept on giving, it was a Sunday, and both the taxis and buses had stopped by the time I was ready to leave. I had to walk the mile home in the middle of a snow shower. That's Karma I suppose with the Neville incident.

I actually sent a version of this story to **Simon Mayo** when he was on Radio. During his programme he had a slot called **Embarrassing Moments** and it was read out.

And the other story – What's My Name?

When I worked at Blue Circle, I had enough money to run two cars: a **Ford Capri** and a **Ford Escort Mk2**. The Capri was on its last legs, so I part Ex'd it for a new van. I kept the Escort as the van was only on a lease purchase. One of the contractors (we'll call him Ian), was moving to the U.S.A. to marry the love of his life. He'd met her a few months before his contract started and didn't want to buy a car for the four months he had left and then have to try and sell it before he emigrated. He asks me, if I get the Escort MOT done and he insures and taxes it, can he use it for four months. He offers to give me 400 quid too, more than it's worth at the time. Well, that's a no brainer. I agree.

One Friday afternoon, he picks the car up to drive back to **Bristol** where he lives. The car is insured/MOT'd, he just needs to tax it on Saturday morning when he gets back home. He comes into work the following Monday and says,

'What's your real name?'

Everyone at Blue Circle and in Upper Beeding to be honest, used to call me Scouse, as I was the only Scouser in the Village! I did have some people think I was Scottish, Welsh, or Geordie, believe it or not?!!! Anyway, on his way home that Friday, Ian had been pulled up just outside

Bristol by the Police, because he had no tax disc. He explained what was happening and the Copper said,

'That's fine. What's the guy's name who owns the car?'

Ian says, 'It's Scouse. I don't know his proper name.'

I couldn't find the logbook, so he didn't have it with him, and in those days, you only needed to sign the forms at the post office to tax a car and put it in your name.

The copper takes a dim view,

'So, you've got a car off a guy who you work with near **Brighton**, who lives in Sussex called Scouse, but he is originally from Liverpool. He's lending you the car for four months and then you're giving it back to him as you're moving to the states to get married. But you don't know his real name even though you've worked with him for two years and you don't know his address either, except that he lives in Upper Beeding?'

Ian says, 'Yea that's right,' which it was.

'Just piss off!' replies the copper. I don't blame him really, that sounded like a lot of paperwork for something that was absolutely true.

I got the car back as expected, but Ian had met someone else over here and tried to break it off with the girl in the states. He was told that he would be marrying the lady in the states as she was the daughter of one of the **Mafia** and if he didn't marry her, he was told that bad things would happen to him. Fearing the worst, he went anyway and told no one where. This made some of my situations, seem quite mundane compared to that. 'Marry her or we'll kneecap you!' He said to me just before he scarpered into hiding. By the way,

"Non so dove sia andato e da allora non ho più avuto sue notizie."

[Italian for: I don't know where he went, and I've never heard from him since].

CHAPTER 6

More Music & Women

When my affair with Lady finished, I had a couple of girlfriends while I was still contracting at Blue Circle. I also started concentrating on playing music again, which came in handy because of what happened one night around the spring/summer of 1990.

It was a Sunday evening and twelve of us mainly Blue Circle Contractors were in **The Castle House** in Bramber and there was a singer using backing tracks which, at the time, was quite a new thing to the pub scene. **Cassettes** were used on this occasion, as **minidiscs** and **CDs** came later. Someone, who knew I played guitar and sang, asked the singer if he minded me getting up and doing a number on my own during the break in between his sets. He agreed and I chose one of the tracks he had (**Love on the Rocks** by **Neil Diamond**). I got up, sang it and it brought the house down! Someone else in the audience asked where I was playing next and that's when I started doing the pubs and clubs as a solo guitar/vocalist. I invested in a sound system, small recording studio and made my own backing tracks. I went on to make them for other people too, using an advertisement in *The Stage* magazine.

There was a recession in the early 1990's and Blue Circle was winding down in Shoreham. I started my music work on a semi-pro basis at first, while still doing basic contracting hours. Singing in the pubs and clubs at night, was normally Thursday to Sunday. Eventually, it became full time when I moved to performing six or seven nights a week. During this transition, a female friend of mine drank in **The Rising Sun**, in Upper Beeding. She was working for a window cleaner, and asked if I could help her start her own cleaning business, which we did for a while. I had the van and some ladders; she had the know-how. She was a single parent with a bastard of a father to her son, and so I helped her. That is all I will say but it's important I mention the window cleaning for when I moved to **Somerset** later on.

The Mirror Woman

When I was cleaning windows there was a house on my rounds. My friend who I worked with would never do it as it gave her the creeps. The view into the bedroom revealed that it was completely decorated with mirrors; on some of the walls, and all of the ceiling, you get the idea. When you went to collect the money, the woman was always in a negligee expecting "extras". Don't worry, I wasn't that desperate, but we called her the Mirror Woman.

Around this time, I met my long time, and very good friend, **Mike Still**. We formed a duo to perform in pubs and clubs. Mike also made one of the first commercial samplers and sold the design for a five-figure sum. Looking back now, I'm sure it wasn't as much as the firm who paid him made over the years. We did a track for **British Telecom** (*613 Express*) that would play in the background of the Top 40 countdown on the phone. The song used to get played in a couple of night clubs in Brighton at one stage too.

*I spoke to Mike in March 2025, and he's still an amazing guy. It was probably 30 odd years since we've seen each other but have talked on the phone and chatted as if it was only yesterday. He told me that the sampler he designed was one of the first Digital Sampler/Delay units. He sold a few units to various well-known musicians in the 80s (one was in **Ultravox***). Mike has always been very clever with electronics and still does a lot of work on the south coast for a member of Pink Floyd amongst other musicians. He also mentioned that he still had one of the original units in its rack mount case until recently when he used it for something else.*

Mike and myself in our duo days in Brighton.

Our duo did well for a while, and we wrote a tune for **Eurovision.** We recorded it in his studio in a shed at the bottom of his garden. Despite being a good song, it didn't get through to the later stages for selection, unfortunately. The BBC said that the lyrics to **Let the Music Last Forever**, that Brian Walker from **Poole**, had brought to us, were too political. Brian also brought us the lyrics of a song called *I am a Child* which we recorded using my melody line. It was about climate change and pollution. We sent it to Green Peace etc, but to no avail either!

On a Wednesday evenings I played guitar and piano at **The Star Inn** in **Steyning**, which was only about three miles from Upper Beeding and Bramber. I used to jam with a guy who used to be in **The Tornados** who had a UK and USA number one hit with 'Telstar' in the 60's. He spent six months of the year in **Australia** with his wife and the other half playing in the UK. He played guitar and was an amazing Harmonica player. Whenever he was about on a Wednesday night he'd come down and we'd play all sorts of stuff. I also got up with him and some of the band when they had gigs at another local pub in Steyning where the fancy dress windup started. I used to get up and sing ***Roadhouse Blues*** with them, a song which I still sing to this day as a jam with other musicians. Somewhere, there is a video of me singing it in **Romania** in 2019 with Bruce Katz (USA) on keyboards at an after-show party at the **Brasov Jazz and Blues Festival** after we'd both played the festival (more of that later).

Word got around about my performances in the local pubs and clubs I frequented who had me on as much as they could, and I got invited to play further away. I went into DJ'ing too, doing a package; a solo live spot and then I'd spin records for all sorts of functions. As well as this, I joined a band in Brighton, but we only did a couple of gigs as they wanted to focus on their original material rather than covers. However, I remember two things about the musicians. The drummer had moved from **Canada** to the UK but the band he left was **Alannah Myles's** just before she released *Black Velvet*. You could tell he was gutted! The other guitarist had learnt to play a right-handed guitar, left-handed and a semitone out so that the guitar was tuned to E flat instead of E. When I first started rehearsing with them, I was watching what he was playing to copy, and I couldn't understand why what I was playing, sounded shit and out of tune. He had an amazing sound which was so different to anything else I've ever heard to this day. He fell in love, left the band and, because no one could actually play like him, the band packed in. There was no way I was going to try and re-learn the guitar, playing it upside down and a semitone out. I did try and persuade him to carry on, but he wouldn't have it. I'd say he wasn't much older than me, when I turned down the Rock Musical audition at eighteen for the love of my life at the time!

I was successfully performing gigs all along the South Coast. I had an agent who got me most of them and this carried on until early 1992 when the whole recession had hit big time. Gradually, pubs and live music clubs/venues were not taking as many bookings, and I was struggling to pay my mortgage. When I was at Blue Circle, the repayments were only one week's wage, but now Blue Circle had shut down and I'd left to be a full-time musician, it was at least two weeks wages, and I was struggling to cover all the bills. I had to sell the flat it was the only way.

Heading North on the M25 to embrace the Zimmer Framers and other stories!

There are so many funny moments from this time in my life, mainly from playing music.

Miming my guitar

At a Pub I played in **Arundel**, a pissed-up bloke pulled the power on the PA because he thought I was miming the guitar. Ha! I had the guitar amp plugged in somewhere else and I carried on playing. He got thrown out.

In the same pub on the same night, a Policeman watched a pissed bloke get into his car and drive off. The copper was, in fact, waiting for me to finish loading my car up and drive off and then pull me over instead. His comment afterwards was, 'Well you're the singer, people buy you drinks.' I said, 'Yes they do, but I've been on Britvic Orange and lemonade all night and you've just watched a pissed bloke get in his car and drive home pal!'

Yes, I've been a stripper… well sort of….

Sat in my local pub **The Kings Head** in Upper Beeding one night. A friend in the pub comes up to me.

'You've got a Batman costume, haven't you?' (Yeah, I know, don't ask why I had one!).

'Yes, I have, why?'

'I booked a Stripper-o gram for my girlfriend's birthday; he hasn't turned up. Will you do it?

'So, you want me to go home, put my Batman outfit on, come back to the pub and strip for your girlfriend?'

'Yes.'

'Hmmm….'

'There's 40 quid in it for you?'

'I'll be Ten minutes!' I was actually 30 minutes.

And I was, with a ghetto blaster, dressed as Batman and did the full monty too! No, I can't remember what I actually did, and I don't know who was more embarrassed; me or the girlfriend. I sort of knew her from the pub but that was it! I got two more bookings from that, including one with the request that I dress as an Arab with a nappy underneath the robe. I'm not sure what all that was about and unfortunately (or lucky for me) there are no photos either unless something pops out (sorry for the pun) after this book has been published.

Miming Artists again

On another occasion, at one of the pubs I used to DJ at each week in **Hove**, there was a duo on in the concert room, but everyone was in the bar. They asked me to see what I thought of the act in the other room. There were two people watching them, three when I went in. The guitar-vocalist was miming! During the lead guitar parts his hands weren't moving correctly and his lips didn't sync up with the words: it was terrible. The only thing that was live was the Sax player who, I discovered later, wanted to go out gigging, but couldn't get gigs on his own, so he had got his mate to just stand there and mime! They lasted one set and got paid off. What's worrying is, I've seen full bands in theatres do that, to a packed audience too and they get away with it!

Yes, I became Black Adder for a night-

Being dressed up as Lord Black Adder 2, Cod Piece and all, for a fancy dress at a residency for **Butlins** staff I used to do every Monday night in Brighton. Yes, it did get messy, and I'll say no more, except that, for every request I played, someone bought me a Bacardi and Coke. I was there for twelve hours! I didn't drive home, just in case you were thinking!

I was the attraction for the night

A pub I played at in Brighton was a gay bar. I don't have a problem with that but, at the time, I couldn't understand (until the Landlord told me), why the audience were all blokes who were all coming up to the front of the stage and staring at me. It turned out to be a great gig, but (and I am sure I speak for all musicians, when I say) that, it would be good to know from which ever agent gets you the bookings, they let you know who your audience are likely to be before you get there. The main reason is to ensure you rehearse the appropriate set list and for what happened on another occasion.

The Zimmer Framers

I turned up at a hotel in **Hastings** for a big function for all the residents who were there from Christmas Eve through to the New Year. The conversation with the agent a few weeks before went like this. 'Phil, you'll have a great night. Although the management has changed from last year, they have most of their regulars staying again. Just do some of the older stuff like **Frank Sinatra**, and **Englebert Humperdinck**, it will be a great night.'

Bear in mind this is early 1990s so Frank and 'Dink have been around for the previous 35 years or so and are still popular with a certain age group. So, I arrived, set all the equipment up and waited for everyone to come into the room. No word of a lie, there wasn't one person under 70 and most were pushing their Zimmer Frames. Apparently, the rest of the residents who normally stayed had heard that the people running the hotel had changed and cancelled their booking. I only had a certain amount of fifties, sixties backing tracks. So, I ended playing 1940s wartime music on the tape decks and dancing with some of the residents, who could actually get up and do some form of dancing, even if it was with the help of the walking frame. A good time was had by all, and I got paid. Phew!

Sad stories too

A friend of mine, who was only in her twenties, died from an asthmatic attack. Her last request was for me to sing *Stairway to Heaven* at her funeral. The church wouldn't let me sing it at the service inside, so I sang it as they lowered her coffin into the grave. That is one of the hardest gigs I've had to do in my life.

Back on the A24 again

Apart from the music, to make ends meet, I did some courier work in and out of London for a company based in **Horsham**. I bought one of those massive mobile phones (second hand, I couldn't afford a new one), you know the ones that were the size of a brick. I rode motorbikes for them too. I think that was the first time I drove quite a big commercial vehicle: a 7.5t truck. I didn't have HGV licence at the time but could drive one of those that size on my standard car driving licence. I'm not sure why

I stopped working for them, but I've never forgotten how cumbersome those mobile phones were back then – how times have changed!

By the end of 1991, Blue Circle had shut down completely in Shoreham, the Bank of England interest rates went through the roof and a buyer for my flat fell through the day we were due to sign the contracts. I remember that night despite drinking a vast quantity of B52 Bombers (Tia Maria, Baileys and Brandy) and downing a bottle of each on my own! It was that or going out and doing something I'd regret! By 2am my ghetto blaster was true to its name (my stereo was broke) as I had **Running with the Devil** by **Van Halen** on full blast. The neighbours hammered on the walls, but I was way-way out of it! I ended up shouting to them, the Tories mismanagement of the economy and my ex-house buyers: "FUCK OFF ALL OF YOU!" In the space of the next six months, I'd lost the flat I owned and moved into a rented one in Hove with my new girlfriend at the time, Lydia – now there's someone, if I meet her in hell, it will be too soon.

I found a photo of myself dressed as Batman, DJ'ing at a Kids party just to prove I did have a Batman costume although I never expected to have to use it for anything other than kids parties.

CHAPTER 7

Brighton, Hove (*Actually*) & Pharmaceuticals

I feel I need to explain the (*Actually*), as it has nothing to do with the **Love Actually** film! The city of 'Brighton & Hove' has a football team with the same name and 'Albion' on the end. When I arrived there, in early 1992, Brighton and Hove were separate towns. Back then, if you asked people who live in Hove, '…do you live in Brighton?' they used to reply, 'Hove actually,' due to Hove being at the posh end of Brighton, a mile apart. Rumour has it, the origin of the phrase came from the local resident (and one of England's finest actors and directors of stage and screen) **Laurence Olivier**. Over the years, it seems the phrase was used with humour by most, and a certain amount of snobbery by others, as the people of Hove 'actually' distanced themselves from their noisy neighbours in Brighton. In the 1990s, Hove Borough Council (which was separate to Brighton's) turned it into a slogan to attract tourism to Hove. However, in 1997 it was decided that the two towns would be better as one, so the unitary authority was granted city status in 2000. Despite Brighton & Hove being one city, it looks like the phrase stuck. Three years later, when residents were asked, 'Do you live in Brighton?' the reply from its Hove residents was, '… yes, well, Hove actually.' I'm sure if I had just put 'Brighton & Hove' in this chapter title, someone, somewhere, would (*actually*) try to correct me!

This part of my life had some bizarre starts, and even more bizarre endings, that began in this part of Sussex and ended in Somerset, late 1995. Before I lost my flat, or should I say, 'handed the keys back', I was still playing music, but gigs were few and far between and I was running out of money. In the early 90s, the recession really stamped its mark

– more so in the Southeast, with the house prices increasing at an insane pace and no one being able to pay the mortgages. The interest rates buyers are paying in 2025 is peanuts compared to what they were then. It seemed like all the banks and building societies repossessed property at the slightest hint of a problem. I'm sure they also made a lot of money, reselling them when the market picked up after the recession during this period.

'For anyone who's interested, by 1992, inflation in the UK had fallen to 3.7%, but unemployment had risen to 9.9%, up from 7.1% in 1990. The economy also entered recession, with DP growth averaging -0.2% from 1990 to 1992. Interest rates on mortgages were between 8 to 9%!'

As I was self-employed, I didn't qualify for the dole (unemployment benefit) despite having worked all my life, and I was determined not to stop working now. I picked up a job through an agency, working at a plastic mouldings company, making the small metal strips that are inserted into the legs of crutches to adjust their length. 99 quid a week take home pay, and the odd gig, meant my finances were getting desperate. It was the first time in my life when I wasn't in a relationship with someone, although good-meaning friends were always trying to get me paired off with a member of the opposite sex.

Spotted by an Elfette

I finally relented when a couple of friends set me up on a blind date. They said, 'She's a lovely girl,' and, to keep them happy, the four of us met in a pub near Brighton. To say she wasn't my type was an understatement. She'd seen me play somewhere in the past and was smitten. I'm not one to hurt people's feelings intentionally (although some may think otherwise), so I went along with the evening.

After a few drinks in a pub, it was decided that we'd go to The Pink Coconut, which was the main night club in Brighton at that time. My 'blind date' and I soon 'saw' that we had nothing in common. But she was still happy to stay with me so, like her perhaps, I counted down the minutes to going home. Suddenly, this spotlight blinded me from where we were stood on the balcony. I was told later that there was this gimmick for the single girls in that club: while they were dancing, if they saw a guy they really fancied, they were encouraged to shine one of the spotlights on them. I was caught in a beam while everyone downstairs was looking up in my direction.

The next thing I know, a beautiful girl/woman/lady comes up to me who, I assumed, was the one who'd shone the beam at me. She was dressed as an elf. I now know that the term is gender-neutral and female elves are referred to as 'elf maidens', but, back then, 'Elfette' sprung to mind and has stayed with me ever since. She didn't have to say anything, I just knew that she was there to ask me out or dance. I could see it in her face, and I was flattered. I looked at her and then at my date. If I'd been a bastard, I would have just walked off with this new admirer and left my date standing. I looked at the Elfette and shrugged my shoulders, while flicking my palms up in despair. I think she understood, as she turned away and I didn't see her again. The evening ended with a shared taxi ride home, dropping my date off at hers on the way. I never saw her again.

I couldn't get the hopeful look in the eyes of the Elfette out of my head and what might be, so I went to The Pink Coconut the following week to see if she was there again. After an hour of waiting around listening to music that I could not stand, I left, deflated. If she had showed up later and I had missed her, who knows what might have been. Another passing point on my path, but, on reflection, because I'd had so much shit with a Fairy in the past, perhaps a relationship with the Elfette might have turned out worse!

The job at the plastic mouldings factory was mundane. After a month, I found a job in the local paper for Laboratory Manager at Custom Pharmaceuticals, in Hove. It had been a few years since I worked in a lab, but with my years at Glaxo and Evans Medical, it was like riding a bicycle, even if it was working in other departments. Their core business was supplying vitamin supplements to the major superstores like Asda, Boots etc. The pay wasn't great, but it was miles better than the other one.

I had met a girl called Lydia at a party in Upper Beeding just before I moved out of the flat. I don't know why I got involved, as she was a party animal and (I might be a bit unfair in saying this, but I don't care) a gold digger. She loved to go to the posh clubs in Brighton, especially The Kings Club which I believe was at the bottom of Market Street. That place was full of rich guys looking for young, fit, gold diggers. I know, because my agent booked me in to play it many times between 1990-1991. It paid good money for acts to perform there, but it was a horrible place. You were stuck in a corner where no one noticed you, and you might as well have been a jukebox. But Lydia loved it. She had an attractive face, a great body and, at first, seemed to have a really nice personality. But I don't think I had enough money for her. She spent a lot of time at my flat and when I said I was handing it back, we decided to move closer to Brighton. So, I paid the deposit, helped by my Mum and Dad I should add, and we rented a top floor apartment in Hove. My music equipment was stored at one of my friends, as there wasn't enough room in the flat. This was a blessing that I didn't realise until later. The new place wasn't cheap, but she was happy (or so I thought).

We had this agreement that we would go out by ourselves on a Friday with our own friends. Well, it was more her idea than mine. Normally she ended up in the Kings Club and came home about 6am, completely arseholed and I wouldn't get any sense out of her all-day Saturday. I thought things were okay between us by making allowances for this weekly escapade, until one evening, when we were invited to a party on a boat. It was actually a luxury cruiser, birthed on the River Thames, in the centre of London. All her circle of friends (who I thought were friends of mine too) were there. Everyone was dressed in designer clothes, and the shirt worn by the 'poorest' looking bloke would cost me over 2 weeks wages. Vintage Dom Pérignon flowed, a celebrity DJ mixed an onslaught of rave/acid/D&B tracks, and I tried my best to blend into the woodwork. Unbeknown to me, Lydia was seeing someone in Brighton, and he was also on this boat. When the party was first mentioned, she asked me, repeatedly, if I really wanted to go. I thought nothing of it at the time and, as I hadn't been on many boats other than the ferries across the Mersey, I stood my ground.

There were two decks, and the main entertainment was on the lower one. Lydia kept disappearing to the top deck. Every time I went to go and search for her, her mates would stop me and say, 'Oh! Phil, you don't want to go up there. She'll be back in a minute,' or some other excuse to keep me away from where she was. I am not a control freak, so I always gave Lydia (and most women I have ever been with) the benefit of the doubt, but I had that gnawing sense that something was wrong.

When we got home, we had a blazing row and she confessed to having a fling with this guy, and, it turns out, he was also the local drug dealer. The reason she preferred these vermin to me? 'Because…,' she told me… 'I was too nice. But, if I'd beat (her) up now and then, (she) would have been happy!' WTF!! She then told me that her father used to beat her up when she was a kid and that's what she was used to. I rationalised it as some twisted sense of affection, which is all very sad. But I believed her. The *Curse of Jane strikes again* or, maybe, it was some karma from my affair with that married woman, four years earlier.

I could never hit, slap or punch a member of the opposite sex just to keep her happy. A bit of bondage now and then hasn't harmed me, but that's something completely different. I've only ever hit a woman deliberately out of self-defence, but that's later on. So, I assume this guy was a (pardon the expression) a Cunt with a capital 'C', and that's why she related to the scumbag. A sad combination, but, as far as I was concerned, it was over with Lydia and I moved out of the flat immediately, leaving behind a lot of my expensive tools and other valuable personal belongings I had accumulated over the years.

Fortunately, a girlfriend of a singer I knew on the circuit had just moved in with him, and she was looking to rent her flat out. He was from Carlisle, and she was from Brighton. It perplexed me that she thought that all of 'up North' looked like the opening credits of **Coronation Street**. Then he took her up there and she saw fields and mountains. Very sad, on another level.

This flat was a tiny bedsit for 80 quid a week rent (and that was in 1992!). But, back then, that was Brighton; one of the most expensive places to rent in Britain outside of London at the time and still is (being the fifth in a table compiled by **Right Move** at the time of publication). I was still working at Custom Pharmaceuticals, and I jumped at the chance to have somewhere on my own. Furthermore, it had just enough space for my recording studio. I started making backing tracks again to raise money towards the cost of this extortionate box. I now had to try and get the rest of my stuff out of the old flat, which Lydia had swiftly invited Mr. Drug Dealer guy (Mr. D) to move into. I phoned her a few times in the day, trying to set up a time to go around to collect everything. Then one day in work, my phone rings and it's Mr. D. 'You leave Lydia alone or I'm gonna come round and do you with a hammer and ….' I slammed the phone down.

'How does he know where I live?' I thought to myself. I hadn't told Lydia, or anyone connected to her/us, but she did know where I worked.

On the way home, I called in to see a friend of mine in the Bikers' Pub (name of which I can't recall). It was at the end of my road where the new bedsit was: one good result of 'location, location', it was a minute's walk from bikes and beer! **Nasty**, a really nice guy, drank there and he was affiliated with one of the main back patch Bikers' Clubs in the country. I tell him the story of Lydia and Mr. D. The next night, I have a knock at the door of my new pad – it's Nasty. I invite him inside. He comes in, closes the door and tells me he can't stop long. Next, he reaches into the back of his jeans. 'Here you go… keep hold of this for now, just in case.' He hands me a pistol and says in a casual, but measured tone, 'This drug dealer who your ex is seeing, get him to meet up with you. When you meet, tell him you've found out, through someone that you know, his boss's name, which is X. He won't be expecting you to be connected with this man. Trust me, he will get you your stuff and not bother you again. If something happens to you, or you end up in hospital before that, we'll take him out.'

I am shocked and a bit lost for words. I've never handled a handgun before – let alone ever thought of needing one for my own protection! I fired rifles at school but that was it. All I could think of and came out of my mouth was, 'But they're on the top floor of a block of flats, with security doors downstairs.' Nasty moves closer to me and, with a deadpan deliver, says, 'We've always got the option of a helicopter!' I thought he was joking at first. But he smiles, taps the side of his right nostril, nods up to the ceiling and then looks back at me and winks his left eye with precision seriousness.

I dial Lydia's number the following morning. Mr. D answers and goes off on one again. I cut him short by agreeing to arrange to meet him so he can do his worst. I suggest the Bikers' Pub car park near my flat. It occurred to me, by this stage, that if Lydia and Mr. D did not know where I lived, where was he going to go to beat my head in. Bright lad then, eh! So, as he stepped out of his car, I walk over and face up to him. Before he can say anything, I stare directly into his eyes and say as calmly as I can, 'Right pal, I know who your boss is, and someone I know is a friend of his. So, you need to either deliver all my kit from Lydia's to the landlord in that pub over there, or you're in serious trouble!' He thinks I'm bluffing until I tell him the name of his boss. I've never seen anyone's cocky attitude change so quickly, and he scurries away like a whipped dog. By the next evening, all my tools and the rest of my belongings are dropped off at the pub. He never, ever knew I lived on that street. A Mr stupid 'Dickhead', and that's being polite. I gave the pistol back to Nasty the following night, thanked him with a few beers and that was that. Lydia eventually moved out of 'our' flat and to Northampton and carried on as a nurse. She got pregnant, but not by me, I hasten to add. I kept in touch with her mum for a while who lived in Rugby. She was my liaison officer while Lydia repaid the flat deposit money. I never got it all back.

Cheeseburger, aerobics and a pointed nipple rally with the Warrior Princess

Anyone who is interested in Brighton may want to know that the bedsit was not far from the Five Ways roundabout. It was in a cul-de-sac, and I used to park my car at the back of that Bikers' pub. Anyway, one evening after work I'm slowing down to the car park when one of my drinking pals shouts out, 'Are you out for a beer?' I reply, 'Just one then.'

Four hours later, we're in a rock club somewhere in Brighton, completely pissed up. We leave God knows when. I remember going to get something to eat, telling the taxi to drive and not to worry about the food I was carrying in the taxi and that was it. The following morning,

I hear loud knocking on my door. I've woken up sat on the couch with my coat on, holding a half-eaten kebab in my right hand. I put my kebab down and go to the door. I open it, and it's a lad who gets a lift with me to work each morning. Whilst adjusting my coat, a half-pound cheeseburger, still wrapped, falls out and onto the floor. We both look down at it. My mate says, 'You had a good night then!'

***

The boyfriend of the girl I'm renting the bedsit off phones me up one day and says, 'There's a new aerobics class starting at the health centre on the prom next week, it's a little different from the others – more down our street. I've been there once. Do you fancy going?' I'm not a fit guy, but I built up a lot of strength and stamina whilst working at Blue Circle and I used to swim when I could, but that was it. Apart from playing tennis in my teens, I had never been able to sustain regular exercise or a gym membership in my life (except once and hated it). I was smoking 20 a day and probably drinking 5/6 pints every night. 'Fuck it!' I thought, 'I'm on my own and what's the worst thing that could happen – I might meet someone or get fit trying.'

'Okay, I'll try it.'

So, we get to this so called 'Aerobics Lesson'. There are only eight other guys there, all either martial arts experts or semi-pro footballers – you get the picture. Out comes this woman in her late 20's, possibly early 30's. In her introduction, she includes the fact that she <u>actually</u> trains the **Special Air Service** (<u>the</u> SAS) Oh FFS! 'We're going out and onto the beach for this session,' she declares, and leads us in a trot down to the seafront. This part wasn't too bad, then it slowly started getting more and more strenuous. Running from the top of one groyne down to and along the water's edge, back up the next groyne to the top and then back along the top on the fine sand. We repeat this not once, but FIVE times!! The guys who were supposed to be super-fit were struggling, but my mate and I are coughing on death's door, and he didn't smoke. After doing some squats, I explained to the instructor, 'I think we've got the wrong class,' and I detail my lack of anything that resembles a fitness regime while lighting up a cig. My mate then informs me that he had been here once the previous week, but it hadn't been as strenuous and was only at the centre and not outside. She was quite impressed by which exercises I'd completed considering I smoked. I don't think my mate ever went back, I certainly didn't.

***

Music seemed to have slipped away from my life again, apart from those odd gigs and making backing tracks for people through advertising in *The Stage*. I had a small **8-Track Tascam**, drum machine and a keyboard, setup in a cramped space near the bed. I had been doing some work with my mate Mike Still, who had the studio in a huge shed at the bottom of his garden. We did the odd duo gig, but it all seemed to have come to a stop. So, when it came to music and women, let's just say I was trying to keep my hand in as much as I could at the time. I had a couple of flings with a couple of girls, but nothing serious.

I bought another bike, a **CB900**. I'd had to sell the CB750 to raise some cash when I handed my flat back to the building society. The **CB900** was more of a rat bike, the starter motor clutch was playing up, and whilst I was trying to save money for the parts, I used to bump it down the street to start it. A bit like they used to do at the TT Races. Now it's either the mechanics push you or you have someone to push you until it fired up.

One night at a party, I met this 6ft female biker called Kaz, who looked a bit like ***Xena: Warrior Princess*** and she had the muscles too. She didn't stand for any shit off people, told it like it was and rode her own bike – a **Triumph Bonnie T120**. I was hooked, well we both were to be honest. Then about two months into the relationship, she told me her full story.

She was an ex-heroin addict on methadone. Her brother and his wife were addicts, and he'd got Kaz on it when she was fifteen. He was eighteen at the time. Addicts tend to lure people to join with them, as it makes them feel better in themselves, justifying that what they are doing is alright. He was in prison at 18 and became the All-England Inter-Prison Bench Press champion from what Kaz told me. But when released, he was always wanted by the police for robbing the money from public telephone boxes to feed his and his wife's habit. Their mum was a Commonwealth gold medallist for shot put in the 1950's and their dad was ex-military, although they'd split up. Kaz had been training as a teenager to run for the Harriers, until her brother gave her heroin, and it all went downhill from there. You know, I should have just walked away from that situation there and then. I didn't, because Kaz wasn't taking heroin anymore, she was on methadone, which is harder to get off than heroin itself. She was a really nice girl, *actually*, and we loved each other, and that was that. She lived in **Littlehampton** with her mum and stepdad. She was not working but was doing college courses to get herself back on track.

Human immunodeficiency virus (HIV) was prominent then. Not only was it high in the public psyche as a sexually transmitted disease, but prevalent amongst drug addicts too. Kaz and I took the HIV test together, so she could prove she was clean, and I could prove that I was clear too.

Then one day she had a relapse. I should have bravely run away, but I didn't. I helped her go through cold turkey, which is awful to watch – and she did it.

By now, I had already decided that I was leaving Custom Pharmaceuticals due to certain things that had happened with the Technical Director, who was a friend of mine by then. Never trust a Managing Director (or MD) who says he will back you all the way when, on his back, he has the **British Medicines Inspectorate** (the **Medicines and Healthcare products Regulatory Agency** today). As the shit hit the fan, he put my neck on the block instead of his. Once the Technical Manager resigned over the incident, the MD expected me to cover for him, as I was the next in line. The problem was caused by an oversight by the MD and I'm sure they are still a very fine company, but I didn't trust the MD. I'd seen it all before with my manager at Evans Medical in Horsham, a 'Mr Farley'. He wouldn't take the blame for anything and tried to get you in the shit instead. So, in September 1992, I left the company. But not before I'd secured a mortgage on a house in Somerset, where I'd decided to live after going down there for a short holiday with Kaz. I commuted for a month before leaving the company.

Finishing this Chapter, there's a story that sticks in my memory prior to moving to Somerset earlier on in 1992.

Kaz and I went to a Motorbike Rally in Essex called **'The Pointed Nipple Rally'**, if I remember its name correctly, which was held one late weekend in January. The plan was to ride back from there on the Sunday morning and up to Liverpool, to visit my parents. It was a cold but beautiful sunny day, until we got about twenty miles south of Rugby on the M1 in the Midlands. We hit freezing fog. Now I know fog in a car is a pain in the arse, but on a bike it is easier. You can see, as there is no glass between you and the fog for the reflection of headlights to dazzle and distort your sight. However, to this day, this was the thickest fog I had ever seen or had to ride through. It was below zero, so you've got the snow and ice to contend with too. I had an open face helmet on, no goggles, just something covering my nose and mouth. The fog was that thick, I couldn't tell which junctions we were going past. Neither of us could see any signs without pulling up and looking. I didn't go above 30mph and none of the cars behind me did either for that matter, they were following me, or so it seemed. Kaz offered to ride for a bit, did twenty minutes, stopped and said, 'I don't know how you are doing that,' and got back on behind me.

It took nearly twelve hours to get from Essex to Liverpool. We set off at 11am and got to my parents at about 11pm. Rugby to Liverpool took about nine or ten of those twelve hours. I can usually do that journey, on a bike, in about three hours. When we got to the end of the M62 at Liverpool, I was in a numb state of mind. I was so cold and hadn't really thought of what I looked like. The fog had cleared coming into the city. We were sat at the traffic lights waiting to turn green and a car pulled up next to me and the driver was staring at me. I bent down to see my reflection in the right-wing mirror. I had icicles on my eyebrows and the rest of me was white with snow. I only needed a carrot for my nose to complete the snowman look. That had to be the coldest and longest ride I ever did. There's no way I could do that now.

Kaz told me to leave her in Littlehampton and start a new life without her in Somerset. Looking back, regretfully, I wish I had done so, as the next three years became some of the worst, best and strangest moments of my life up to autumn 1995. If I hadn't felt so bad leaving her, or cared about her so much, things might have developed completely differently if Kaz hadn't come down to live with me in Somerset. Again, another huge decision that, quite frankly, shaped the next sixteen years of my life.

By November 1992, we'd moved to Chard in Somerset. I didn't work for Custom Pharmaceuticals anymore and set up a small motorbike business at the house that I'd bought.

CHAPTER 8

Addicts, Alcoholics, Bikes and a Police Informer

As well as Kaz, I also took someone else down to Somerset with me, who I had become very close to. His name was **Tyson** or **Tysie**, and he was an Alsatian/Doberman cross dog, weighed around 7 stone/44.5 kilos and lived at Kaz's mum's house in Littlehampton. I'm not sure why or how he ended up there, but he was neglected, unloved and left outside all the time. We became friends, and I offered to bring him with me, as no one wanted him. The next three years in Somerset were more like a Hollywood movie a scriptwriter would make up. If anyone wants to make it into a film, I want a hefty advance!

So Kaz and I moved to Chard; 'The Birthplace of Powered Flight' it says on the signs as you drive in.

It also had the reputation at the time, by people who lived in the town, as having the highest percentage of drug addicts in Somerset living there, which I didn't know (no Google then) – if I had, there was no way I would have moved there, or taken Kaz with me. It's a very nice town now.

The plan was to carry on singing in pubs and clubs, while establishing a second-hand motorbike business in the garden of my house. If you are unfamiliar with the British description of a 'terrace house', it is one of many in streets of houses all joined together. An alleyway or ginnel (in various Scottish or northern English dialects) runs down the back of the houses, parallel to the street or main road at the front. These passageways allowed access to the gardens or yards at the rear of each house. Earlier in the 1900's, all terraced houses only had toilets as standalone, small, bricked, shed-like structures in the yard. Eventually, we became more civilised, and toilets came inside the house. The last houses at the end of the street were termed 'end of terrace'. These usually had a larger outside area at the back. Some had a garden down the side of the house as well as the rear, and these were more expensive to rent or buy. A lot of these terraced properties were originally built by local councils. The house I bought was an end of terrace, with a big garden on the corner of a main road junction, which worked well as drivers passing could see all the bikes I was working on.

Quite a posh row of terraced houses and, below, a typical ginnel.

I used the 30 quid I got for selling my microwave and bought a Honda C90. Did some work on it, sold it with the MOT for 120 quid, then bought two more and my business raced from there. I advertised for lodgers, as the house had three bedrooms upstairs where the bathroom was. Below had three large rooms. The kitchen contained a double Aga oven (which provided the hot water and central heating), and the roast dinners cooked on it were amazing. The front room ended up being our bedroom later and had a wood burner in it. There was an open fire in the main living room, which was between the front room and the kitchen. At the back end of the kitchen was a utility room and a garage where I did all the work on the bikes. When it was too cold in the winter to work out there on engine rebuilds, I used to do them in the kitchen, as it was big enough and warm.

Meanwhile, Kaz was off heroin but had gone back to taking methadone, which I was hoping to get her off eventually. While I was still looking for paying tenants to help with the mortgage, I got myself a job as a window cleaner. I saw an advert in the local paper, as I had the experience. After an interview with the owner, he said, 'Start Monday.'

Never Play with Matches

When we first moved in, the Aga didn't stay alight overnight properly, and I had to put a bit of petrol on the embers each morning just to get it going again. I know it's not what you should do, but I never had a problem until one particular Monday morning. Kaz had a habit of putting used matches back in the box. I opened the door of the Aga, put some petrol in out of the small can, took a match out, but all the matches in the box were used ones. I shut the door of the Aga, went and got another box of matches from the living room, came into the kitchen, struck a match and opened the door of the Aga. As I threw the match in, I realised (after the event) exactly what happened next. The petrol had vaporized in the warm oven, a fireball came out of it and 'WHOOSH', the hot flash passed over my head. I stood up and blinked, the whole kitchen was covered in soot. 'Bloody Hell,' I thought to myself, 'Kaz only cleaned the kitchen spotless recently, she'll be livid!' I looked in the mirror. I had no eyebrows, and all the top of my hair was singed. I was covered in soot and my new boss was picking me up in 30 minutes. In a panic, I tried to get as much of the soot off me but to no avail. What was left of the front of my hair was black and the remnants of my eyebrows were burnt toast black. I changed my overalls, wrote a note to Kaz apologising for the kitchen and stood outside waiting for the pickup. He drove past me three times before he realised it was me. 'What happened?'

'Don't ask….' Problems with the Aga were unresolved until later!

***

I did that job for a few months until I had built up the motorbike business. Chard, in the early 1990's, was a small town and you used to get a few guys riding motocross bikes, without registration plates, up to the local fields with a gallon of cider strapped to the back. Not a clever thing to do, but all the traffic cops were stationed in Taunton (fifteen miles away) and very rarely came to Chard. What had started with a couple of mopeds, was turning into quite a good business. I even had a Puch moped (remember them?) for a company bike before I got a van to pick up parts from the breakers. Tysie was a great guard dog. To say he was strong is an understatement. I was in the kitchen one day and heard all this noise in the garden. Tysie used to be on a long chain attached to his kennel in the garden. I went outside to see him chasing a cat around the garden, while dragging the kennel and a couple of bikes along behind him. On another occasion, Tysie cut his paw on a piece of glass in the park. I took him to the vets. He didn't like anyone in a uniform – postmen, vets etc, some dogs don't. The vet says, 'I'll sort him out in the other room,' while I have my hand clasped around his snout and he's growling.

'Do you want me to come with you?' I say.

'No, I'll be fine,' replies the vet. Twenty minutes later, after half a dozen staff and a muzzle have gone into the room, the vet comes out exhausted and declares, 'That's one strong dog!'

'I did warn you.'

***

The motocross bike riders got word that I was doing repairs as well as sales, and I began to get jobs in the likes of re-bores, chain & sprocket replacements etc. I'd only ever worked on 4-stroke engines before, but an engine is an engine, and I discovered that 2-strokes are a damn sight easier to rebuild than 4-strokes, although they tend to go wrong a lot quicker due to them being hammered (and not with cider).

While all this was going on, Kaz had met a guy called Dave at the chemist who was picking up his methadone, like Kaz. He was looking for a room to rent. He was unemployed, but, in those days, the landlord got the cheque for the rent, so that was fine. The problem I had was that he was, or had been, a heroin addict too, which made me hesitant to say yes. Kaz explained that he wanted to get off methadone too, get a job etc, and that it would be better for the two of them to do it together. He was a nice guy, so I said 'Okay.' That was a mistake, because within three months, they were both back on heroin. I now had a lodger and my girlfriend on heroin (albeit only smoking and not injecting), but both of them were out of it and laying around the house most of the time.

I used to go to the local pub, **The Queens**, a few evenings a week playing pool, and one of the regulars was looking for a bedroom to rent. I can't remember his name. He liked a drink, smoked a bit, took a bit of speed and that was it, but he did have a job. So, he moved into the third bedroom, and I had someone I could talk to about what was going on with the other two. Don't get me wrong there was never any hassle, but I'd seen what happens with a heroin addict for the past nine months. This might sound a bit harsh, but for a while after this episode of my life, I would have been quite happy if someone had wiped all heroin addicts off the planet. I wouldn't have batted an eyelid. I'm sorry, but that's how I felt at the time.

So, I had two lodgers bringing in enough money each month to cover most of the bills and Kaz got unemployment benefit too. I wasn't earning enough yet for the social to say she couldn't have the benefit. I was still self-employed as the PAYE job with **Custom Pharmaceuticals** was only an interim thing, so I couldn't claim anything anyway. I started getting a lot busier with an increasing number of engine rebuilds. I needed to turn these around as quickly as possible, as some of these bikes were their owner's preferred mode of transport to get to and from work. Buses were an option, but there are a lot of country roads in Somerset and, although this public service was good, it took ages to get to anywhere like Taunton,

Bridgewater and other places where the major employment was. That's when I re-started taking amphetamine or Speed. I took it for a while in the 1980s when living on the Wirral, but I'd packed it in and hadn't touched it since I'd moved down to Sussex. I wasn't addicted to it, but I did enjoy taking it socially. I enjoyed a drink and that was enough up to this point. So, I took some to keep awake through the night rebuilding the odd engine, but after a while I'd have a bit of a get together with my lodgers on a Friday night and I'd have it socially as well.

Chimney fires and part time firemen

Unbeknown to me, there was a blockage in the chimney to the Aga. I'd looked inside the top panel above it with a torch but could never see anything wrong. On one of those 'social speed evenings', there was a few of us sat in the living room with a roaring, open fire on the go. I got up to go to the loo. I came into the hall and could smell burning upstairs. I went into the back room to discover the wallpaper was starting to go brown with the heat. SHIT! I'd left the air ducts open on the Aga. I went into the kitchen: I'm surprised the cooker hadn't melted. I closed the air vents and went outside. Yep! Just as I thought – a chimney fire!

I have the deepest respect for our fire service, they see some terrible things and deal with a lot of shit, as all our emergency services do. So, I phone the fire brigade. It's a small town with only a part-time fire service. It's Friday night and most of the firemen are in the pub. They get my call, and the fire engine turns up, 'OK,' says the chief, 'Let's get this put out.' He turns to me, 'Only one chimney, we can't go wrong with that. Last week, we put out a chimney fire and pumped the water down the wrong chimney, and an old dear next door was wondering why there was water pouring into her living room!'

After the fire gets put out, most of the crew are standing around outside waiting to go back to the pub. I'm inside with the chief and his assistant, who have a look inside the bottom of the chimney above the Aga.

A brick had fallen down into the flue, and all the soot built up behind it had caught fire. That's why it never worked properly overnight either. Fantastic, problem solved.

'We'll sweep the chimney for you,' the chief says. I'm having a chat with him and I'm watching this other guy put loads of rods up the chimney.

I say to him, 'Are you sure you're not out of the top of the chimney yet?' The chief repeats this to the rest of the guys outside, who are supposed to be keeping an eye on things.

'STOP! STOP!' they shout. We go out and onto the other side of the street to see the chimney pot about three feet above the chimney breast, sat on top of the rods with the brush.

'Best put our hard hats on now guys,' says the chief.

The whole incident was one of the funniest and bizarre things I've ever seen – like something out of a **Buster Keaton** comedy. Fair play to the fire brigade, they came back the following week and put the chimney pot back on. …. and the Aga worked fine after that.

***

Anyway, coming back towards the M5 (seeing as we're in Somerset)

The Queens pub used to put on the odd band or soloist. I still had all my gear, so I asked the landlord if he would like me to do a gig there. He agreed (for a good price too) and I performed there a few times. One night, I got on stage with **Dave Green,** who was a soloist. Dave had played for many well-known bands over the years, and he came back to do a gig with me and his son, **Chris Green**, joining in too. Sadly, Dave passed away a few years ago and I never saw him after those gigs in Somerset. A few years ago, I got back in contact with Chris who lives in the U.S.A. He used to be in the New York based, hard rock band **Tyketto from 2014 to 2023**. Great band, check out their music.

While I was doing these gigs, over a couple of months or so, I was getting twinges in the lower part of the right-side of my torso. I dismissed it as a pulled muscle at first, but when I did a gig in **Axminster** at **The Castle Inn**, I was in agony by the end of the set. It turned out I had a groin hernia from lifting some of the larger motorbike engines out of the frames, amongst other things. This put a stop to me performing for the next three years.

Before I go into detail with this next part, I need to say that I'm not proud of some of these events. Once I left Somerset, I realised how stupid I was getting involved in certain… let's say… misdemeanours. Since then, apart from speeding tickets, I've never gone down that road again. I was thinking about leaving a lot of this out, but I can't. It's what's made me into who I am now, and I hope for younger readers, it will help you not make some of the mistakes in life that I have. If people want to judge me on these years, then so be it, but it has to be told.

To begin with, I need to explain about my best mate down there, Pat (not his real name). There were a lot of things that happened during those three years with Pat, some good, some bad and maybe one day I will fill a book about them.

I think we first met when he came round to buy some bike parts. Pat was no saint but looked after his mates. Although he was occasionally paid by people to 'put the frighteners' on certain others, if you know what I mean, he was actually a really nice guy. He was doing a very similar thing to what I was doing, but with cars rather than bikes, and he lived about ten miles away in a small village. I'd go round a few times a week, sometimes with Kaz but often not. He didn't like Kaz that much, which I think was to do with her connection to heroin. We were so similar in many ways and looks that some people thought that we were brothers, that's how close we got.

Pat used to pick up some speed from a notorious gang in London, and I'd get some off him and I'd share it out with the guys at my house and a few friends. If they were going out and selling it to other people, I didn't know and I didn't ask questions. Any 'dealing' was tiny and only amongst a small group of mates, but I was not proud of what I was turning into, Furthermore, the whole situation with Kaz, the lodger and trying to keep myself sane, was all taking me down a road that (when I look back) I was very lucky to get off. One day, I received a phone call from Pat. He'd broken down just outside London and asked if I could pick him and his bike up in my van. I had an idea of where he'd been, and I didn't ask any questions. Even though we were both pretty strong, it was a struggle to get a **Harley 1340 Evo** into the back of a van without a ramp. When we got back to Somerset, he revealed he had a kilo of speed on the bike and needed a safe journey home! Can you imagine, with what he had stashed on the bike, if the police had stopped to check him out while waiting for breakdown or having to leave the bike in the services where he had stopped – what would have happened?

Pat did have a problem with the police. A year or so before I knew him, a policeman had tried it on with his wife in their house. The sequence of events started when the policeman had called about a motoring fine and left to find his vehicle had broken down; with Pat not being there to help, he had to wait for its recovery. While he was waiting for the recovery vehicle, Pat's wife offered him a drink as he wouldn't be driving. It was close to Christmas, and the fact he didn't have to drive now with his vehicle broken down, he put 2 + 2 together, made 5 and got the wrong idea. Once Pat got home and his wife had told him what had happened, he went down to the station where the policeman was based. Let's just say there was an 'altercation' with this policeman and Pat got the better of him in the foyer of the police station. However, no charges were ever pressed against Pat, but he used to have detectives stood at the end of his garden path, trying to antagonise him to snap. He never did, but they got him another way instead.

There was a guy called Fisher (not his real name) who was another biker we both knew in Somerset. I called round Pat's house one night. While we were sat in the living room having a beer, he said, 'Have a look down the side of the couch.' In between the couch and the wall of the living room, there were two large, clear bags in a large shopping bag. One had a kilo of speed and the other a kilo of cannabis. Pat says, 'Fisher has just dropped it off and asked me if I can keep hold of it for a couple of days as he's nowhere to put it. However, I smell a rat, so I'm not touching it.' I thought it seemed a bit strange and didn't touch it either. The next day, I get a call from his wife. 'Phil, the drug squad came around this morning and arrested Pat. They barged into the living room and went straight to the two bags. I think he's been stitched up.' Obviously, the police wanted to get back at Pat for that 'altercation' above. Fisher, who we both thought of as a friend, was, we discovered, a paid infiltrator/

informer or 'snout' working for the police. Fisher wheedled his way into bike clubs and other similar gangs and set them up. It came out later that he was a heroin addict too, and grassing up others paid for his addiction!

The police found Pat's fingerprints inside the bags, and even though Pat swore he hadn't touched them, he was sentenced to five years in prison for the supply of Class B drugs. Pat owned a bike that he bought from money left to him by his gran when she died. The courts insisted that it was paid for from the sale of drugs, but they couldn't prove it. So, when they couldn't find his bike (I had it stored for safekeeping) to recoup the money that they couldn't prove he'd made, the judge gave him another two years. Yes, Pat did deal a bit, but to get someone to stitch him up like that, well you can come to your own conclusions. I spent every day of that court case in the public gallery, watching it all unfold; it was so evident it was a set-up.

After eighteen months inside, Pat got an appeal at the High Court in London and his sentence was reduced to three years. He was told that if he had gone for a quashed verdict at the first hearing, he would have got it, due to the judge being biased from day one. It had been rigged from start to finish.

***

Strangled by love

I called the bike business **Wrecked'Em Motorcycles**. I thought the name was quite funny, as proved by one of my customers. I advertised in the local paper and also in the *Yellow Pages* (remember them!), and he told me (while still laughing) that when he phoned directory enquiries for the number of Wrecked'Em Motorcycles, the operator hung up because she thought he was being rude.

I was buying some really nice bikes, and cheaply. It's amazing what people will keep in the field next door to their house. For example, I had a **Peugeot 504 Pickup** for a while (remember this vehicle for later) and went to look at a **Suzuki GS850** that had been stood in a field for three years. 250 quid and it's on the back of the pickup. On the way home, somewhere on the A303, my clutch went. SHIT! I knew that if I left the pickup with the bike on, it would be gone by the time I got back. Kaz was with me, and phoned Trevor (*someone who I knew on the Wirral, only to find him living 5 minutes from me in Chard some 12 years later and who became one of my drinking buddies*) who came down with a helmet, gloves and jacket for me. While we're waiting, I get on the back of the pickup. This bike hadn't run for three years, but I've had quite a few bikes like that. A bit of new fuel (which I always kept with me), jump leads and I give it a go. A quarter of an hour later, I had the bike running. My little air compressor pumped the tyres up and once it was off the back of the pickup, it was ready to ride. I had traders' insurance then, so although it didn't have an M.O.T certificate, it was the only thing I could do. I didn't have breakdown cover. Fuck me! I had my own breakdown truck, but no one else could drive it! Anyway, Trevor turned up and took Kaz home, and I rode the 30 or so miles back on the bike and went back and got the pickup the following morning.

That was how everything was with me then. I could fix anything, I had a good business, things had turned out a bit shit for Pat (his bail had been revoked at the time), but Kaz seemed to be sorting herself out. For a while, all was well in our home until her brother and his wife came to stay. Don't forget, ladies and gentlemen, Kaz's brother and sister-in-law were both heroin addicts. They satisfied their habit courtesy of change from public telephone boxes. This guy was a doorman at fifteen years old in London and was built like a brick shit house, even as an addict. I pleaded with Kaz not to let him come down and stay. Even after all the shit things he'd done to her over the years, she implored me with, 'But he's my brother.' Heroin addicts stick together; it doesn't matter what they have done, it never makes any difference. If things got out of hand, I know I could have got a few guys like Pat, and we could have sorted him out. But I'm there living with someone who I still love and, well it's so difficult to explain. I understand now, to a certain extent, how women in abusive relationships must feel.

One night, a week or so before her brother is due to visit us, Kaz and I had a row in the pub. I went home and slept in the spare bedroom. I was woken at 2am with her fingers around my throat strangling me, and

I mean full on thumbs on my windpipe, not a bit of shaky, shaky around the neck. That is one of the few times I've ever hit a woman. I was nearly unconscious, and I honestly believe that if I'd lost consciousness, she would have finished the job. She was built like an Amazonian and fought like a bloke. She laid out four Marine Cadets in Taunton who tried to take her taxi FFS! Yes, I lost it Berserker style for about five minutes. I was in that tunnel I told you about with the Hells Angel prospect. Afterwards, Kaz was curled up in a corner of the room, cowering, while I was shouting 'YOU WERE TRYING TO FUCKING KILL ME!'

It took a few years after that before someone could wake me up suddenly, without me grabbing them by the neck. I wasn't proud of what I did. But, given this and the fact that this was a woman who had wanted to 'deck me' and had, also, once hit me in the face, smiling and jumping about saying, 'I think I've bust his nose!' After that, I lost all respect for her and knew things were getting worse. She still had her brother and his wife coming down to stay at the house. By this time, I was spending more and more time at The Castle Inn, where the next part of this unbelievable tale carries on.

The photos below are ones I've copied onto my phone from the originals, which are now a little worn.

The motorbikes in my garden.

The GS850 I rescued from a field.

My faithful Peugeot 504 truck.

CHAPTER 9

The Bodyguard and the Nuclear Dump

The Castle Inn landlady, Kathy (not her real name), was one from 'the North' – hardworking. She got some money together, bought a pub, sorted it out, sold it and then bought another and so on. The first time we met, there was a connection straight away and everyone could see it – including her live-in manager Geoff (his real name). I found out later she had a one-night fling with him, that was a mistake, but he didn't see it that way. To top it all, he was a raving alcoholic and a violent one at that. I could tell there was something wrong and the more I went to the pub, the more Kathy told me, and the more Geoff was getting pissed off. I told her of my predicament at home and the strangulation event. Within two weeks, I had moved all the bikes down to her outbuilding next to the pub and was working from there. So, just before Kaz's brother arrived and after another blazing row about it, I walked out of MY HOUSE and went to Axminster.

Now I say 'moved' to Axminster. The bikes were there for the business, but I wasn't living anywhere as such. However, I had started sleeping on the benches in the bar of the Castle after an incident one night. Kathy was being threatened by Geoff most nights, and by pure chance, I was pissed and fell asleep in the pub, and he didn't do anything because I was inside the pub. That was how it started. I was there all the time, bikes next door and sleeping on the pub bench in the bar every night. I'd go to the local swimming baths every day for a swim and a shower, work on the bikes and then sit in the pub each evening keeping an eye on him, which he hated. This went on for about three months. A lot of the punters knew what was going on, but many of them had their own problems. Axminster had the highest suicide rate in the southwest at the time. I'm not sure why. There was a nuclear dump down the road which did make me think if that had something to do with it. One day, a guy sat at the bar was going on and on about killing himself. The state of mind I was in at the time, and the shit I'd been through, I just blurted out, 'Will you stop fucking going on about it. If you're going to do it, just go and bloody do it!' I shouldn't really have said that. The guy left the pub, and we never saw him again! There was nothing in the paper about anyone deciding to end their own life and he wasn't a regular. I shouldn't have said what I said. Apologies to his family if he did heed my words, but I need to explain that with what was going on with Kaz, the house and her brother, if there was anyone who should be thinking about taking their own life it was me, and I certainly wasn't going to give anyone that satisfaction of tipping me over the edge.

Anyway, the punters used to choose the soundtrack to the film **Robin Hood: Prince of Thieves** on the juke box, you know, the one with the **Bryan Adams'** *(Everything I Do) I Do It for You* which was a massive chart hit in 1991. That's what it looked like: me, the proverbial knight in shining armour, helping a damsel in distress. It was all very surreal. Kathy would look at me, I'd look at her and yes, we were falling in love. She would come down from upstairs some nights after the pub was shut, kiss me while I was sleeping on the bench and then flee before he knew she had left her room. There were times when he kicked off, and all I had to do was shout up the stairs and he'd stop. He was a bully and a coward and lied about giving up alcohol. Kathy should have got rid of him as her manager, but he had this hold over her. That one-night stand (many moons ago), in a court, would not have looked good in a case for unfair dismissal. We decided we had to wait until he really lost it and then he'd be out. Which he did one night.

This particular evening, all the punters had left, something was said, and he kicked off smashing glasses and wrecking the pub. Enough was enough! I'd spent too many nights listening to all this shit coming out of his mouth and his cruel behaviour, so I threw him out of the pub, locked the door and he was gone.

You'd think 'YEAH!' that's the end of the film, but no. Yes, Kathy and I slept together that night and I will never regret that. It was like a weight had been lifted off both of us and it was just like a movie. I got up in the morning and went to go and check on the house, which I did now and then, as well as pick my mail up because I didn't have a new mailing address. Normally, Kaz and the other two were out of it and still asleep. One of the lodgers used to see me and we would go outside. He would tell me what was going on. That morning, I rode back to the pub about 1pm. Guess who was standing behind the bar as I went inside?

FUCKING GEOFF! There are not many times I'm lost for words, but I was dumbstruck. He stood there with this cocky smirk on his face. I didn't know what to say. I looked at Kathy and her expression said it all, but I understood. He had some form of hold over her that Kaz didn't have over me. Very similar circumstances, but different at the same time. I hope you understand that before you shout at me for being a cock! I walked out that pub, but I couldn't just walk away – I had all the bikes there, my business, so I had to grin and bear for a while until I could sort things out.

This did take a little while, because…. well, let's look at the predicament I'm in:

1. I've moved out of my own house because it's full of heroin addicts.
2. All my business is in an outbuilding next to a pub.
3. A pub where I was living on one of the benches.
4. I am bodyguarding the landlady, who has just blown the whole situation we were aiming for overnight.
5. I couldn't go back home until I'd sorted out all the shit that was happening there.
6. What a fucking mess!

I found somewhere to stop around the corner from the pub. It was in the upstairs of a half-built warehouse. It was being converted into offices, but the owner had run out of money and all construction had stopped. It was a temporary place to sleep with toilets, but no hot water or heating. Meanwhile at my actual home, I heard that Kaz's brother had left. His wife had already gone back to Sussex. The police had found out where he was, but he avoided capture by jumping out of a first-floor window. Her heroin addict lodger had left because he couldn't handle all the shit going on with her brother. This meant Kaz was alone. Then, out of the blue, my other lodger came down to see me and told me Kaz had gone and asked if I would come back – which I did. I moved everything back to Chard; Tysie was still there, and I only had one lodger but that was cool.

Kaz had signed herself into a psychiatric hospital in Taunton. After a few weeks, she signed herself out. She got on her Yamaha SR500 (which I'd bought for her) and returned to Sussex. Music had gone right out of the window. I couldn't sing because of the hernia and my electric guitar (**Epiphone Coronet**) had been nicked at the Castle one night. This was after an impromptu gig, which just about killed me with pain. I'm sure Geoff had something to do with the guitar going missing, but I could never prove it. It was worth quite a bit of money. Pat, by this time, was inside for the stitch up and I used to go and see him in **Weymouth Prison**. He had to fight his way through the ranks in there to make sure he was left alone. I've never been inside, thank God, but I can imagine from what he described that that's what you had to do.

I found a unit near The Queens in Chard and moved all the bikes there, as well as the cars I'd acquired by then too. I didn't stay there long; it was too expensive, and I think the buildings were getting sold for a new development, so everything moved back to the house.

Off on a Tangent

People part exchange some amazing things to buy a bike or a car. I had a **Kawasaki Z1000** racing outfit in exchange for the **GS850** I mentioned, plus cash I may add, and an **XS750 Yam** – all in one deal. The GS was worth quite a bit of money, even then.

∗∗∗

I sold a Honda **CBR500**. I had paid the customer what he wanted for selling the bike and still had a small boat, trailer and outboard from the sale, and an **Opel Manta** (remember them?). Things were good again. I lived by myself for about three months, until I got a lodger who was in another back-patch club down in Somerset. He was a shepherd and just needed somewhere to live until he went back to Scotland for the shepherding. I started teaching guitar to a couple of brothers, aged ten and eleven. They could play already but wanted to learn songs that they liked, rather than what the school was trying to teach them. So, they used to come along with a tape of the songs they wanted to learn, and I'd show them how to. These included: **Hotel California** (**Eagles**), *Stairway to Heaven* (Led Zeppelin) and **Little Pig** by **Green Jelly,** an awesome song. The funny thing was, they never told their music teacher (Mr Rocket) about the lessons, so he thought they were both geniuses.

On the female side, I ended up in a situation (again!) where I would go to the pub on Saturday nights, and this lady would take me home to her flat. She was about ten years older than me but, hey, I was single. I was still frequenting the Castle on and off, foolishly hoping Kathy would have changed her mind and sorted things out but, no. That's when I did two stupid things.

Toy Run, Racing and another distressed damsel

Two of my friends (another Geoff and his partner who will remain nameless) were a couple who lived down the road from me in Chard. We had all gone down to **Lyme Regis**, with loads of bikers taking toys and presents to a local children's hospital for Christmas. It's known as a Toy Run. When bikers do it at Easter, it's called an Egg Run. After dropping the toys off, we were all sat in the pub just outside Axminster where a **Boss Hog Chopper** was stored opposite. These are huge motorbikes with a Chevy engine!

I was on an FZ750 Yam that had had a hard life. Fork seals on the way out, rubber band holding the gear selector on. It was the only bike I had at the time that was legal, and I could ride on, down there. Geoff hated me, I'm not sure why. He always said we were friends, but there was something not right. I know his partner fancied me and maybe that was the problem. He owned a bright yellow 1000cc **Moto Guzzi** Le Mans that held the 1977 **TT** Lap record. He had the certificate, and it had featured in *Classic Bike* magazine. It was the works and we'd both had a drink.

'I'll race you to Chard boundary sign,' he says, which is about ten miles away. I don't say anything.

'You're a chicken!' he says loudly.

Now, bearing in mind, I'm sat in a pub with over 100 bikers listening, most of them know me and have heard all about the shenanigans that have been going on in my life over the past year or so. What do you do?

'Okay, you're on, but we stick to the speed limits until we get out of Axminster and onto the national speed limit roads,' I say.

We agree. I've just agreed to have a race with a guy who's got a bike with the TT Lap record from 1977. I am using a worn out **FZ750** Yamaha, which was still quick, but has elastic bands holding bits of it on and one front fork leaking oil, which is really shit for handling and braking.

Off we go and everything is all above board until we hit the national speed limit, and off I go. His girlfriend is on the back of his bike, but despite this added weight, he's got a bike that should piss all over mine and after all, he challenged me. Coming out of Axminster, there's a bridge on a bend which you shouldn't take at any more than 40mph. I took it at 65mph I think. Out of the seat, the bike was sliding across the road with a car coming the other way and I thought, 'SHIT! This is it.' But the tyres gripped, and I kept going. I come to South Chard boundary, and we have another four or five miles still to go. But it is a 30mph speed limit for about half a mile. Remember the agreement. I slow down; he fires past me, with his girlfriend sticking two fingers up at me as they go past. He was beat, but he had to cheat. Off I go and he thinks I'm way behind now – we hit the Chard Boundary sign, and he looks in his mirror to see me sat right on his back wheel. He won, but he knew he cheated, and a decent rider would have hammered me with that Guzzi. I'd done that road before testing out a **RD350LC** 2 stroke and had done the five miles to South Chard and five miles back to Axminster in twelve minutes. I knew the road well. It's not big, it's not clever, but I have to put it in because of what happened that New Year's Eve.

That night, the couple I'd had the race with were in the **White Horse** in Chard. This is where I am sat too. It is also where Kim the future mother of my children, frequented. But she was going out with another guy at the time, so I didn't even consider it. I always seemed to be helping damsels in distress back then. Now, bear in mind that I knew the two of them reasonably well. He was becoming quite aggressive to her and, from what I found out later, he was like this at home too. I wasn't sat with them, I wasn't causing the problem, it was just him being a twat. It ended up with a couple of us throwing Geoff out of the pub, as he was threatening to hit her. The doors got locked and he was hammering on them, but he wasn't getting back in. She's in a mess of emotions. After a while, I get a taxi and take her back to mine, as she's worried about what he's going to do if she goes home. She sleeps on the couch. I'm sure nothing happened, but it's a long time ago and both of us were pissed – however, she did pour a lot of feelings out about how she felt about me. Here we go again.

When he comes around in the morning, she doesn't want to see him. She's already explained to me everything that's been going on with his drinking and emotional abuse. I don't think he ever hit her. I tell him to fuck off and never go back to her house. It was her house, but he lived there on and off. It was a strange set up. I only found a lot of this out on New Year's Eve. I also found out he had a wife, for fuck's sake! I took her back to her house that day. I cannot remember exactly what happened after that. She came around explaining that it was all sorted and not to worry about her, even though at mine on New Year's Eve, she was declaring her undying love for me. I'm not saying any more about that situation, except that, although I was a knight in shining armour, the heart on my sleeve happened again. I will say no more.

So, back on the M5 as I'm still living in Somerset

I remember one foggy night going up to the **Ship Inn**, which was another public house not far from my house, heading out of Chard towards Taunton, and Kim (not her real name, short for 'Kids Mum', and who became my partner for fourteen years) is sat in there having a drink with a friend of hers. I find out that she's split up with the boyfriend, I ask her if she wants to go out for a ride on the bike and that's how our relationship started. Over the first month or so, I'd just call round after being down at The Castle or sorting something or other out. No matter where I'd been, I'd make the call to see if she was at home and go and spend the night there. While our relationship developed, one of the lodgers told me one day that he had gone to The Castle and told Kathy that I was seeing Kim; she said that she should have kept what she had found at the time, and soon as I had met Kim, she knew I was gone from her life for good.

After all that, to be honest, I'd had enough of the Casanova shenanigans that had happened for the past year or so. Kaz had been gone from the house for over six months, and, apart from a few clothes, she had taken everything with her. Kim spent more time at mine than at her flat and the cats moved in, much to the alarm of Tysie. He settled once Blackie (Kim's huge male cat) had punched him across the nose with a paw. It's funny watching a 7 stone Alsatian/Dobermann cross sit there whimpering, after a cat had just told him who's boss by smacking him on the nose. They became best friends.

I need to go off track now, but this is a biggy. I'm going to go around every single motorway in the country!

There's nowhere else I can put all these stories except here, so here we go.

Tysie Dog was something else, I'm sure he was a human trapped in a dog's body. I came home one night from the pub with an Indian curry for my tea. I walk down the side of the house to the kitchen door, and peer through the gap in the curtains of the living room window, only to see Tysie sat bolt upright in the armchair watching the snooker on the TV! I used to leave the TV on for him. Anyway, I come into the kitchen, put my food on a plate and he still hasn't come out to greet me – must have been a good game of snooker. I walk down the hall with the plate and, yes, I hadn't put the light on, I trip over a bike tyre that seems to have been left in a convenient place, considering it had been stood up in the kitchen before I left for the pub. I go flat on my face, drop the plate of curry and Tysie is waiting by the stairs and eats the whole bloody lot!

* * *

I had a unit for a while at the top of the road near the Queens pub, as I mentioned earlier. I used to have Tysie on a chain outside the unit. There was a car dealer next door who would sell anything to anyone, even if it meant he would be selling his soul to the devil to get the deal. People used to drive across the front of my unit so fast, and Tysie used to run out on the chain and bark at everything. One guy was a bit close one day and Tysie ran out, and the **Scimitar** *(remember them) he was driving hit Tysie. 'Oh no' I hear you say. It didn't bother Tysie; the body of those cars were fibreglass. Tysie just stood there growling at the bloke, while he looked at the dented wing. There were a few heated exchanges, and he drove off. The dog wasn't hurt at all.*

***

I used to hate that car dealer. I did do some work for him on a **Ford Sierra**. I spent ten hours on the floor, in the rain, trying to weld its bloody chassis back together. The idiot had promised the buyer it would pass an MOT when he sold it, six months previously. The bloke came back with the car when it didn't – I told him to forget me doing any more work for him.

A guy came to my house one day, and asked if I could rebuild the engine of his **Honda Silver Wing**. He'd taken the engine apart already and all I had to do was put it back together for him. Now for anyone who has rebuilt any type of machine, you know it's a lot easier taking it apart and putting it back together yourself. When he said it was in bits, IT WAS IN BITS! Every single nut, bolt, cog, bearing, piston, it all came in boxes. He told me that it just stopped running one day, so he took them out to sort it. This guy used to be in the REME (Royal Electrical and Mechanical Engineers, my dad was in them in the 1950's). God help the REME when he was there, that's all I can say. I tell him how much it will cost for me to rebuild the engine from parts in boxes, as it was going to take a long time. He hadn't labelled anything but agreed, and I started rebuilding this engine. Meanwhile, I get a note through the door that he's left his wife and gone to live in Spain with some girl, but to still sort the bike out and give the money to his missus who only lived just up the road. On and off, I spent a month fixing this bike. I sorted the engine out and put it back in the bike. It wouldn't run, so I took it back out, thinking I'd done something wrong, believing the problem was the engine. Me and a mate towed it behind a van down Cricket St. Thomas

Hill (two miles) and it still wouldn't run. I eventually bought another set of carbs for it, and it fired up straight away. There was nothing wrong with the fucking engine in the first place, it was the diaphragms on the carbs. I sold the bike, took what it owed me and gave the rest to his ex, only to find out a few weeks later that he was back from Spain, and was bad-mouthing me in the pub about how I'd ripped him off. I phoned him and told him I didn't know how he'd ever got in the REME. Okay, so I should have looked at everything else on the bike to solve the problem, rather than listening to him. Lesson learnt.

About six months later, the bike came back to me from the customer who bought it. He cooked the engine (Silverwings are water cooled) and so I had to rebuild the whole bloody thing again.

***

There was a tyre fitting company just down the road that let me use their equipment to fit bike tyres. One day, I was stood outside of the unit having a cup of tea and a smoke, and just happened to watch this **T5 Volvo** *on the road go behind the building in front of me, but not come out the other side, except for a wheel. The driver had just come out of the tyre place with four new tyres, and both fitters had thought the other had tightened the nuts up on all four wheels. He'd gone 200yrds and one wheel was off, and the others weren't far behind. What was more embarrassing was that the car belonged to the editor of the local paper. Whoops!*

Now for the Biggy

One particular night at The Ship Inn, I was with a mate at the bar and these three guys came in. You knew they were looking for trouble straight away. One was a bareknuckle fighter, and they were from a permanent Travellers camp about five miles away. They poured a pint over the landlord's head, and it all kicked off. The three of us, the landlord, my mate and I, got them out of the pub after a few punches were thrown and locked the doors. The last thing one of them said, with a finger pointing at me, was, 'We know where you live, you'd better watch out!'

I happened to mention this to a couple of Pat's friends, who had called around while I was there, when he'd come home on leave before his release. Unbeknown to me at the time, one of these guys was an illegal firearms dealer. He said with Pat going back inside for a few months, here was his number and if anything happened to me, to get someone to phone him and he would sort it out, and that was that. I told him where they lived. Bit of déjà vu, me thinks, from when in Brighton and Nasty. Anyway, the Travellers thing sorts itself out, as the main guys from the camp apologise to the landlord and tell him to press charges – the three get jailed for the incident.

A year later, not long before Kim and I are moving back up north, I'm around at Pat's again and these two guys turn up for a drink. The same guy says to me, 'How are you getting on with the Travellers?' I tell him it's all sorted and thanks, but he says, 'You should have let me know because I've had a van with a mortar bomb in the back sat outside the camp for the past year. If you'd ended up in hospital, I would have just assumed it was them and I would have gone and set it off.' From the immortal words of Black Adder, I think the phrase rhymes with 'Clucking Bell'. I never knew the guy's name nor his mate, but I found out afterwards that they were notorious in the underworld. It's not what you know but who you know, I believe the saying is.

Anyway, back on track

Kim used to work for the Ministry of Defence (MOD) then. She was a very good artist and did all the shipping charts for them, amongst other things. No computers, all hand drawn. One day, she said to me that she was waiting for the right person to come along to have kids with, and that it was me. I will always remember that. For a female to say that to a male, it strikes something in your heart and is rather flattering. I hadn't even thought about kids until then, especially after the fiasco with Sharron and losing Rebecca. I think the fact that I'd inadvertently, a few days before, when I dropped her off at work, said that I loved her, when I was supposed to have said 'see you later', helped in her decision. I felt embarrassed when I said it, but she replied that she loved me too.

Maybe after all this shit over the years, especially the past three years (including the six months before I moved down to Somerset), things were now sorting themselves out and the curse of Jane had gone for good…or maybe not?

My Kawasaki Z900 Low Rider being built.

The SR500 I had to give to Kaz at the time.

CHAPTER 10

The Knife attack, The 'Postman' and other fraudsters

While Pat was inside, before he got his appeal through, he asked me if I would do him a favour. One of his mates inside was coming out, had nowhere to live and would I take him in as a lodger?

'Not a problem. What's his name?'

'Roger, and thanks Phil.'

Ha! Roger the lodger! He'd been inside for fraud or something like that, but nothing heavy-duty. Kim and I used the front room as our bedroom, so there was a spare room upstairs. I was still going to a mate of mine in Dorset for some speed and Kim used to smoke a little bit of cannabis to ease her arthritis, that she'd had since she was a teenager, but that was it. We were both settling down comfortably with each other, until one Sunday afternoon.

Kim and I are in the Ship Inn having a quiet drink when the phone rings in the pub.

'It's for you, Phil.' It was one of the lodgers.

'I think you'd better come home. I've just seen Kaz riding up and down the high street completely off her head, no crash helmet. She spoke to me saying she'd knocked at the house and there was no-one there and that she's coming back round to the house in an hour to pick the rest of her stuff up.'

Great!

There were only a few clothes she had left in the house, which I'd put in the utility room in a bag. It was the fact that she was back living in Sussex (120 odd miles away), she was now in Chard, had no helmet on and 'completely off her head' that worried me. Kaz had left six months before. I had only popped up to Sussex once to see how she was getting on, and if she had sorted herself out mentally. She was clean and back in college, so I'm not sure what had happened since then. But then heroin is a funny drug, and I am not talking about laughing.

Kim and I finished our drinks and went home. Soon enough, Kaz turned up. Kaz and I end up having a blazing row about something I can't remember, but I don't think it was to do with Kim. I turned around and went into the utility room to get her bag, came back out and Kaz had Kim pinned to the wall. They both had hold of the handle of a bread knife, which I don't know who has pulled on who. I didn't think about that, I just grabbed the serrated blade with the full grip of my left hand. Kaz has more power and pulls the knife backwards out of my hand. I cannot describe the pain and the damage that a serrated knife has on your fingers. Kaz and I tussled to the ground and blood seemed to be everywhere. I lost it again!

'Call the police!' I shouted to Kim, while I held Kaz in a head lock.

'I'll punch the fucking living daylights out of you if you move!' I scream into Kaz's ear. She doesn't move until the police arrive and take her away. The hospital sorted out my fingers. I didn't play the guitar again for over twelve months. Luckily, it was mainly my third and fourth fingers, but when I look closely, I can still see the scars at the tips of my fingers from the wound. It took ages for the sense to come back so I could fully feel the strings again.

The police called back for a statement and charged Kaz with GBH, and that was the last I heard of it for a while. While Kaz was on remand, Pat came to see me. He was out of prison on a home leave, before being released completely after his appeal. He told me he had a letter off Kaz in which she wrote, 'I think I've gone a bit too far with Phil this time.' I told him all about the incident and I assumed it was to do with the knife attack. Pat went back inside for the last few months of his sentence.

The police didn't tell me about what was happening with Kaz, but I find out off someone else that she had been released and had returned to Sussex. This all smelt of something and it wasn't roses. You know when you've got a feeling something is going to happen? I dismissed it.

Big mistake.

Who is the real Fraudster?

One morning, I had to travel down to Cornwall to look at a motorbike that was for sale and had caught my eye: price versus condition. I dressed and went out to the garden to get Tysie ready to come with me. It is about 7.30am; a beautiful, clear day, sun in the sky, birds singing – perfect!

I used the kitchen door, as we never left the house via the front one when we didn't need to. I walked around the corner and got in the van parked on the main road. As I drove off, I noticed a **Vauxhall Cavalier** facing the wrong way a little further on down the road. The five blokes were staring at my house. I still wonder to this day what would have happened if I'd knocked on the car window and asked what they were doing. As I drove up the road, the more I thought about it, the more I felt sure they were coppers of some type. I pulled over at the top of town and used a telephone box to call Kim. She told me,

'You'd better get back here quick Phil, there's police everywhere.'

I jumped back in the van, drove back down to the house and came around the corner to absolute bedlam. There was a police dog van, a DVLA van (or DVLC as they were called then) and a couple of other police cars and vans. There were coppers everywhere. I left Tysie in the van and went into the house. They didn't know who I was as I walked in. This all seemed very strange.

Kim told me later that there was a knock on the front door. She opened it to find a postman stood there. 'Parcel for Mr. Baker,' he said, and barged his way in without showing a warrant or anything.

He was the Head of the Operation from the Drug Squad. Apparently, I find out later, the first thing he said was, 'Where's the dog?'

I smelt a rat, and it's called Kaz.

If this was a planned operation, they would have known:

1. What I looked like. For fuck's sake! I'd just walked out the house 30 minutes before and got in my van in plain sight of their car and they didn't recognise me!

2. What the dog looked like.
3. We never used the front door, even the usual postman knew not to. He always knocked and said 'Hello' at the back door.

Anyway, I entered the kitchen, and they were all panicking about the dog. I wish I'd brought him in now to be honest. They found a $1/8^{th}$ of an ounce of cannabis (about 10 quid's worth) in the kitchen which was Kim's, and she had already been arrested. Kim would have lost her job at the MOD if she had been charged, so I say it's mine. The female officer turned to Kim and said, 'I am de-arresting you for possession of cannabis resin.' Then the officer turned to me. 'Mr. Baker, I am arresting you for possession of cannabis resin.'

Roger came running down the stairs shouting, 'Phil, don't let them pin it on you!' They had already been upstairs and gone through the lodgers' bedrooms and had found some dried magic mushrooms that were Roger's. He told them that they were his, but they brought them down to try and charge me for them too. Dried mushrooms are Class A drugs and that is serious. The police realised that this was a bad idea, especially when Roger is stood there telling them that the mushrooms were his. They never charged him.

I got taken outside to the garage. The guy from DVLC Vehicle Fraud Squad is there. He was looking at the outboard motor I have stored there, which I'd been trying to get going for weeks.

Now, I have never bought or sold stolen vehicles. I knew that the boat that it had come from was a part-ex of a car I sold, and both were legal. The boat was sat in a compound up the road at a taxi rank. I paid rent to keep vehicles, that I didn't have room for at the house, in the taxi compound until I sold them, but I'd brought the outboard motor back to try and repair it. The day before, there was a serial number on that motor. That morning, the serial number had been removed and (by coincidence) a rasp file was sat next to it on the bench.

'Well, what have you been doing here then?' he said, pointing to where the serial number should have been. What a Bastard! He took me to all the bikes in the garden and said, 'One of these bikes is stolen.' I thought,

'Shit! Which one? Because I always check and make sure that all vehicles I trade in are all legal.'

'It's the Kawasaki AR80, we'll be arresting you for that.'

I say, 'Well that's in for a repair and isn't mine, I'll give you the guy's address.'

He looked at me as if his world had imploded. There had to be at least ten police, from God knows how many departments, all trying to get as much on me as possible. They were not interested in anyone else, except for Kim at first, because I wasn't there at the start. Even one of the other lodgers who had a chillum pipe that had been used to smoke marijuana. He told the police officer who went into his room which drawer it was in. They weren't interested.

They took me to my bedroom. Now I have always folded crisp packets up into triangles; it's so much tidier in a pub before putting them into an ashtray, rather than ramming them into a pint glass. I did it at home too. The 'postman' declared, 'Oh, so you're making wraps.'

'They're Hula Hoop packets,' I reply, matter of fact. He didn't believe me and proceeded to empty the bin.

'Oh, they're Hula Hoop packets!' he admits.

'Told you,' I think.

I said he could search the whole room if he wanted to, but the only drugs in the room were half a gram of amphetamines, and I revealed it to him. I could tell, from his face, that things were not going very well.

There was a set of scales on the mantel piece I used to check what I was buying, but they were more of an ornament. They got taken away and tested, and nothing was found on them.

By noon, and after all that had gone on that morning, all they had on me was:

1. A stolen bike that was a customer's in for repair. I had given them the owner's address.
2. A motorboat outboard engine with some filed down serial numbers. Although they took it and other stuff away, I never got any of it back and I was never charged for any stolen goods.

3. About 30 quid's worth of personal drugs, half of which wasn't even mine, although I had said it was mine to protect Kim.

Meanwhile, sensing that I was about to be taken to the police station, I said I had to get the dog out of the van and put him in the house. Every officer there then went into panic mode. Tysie had been going mental watching all this. There was no way anyone else could have got him out of my van.

I was taken to Chard Police station. Sat in a cell, I was thinking, 'Shit! This isn't good!' I tried to work out how it had all happened. Then I remember Kaz's letter to Pat, saying how she had gone 'too far'. The penny dropped. I spent two hours being interviewed. I explained that Kim and I have a smoke now and then and share a bit of speed between us and the lodgers, only in the house. That was it. They asked me to tell them where I got it from. I refused to. They bailed me and I went home. Next morning, the local coppers came round for a chat over the wall. I serviced these guys' motorbikes. 'I hope you didn't think it was us?' they ask.

'Of course not.' I say.

Bearing in mind I had been told once that a couple of the local police officers used to allegedly smoke a bit of weed at the station (believe it or not), I had never witnessed this. So, after a bit of digging, it transpired that Kaz, to get off the GBH charge, told the police that I had kilos of drugs at the house, stolen bikes, a huge vicious dog, the works. About a month later, I got called back to the station. I am charged for the following:

1. Social Supply of Cannabis.
2. Social Supply of Amphetamine.
3. Possession of Cannabis.
4. Possession of Amphetamine and…. wait for it,
5. Allowing cannabis to be smoked in my house.

Social Supply is handing someone a spliff or something of the sort, I'd never heard of it before, or, for that matter, charge 5. After all that hassle at the house, Kaz had stitched me up big time. They knew it and were determined to charge me for as much as they could, and I couldn't do anything about it. I also wonder if they had been following Pat when he came out on home leave. Saw him come and see me at the house and decided to have go at me too, hence they knew about the dog etc. It had to be Kaz.

On top of all this, things were starting to get 'a bit hairy' as they say.

Fisher, who had stitched Pat up, but we couldn't prove it, moved into a house not far from me and set up a motorbike business. I'd come across him a few times while Pat was inside. He was, to put it bluntly, a nasty 'FUCKING CUNT'! I'm sorry, I've been trying not to swear too much, but there are no other words to describe him. Fisher robbed the flat of a blind friend of mine who lived in the local council estate in Chard. He recognised his smell, as blind people do. Fisher never got charged. I think Fisher also killed his dog at some stage when he tried to press charges, but there was never any proof. The dog was found dead outside the flat. When I found out, I did burst into a pub one night where I knew Fisher drank. I had Tysie with me. I'm glad he wasn't there because I probably would have done time for that. I was so angry.

Anyway, on one of my prison visits to Pat, he tells me that there's two guys who are being released soon that Fisher had stitched up too. This is how Pat found out what had happened to himself. Fisher had been doing this all over the country apparently, and did what he wanted, including robbing blind people in their own home. The police were happy as they were getting results. I'd told Pat that I knew where Fisher had moved to. I gave Pat his address to give to the guys. Fisher disappeared a couple of weeks after the other guys came out of prison. I never saw him again. I try not to wish bad on anyone if I can help it, but whatever happened to him, he deserved it. Looking back, I have no qualms about handing over his address – he was the scum of the earth.

As for the Drug Squad bust it's a good job Kaz never knew about a lock up I was paying rent for around the corner in the local council estate that I used to keep motorbike spares in and other things just in case.

Enough said.

***

I'm sure there will be a few, or maybe many, after reading this chapter of my life that will judge me on the events of those three years. I will just say this: if you've never been in a position like that, or up to the hilt in something that is out of your control, sometimes you can't be judgemental, as you will never know what it's like or how difficult it is to change anything for the better until it's all over.

CHAPTER 11

Up North, Courts, Birth, Hernia and more scraps!

It was a while before I got a court date for the charges brought against me. I couldn't tell any of my family about these episodes, not even my sister. The first they will know about that part of my life is if they read this book. I'm sure my sister will, but my Mum has now passed away and will never know. My kids know a lot of it, as I've told them most of the stories many times already.

While I'm waiting, Kim and I decide to move up North. Kim comes from Swansea but was quite happy to move to Lancashire. By now she's pregnant and I've just about had it with Chard and all the shit that's happened. Pat's out of prison now. He's gutted after I tell him.

He says, 'You're the only person I can trust down here anymore and you're buggering off.'

I really felt bad for him. He'd had some shit going on in prison, but I reckon I'd had my fair share of it outside too.

'I need to go back up North and start again mate.' He understands. I start looking for somewhere to live in Lancashire. I suppose I was brought up in Lancashire when Liverpool was part of that county, before Merseyside was formed, and Lancashire seemed like a good place to be. The main problem I have is that I've got about fifteen motorbikes and a few cars, including a 1936 vintage shell that's worth quite a bit. Oh! And a 7.5t truck's worth of bike spares and a Beavertail car transporter.

I still haven't had the operation for my hernia either and it's really starting to hurt. The doctor had told me to 'just stay off work until the op'. I find an industrial unit in **Thornton-Cleveleys**, sort out the application and I can move into it three weeks later. However, a few days before I've got everything ready to move (business wise that is), the agents tell me that the owners have given it to someone local! I start the search again. The house sold for about the same price that I'd bought it for, due to lowering house prices in the area. Yeah! I end up selling a couple of cars in exchange for an old library bus that's been converted into a camper. It was the best I could do at short notice. I find a potato storage place in **Great Eccleston**, part of the rural area of **Garstang**, Lancashire, that I can keep everything in for a month while I find another unit. I locate one at **Alty's Builders Merchants** in **Hesketh Bank** (7 miles from **Southport**) and everything then gets shifted to there. The whole thing was a logistical nightmare, let alone trying to get all the possessions in the house moved too. I had to sell the Z900 low rider I'd built to pay for it all. I was gutted.

Kim's pregnancy was planned, but we weren't expecting to do everything else we had to do at such short notice. One moment, we were living in a residential, three-bed, end terrace with plenty of space inside and out, then suddenly we are squeezed into a converted, mobile tin can parked outside an industrial unit. And don't forget Tysie, and Kim's cat too! It's no surprise Kim chose to stay at my sister's quite a lot, which was only about ten miles down the road. We were both grateful to shower at sis's most days anyway. I was 'officially' living at the unit to be able to qualify for unemployment benefit (bit like the government hoops you still have to conform to these days). We had no income whatsoever, and after the estate agents' fees, and whatever else you get stung for when selling a house, there was no money from the house sale.

I had started work straight from school, and apart from 'signing on' (dole) for two months* after I took redundancy from Glaxo, I had never claimed a penny from the state. I've always worked, and I always will, that's how I am.

*I did so for the 40 quid a fortnight off the **Business Enterprise Scheme** when setting the discos up in the 1980's, a scheme that the government had started because of the number of people trying to start a new business.

I'd been claiming dole for about a month when I get a visit from the **DHSS**. They ask me about the bikes, and I explain my situation.

Although I'm sat there waiting for customers, that are few and far between, I am available to work should the Job Centre phone me. They take my **UB40** certificate off me and that's that. It was strange that, a month or so later, the Government announced a drop in the number of unemployed by 100,000. It looked like they were going around trying get as many people off unemployment benefit as they could to manipulate the figures, which governments of all political persuasions do (not just one party, I should add).

The winter of 1995. Cold on so many fronts, with a slight bit of déjà vu!

By now, Kim has only got a couple of months before her due date.

'Kim?' I say, 'I've never done this in my life, but you go and find a local place to rent and claim as a single parent for now. I'll still live at this address but will call round as much as I can.'

She agreed it was the best for the child and moved to a small flat above the Spar in Hesketh Bank, about half a mile from the unit.

While all this was going on, I had two other problems. The first being my hernia and the second, I really needed to get back into performing music again. The operation was finally re-scheduled to be at **Ormskirk General**. They had offered me a slot at **Taunton General Hospital** when I was still living in Chard, but it landed right when we were moving back up North. I had to cancel it after waiting for nearly two bloody years! The other pressing matter was my impeding court case. Before we left Chard, I'd attended the Magistrates Court in Taunton and had pleaded guilty to all the charges, expecting some form of community service. They wouldn't deal with it because it had 'Supply' in two of the charges, even though the court was told that it was a casual thing between friends. My case was referred to the Crown Court. This was bad. I remember the solicitor telling me, 'I don't know how you've pissed everyone off, but they want you to go down!' It made me wonder if Fisher was trying to get me out of the way, just so he could build up his bike business. This all seemed like a slight bit of déjà vu.

I'll explain the rest of this in one go and then I can carry on with the rest of my tale. Kim is close to dropping when I had to go to my first appearance at the Crown Court. I was shitting multiple bricks. I rode down for the hearing on one of the bikes by myself. I arrive at 10am. The judge comes into court with his wig slightly cockeyed. I hear him saying to one of the barristers, 'that was a great party last night!' or something of that ilk, and he still looked a little pissed. I plead guilty and the prosecution presents the evidence – the scales, the small amount of drugs and some magazine paper. All this was their evidence to support their case that I was weighing the drugs out before putting them into wraps. After the prosecution had finished, the judge asks, 'Why has this come to Crown Court? There is no proof of any money being made or changing hands, it is the smallest number of drugs I've ever seen in a Crown Court and the scales have not tested positive for any residue of any drugs whatsoever!'

My defence barrister then brings up the mitigating circumstances, the fact that I have a pregnant partner and a sole trader motorcycle business 'Not in a very good state at the moment,' I think to myself. I've moved back up North to put all this behind me. You get the idea. The judge wants to adjourn for a couple of weeks for reports, as they do. The prosecution wants to deny bail, which the judge, doing his best to suppress a laugh, denies. My solicitor is still convinced it might be a jail term though. Off I ride back home to Hesketh Bank. A few weeks later (25th November 1995), Kim comes with me as it's the sentencing, and she's as apprehensive as I am. I go to the court; she heads for the gallery. I'm asked to standup by the judge, and it went something like this.

'Mr. Baker, as I said at the last hearing, the quantity of drugs found is so small, I cannot sentence you for the Possession charges in the Crown Court and this whole case should have stayed at the Magistrates Court. Although I am not condoning using drugs, I will say that there are your personal circumstances to consider. I see you have your partner with you today and that you regret this misdemeanour. Furthermore, you have never been in trouble with the police before. On the other three counts, I therefore sentence you to 140 hours community service for the two Social Supply charges to run concurrently. 40 hours community service for knowingly letting cannabis be smoked in the house running concurrently too. The probation service has told me you fix motorbikes, and there is a scheme near where you live which will benefit from you showing your skills to young offenders.'

That was it. Kim and I, after having a chat with the probation service who were there, drove back up North.

The only time we ever came back to Chard was now and then to visit Kim's mum, as she had lived down there for a while after splitting up with Kim's dad. For the next six months or so, I attended a unit in **Skelmersdale** for my community service. The young offenders there were trying to learn new skills to help them get a job and stop them from getting into trouble with the police, so at least something good came out of it. What pissed me off was when I got the papers through from the court. On my criminal record, I had been sentenced for the two possession charges, the same for the social supply, which was not the case in court. That criminal record should have disappeared after five years, with it only being community service. How wrong I was, and I didn't find out that it was still there until 2002. That will all be explained later.

We arrive back in Hesketh Bank, and I start to think about the best way of moving forward. The bike business was not making a lot of money. If Kim hadn't been living 'by herself' for a while, I would have struggled to pay for everything at first. Christmas passed and then on the 28th January 1996, our wonderful son Jonathan was born at **Christiana Hartley Maternity Hospital** in Southport which is now unfortunately closed down.

Off down the M6

Kim had a lucky escape before the birth. I was watching the pethidine get pumped into her by a machine, when I noticed air in the line! When I questioned it, the nurse didn't take me seriously. I'd worked at Glaxo for God's sake, I knew what I was talking about. They had just changed the drip bottle, and I reckon that's how it happened. Kim's completely out of it, as you can imagine, unaware of the impending air in the pipe which would kill her. I ask the nurse again when she comes back into the room, she looks and runs to get the doctor, who immediately sorts it out. They don't say a word to me about it. That was a big mistake on their part. By the way, there were no compensation claims made. Take note. It's not all about money, although it sems to be for a lot of people these days. On a different note, if the worst had happened and Kim had died, my life again would have changed in a major way and probably most of what is written in the next 13 chapters would never have happened.

Anyway, **Jonathan** is born safely and all's good. I go into hospital in the spring of that year for my hernia operation. Today if you have a hernia, it's sorted within six months; a general anaesthetic, a little snip and in they go, done and you walk out the following morning. They might even do it while you're awake too!

I've had this hernia for nearly three years, and I've been working with a constant nagging pain in my groin for most of that time. I go into the day ward in the morning and handed a gown and a razor to shave my pubic hair with. 'Hang on a minute, no water or soap?' I ask. Apparently not! It hurt and was awkward. I didn't do a very good job. Someone else must have completed the task, as I was totally bald down there when I woke up about 1pm.

It felt like someone had opened my legs and smashed a sledgehammer into my balls, or gentleman's balloons. The pain was just indescribable. The nurse just chucked my bag of clothes into the room and said, 'You can get dressed now.' GET DRESSED! I couldn't even move in the bed, let alone get out of it. Eventually, the surgeon comes to see me and explains that he hadn't seen a hernia that bad for a long time, and that he had to lattice the muscle as well as having mesh put in too. That's why I was in so much pain. Any pain relief had worn off and I hadn't been given anything else – not even some water. The nurse apologised after my sister had been in and kicked off after what had happened. Remember, my sister is a qualified Sister in the NHS and has, for example, run the Trauma/Neuro Ward at **The Walton Centre**, before moving to the **National Hospital for Neurology & Neurosurgery in London**. I was kept in overnight and my mum had to pick me up in the car the following day. I still couldn't walk properly and, to top it all off, it took three weeks for me to sit down on the loo. That was a relief, I can tell you.

Once my gentleman's balloons (testicles) had shrunk back to normality, I got back to the bikes and started thinking about my musical career again. One day at the unit, I was on a fag break when two policemen came in. The court case comes flooding back and I'm thinking 'Here we go again!'

'Mr Philip Baker?' says one of the officers.

'Yes.'

'Did you used to own a Peugeot 504 Pickup, registration XXXX XXX?'

'Yes.'

'The registration of the vehicle has been used in an armed robbery, and your name is still on the logbook.'

I'd sold the pickup to a guy in south Chard in exchange for a van that had a police siren as a horn, which was great if you wanted car drivers to get out of the way. The buyer, in due course, sold the pickup to the scrap yard next door. However, it got nicked from there a few weeks later but only got 200 yards down the road where the thieves wrote it off. It transpires that there was a dodgy guy working in the scrap yard who was selling registration plates off scrap vehicles to criminals, and the plates off my pickup had been used in this particular armed robbery. You couldn't make this stuff up. Luckily for me, I had a receipt of sale of the pickup, and I went to the station to sort it all out. While there I pointed to where the scrap yard it had gone to on a map. That's how we found out about the registration plates because, up until that point, they were looking at charging me for armed robbery because the bloody pickup was still in my name!! As I said at the beginning, I never really do things in halves do I!

Anyway, back to the story.

CHAPTER 12

Music, Agents, Rats and Door Fitting

In 1996 to get my musical career going again, I needed an electric guitar. I only had an acoustic, after my **Epiphone** had been stolen down in **Axminster**. My fingers on my left hand were now back to normal after the knife episode. I found a Yamaha RGX312 for sale in **Blackpool** for 140 quid including a hard case. I have only ever seen another one of these guitars and that was one I bought later on as a spare, but it never played the same as the original and I sold it.

I still have the original RGX although I don't play it that much these days. The pickups need a rewind, and the original fretboard is worn out and needs replacing. I played that guitar for over fifteen years on average two hours a day, five sometimes seven days a week while gigging.

I still had my tape decks, backing tracks, a small PA and so, when things were quiet in the unit with the bikes, I'd practise the songs again.

It was my Mum and Dad's Ruby wedding anniversary, and they'd asked me if I would do a show for them at their 'do'. A friend of my dad's, at the party, told me he knew an agent called Doreen. He must have been something to do with **West Derby Bowling Club**, which unfortunately closed not that long ago due to lack of support. My dad was a member, and he mentioned that Doreen used to book acts for the club. In due course, having contacted Doreen, I did an audition at a club one night and she was my sole agent for the next two years. I played all over the Northwest. She also got me on a few talent shows including one on **Magic Radio** station in Liverpool with **Billy Butler**. More on that later.

The unit was badly located for my bike business, which was just ticking over keeping our heads above water. A couple of old boys on mopeds used to come in all the time to get their **Honda C90**'s looked at and a chinwag over a few cuppas. They were in their seventies and lived on a caravan park just outside Southport. Because of the terms of using the campsite, they could only live there for nine months of the year. For the other three, they used to jet off to Benidorm and party with all the youngsters from January to March. They were ace. Another set of customers pop in one day and say there's a load of bikers meeting at a pub nearby with a view to setting up a **Motorcycle Club** or **MCC** bike club. MCC is a motorcycle club that raises money for charity and only wear front or side patches.

This is distinct to a Motorcycle bike club (MC) who are all backpatch clubs. It would take too long to explain the differences between them and the sub-culture of Outlaw Motorcycle Clubs. I have experience of most of them and your own search of the internet will help you if you are interested to know more.

I agree to come down to the meeting at the pub, I've never been in a club as such, I'd ridden with other clubs, but have never been part of one and, to be honest, I wasn't particularly interested in joining one. I thought it might be good for business as much as anything else. I go to the meeting and come home. Kim says, 'how did you get on?'

'I'm its chairman!' And I was for the next two years. This is one of those times in your life when a decision like that affects many things.

Kim and I hadn't really thought about where we were going to live once Jon was born. We were still in her small flat, but it was the three of us and Tysie. I needed to pack the bike business in and find another job, until the music took off again.

River Rats MCC, had some great guys in the club. A lot were self-employed like myself.

Ian, who was the Rally Secretary, fitted industrial doors, Roller Shutters, Sectional Overheads: the full monty. The guy who had been working for him had got himself another job and left Ian with a problem. You can't fit doors like that by yourself. I said I'd give him a hand for a couple of months while he found someone else.

I ended up working with him for eighteen months. I only packed it in because I was getting so busy with the gigs. I couldn't afford to be stuck on a motorway coming home from **Southampton** or wherever and miss doing a show.

Initially, I shut the unit but carried on paying the rent on it, and I go over on a small 250cc motorbike every morning to Ian's who lived in **Chorley**. It was about 15 miles. Fine in the summer but, in winter, if you need to be there for an 8am start, you had to allow an hour or more for the journey especially if it was snowing! If we were driving to, say Southampton for a 8am, it was a 3am start from Ian's.

While I was away working one week, Kim and my sister found a house in Chorley that was up for rent; a four-bedroom semi, with a massive drive-through garage and huge garden. I'm a bit hesitant at first about something that big. But I had all the motorbike spares, motorcycles and a Daimler I was trying to make into a motorcycle trike. These are all in the unit I was paying rent for. So, the whole lot came with us just before Christmas in December 1996, when we moved to Warton Place, Chorley. We stayed there as a family for nearly ten years.

Before we moved to Chorley, the family had been getting increasingly worried about my dad. In 1976 he had a stroke. We didn't know he'd had the stroke; we were told it was a nervous breakdown by the local doctor. I remember him phoning my Mum from our newsagent shop, to say he didn't feel well. When my mum arrived, he was just stood there staring into space and one of the paperboys trying to look after serving our customers. What was amazing was that through all the trauma of having the stroke he remembered our home telephone number to phone to say he was ill. It's curious how the brain works.

After that, every now and then, he'd have a funny turn. Unfortunately, when one occurred on holiday, the foreign medics didn't have access to his medical records and, of course, Mum would be told that it was a relapse of the breakdown, when in fact it was another stroke.

One Saturday, my dad had been dropped off at our flat by mum to see Kim and baby Jonathan. Mum said she'd come back in a couple of hours after she'd been to see my sister. I was at the unit which was only a ¼ mile walk. Kim phones me at the unit and says she is going shopping with Jonathan and my dad has set off to see me and will be there in ten minutes. An hour goes by, and he still hasn't arrived. I go to the flat in case he turned back but no one is there. All I can do is ride around trying to find him. Eventually, my parents' car is coming towards me, and he is in it with mum. Dad had had another relapse and started walking back home to Liverpool, about 25 miles away! Again, we put it down to another relapse, he had all his faculties he was just coming up with weird ideas like walking home 25 miles was good exercise at 64 years of age!

So, we moved over to Chorley just in time for dad to have a massive stroke on Boxing Day. He was rushed to hospital, and once he'd been examined, they said that since 1977 he'd had fifteen minor strokes, five major strokes and ten percent of his brain was dead. They were perplexed that he was still alive. He went blind for two days after this one: that's how bad it was. If it had been diagnosed correctly in 1977, possibly none of these other strokes would have happened. In 1997, he was 9 months from retirement as a Court Usher. He wanted to buy another motorbike, and both my parents were going to relive their youth riding around Europe. His licence was taken away and he never drove a car or road a bike ever again. But he was back to his normal sarcastic self after a few weeks. However, all was not right, because of other ailments, which we'll come to later.

I'm going to get a funny story out of the way from the bike club so that I can concentrate on the music and all the other shenanigans that have happened since 1996, so off we go down the M61 now (which, by the way is near Chorley).

The River Rats MCC set themselves up at **The Leisure Lakes** in **Tarleton** just outside Southport. We'd meet there every week, and Leisure Lakes had a vast expanse of land. We decided to hold a rally the following spring and utilise the military tanks that were on exhibition there.

It was decided to have a raffle at the Rally and the first prize was to use a Chieftain Tank to crush a **Volvo**. For any non-bikers, there was always this thing about motorbike accidents and Volvo drivers and the fact that Volvos were highly regarded for the safety. Hence, Volvo drivers were cocooned in protection. Back then there was a saying 'Volvos are built like tanks' and that because Volvo headlights (like all Scandinavian cars) were on all the time, that even in the scrap yard with the battery dead, their lights still worked. For any of you who may believe this was a myth. I had a 244 Volvo that was on its last legs. So, we took the engine and gearbox out and got it towed to Leisure Lakes for the Rally. The prize was drawn and the guy who won got in the tank with the owner and, after a drive around for a bit, went for the Volvo. Now, please bear in mind this tank, even decommissioned, weighs some 50 tonnes. It climbs up onto the roof of the Volvo and yes, not all the weight was on the roof of the car but not far off. The car just sat there. 'SHIT!' I thought the bloody car had won. Fifteen seconds later, suddenly the whole car collapsed under the weight, and it was flattened. I had a photo of this and although looking everywhere, sadly, I can't find it to share with you.

A great weekend was had by all and that was Jonathan's first rally, aged twelve weeks old. He went down in the sidecar of a **BMW** motorbike I was selling for someone and still had it at the time, even though we'd moved to Chorley. Obviously, Kim was sat in the side car with Jon just in case I get trolled for having a 12-week-old baby by itself in a side car. The things you have to do these days with social media!

I remember the 'Christmas Toy' and the 'Easter Egg' runs to the hospitals for the kids in Southport. I still have one of the Egg runs on

VHS as Kim filmed it all in the side car. After a couple of years, it all started getting a bit political, as clubs do, and I called it a day. Apart from that, I was now starting to get really busy with the music which was where I wanted to be.

My River Rats patch that we used to wear on our leathers. About 3 inches in diameter and worn on the top half of your arm or on the front left of your leathers.

*What I'm trying to put over here, is that if I hadn't gone to that meeting about the bike club, I would never have met Ian and moved to Chorley. Furthermore, I certainly wouldn't have set up my **Pink Floyd** tribute band to help raise money for **Chorley Little Theatre**: in short, I would have gone down a completely different musical career to where I am now.

CHAPTER 13

Births, Depression and Challenges

While we settled into our house in Chorley, I started drinking at The Gillibrand Arms on Collingwood Road in the evenings when I wasn't working. It closed in 2015 and was demolished. I can't believe that they've crammed about 30 houses onto the same site. However, back then, I got to know a couple of musicians who drank there.

Neil played drums and was having a hard time. He was off work due to a breakdown that had happened as a result of pressure from work, which he eventually got compensation for. Peter (aka stage name Max Peters) was a singer, who in the 1980's had been in some pretty good bands in the states and was still getting royalties every now and then from various songs on compilation albums he recorded. He's the one who mentioned me going off down the motorway. He also did the pub and club circuit which I started working in again and did for the next twelve years. We three, had a chat one night and decided to form a 1980s tribute band. We called it **Out of the Blue**. I'm not quite sure where the name came from, but it must have been from a song or something from that decade. It took a while for the band to get together around 1997 the year before Elea was born.

Jonathan (Jon) was now a year old and was fine, but since we moved into the house, Kim didn't seem to be in a good space. I think it had come from post-natal depression. She seemed to be getting more and more depressed.

We decided to have another baby. We read the theory that having another child can cancel out post-natal depression and we really wanted a little brother or sister for Jon. We also decided to have our next child's birth at home, as this was less stressful for the mother as much as anything else and as long as there were no complications with the first.

The midwife was quite happy for this to happen, unlike our local Doctor which I'll come to later.

I was working away sometimes through the week with Ian and gigging on a Friday through to Sunday. However, our band was starting to receive requests for playing further afield. The cost of renting a larger house, is larger bills. For the first few years I was trying to earn every penny I could. Kim was in no fit state to work.

Early hours of 6th April 1998, Elea was born. Her full name is Eleanor from the star-shaped flower that grew in the forest of **Lothlorien** in the book *Lord of the Rings*. It was fortunate that we had a home birth because when Kim's waters broke on the morning of the day before, I had a £80 gig that afternoon in Garston, Liverpool. The Midwife said that it was going to be a least twelve hours before the baby would be born even though she was two weeks overdue. My parents came to look after Kim and I arrived home about 7pm for the birth to happen 6 hours later, while Jonathan was fast asleep in the bedroom next door. Elea weighed 10lbs and there was a lot less stress than having to rush to hospital and, if you have other kids, arranging a babysitter, not knowing how long you'll be at the hospital, I could go on.

I continued working with Ian, but it was becoming physically tiring and logistically demanding to gig while working away. The labour-intensive work we were doing was a young guy's game and I was 38. Similar to the work I did as a contractor to Blue Circle, health and safety tended to go out of the window to a certain extent. For example, carrying a three to four-metre-long roller shutter drum is hard. Together, you may have to climb two separate sets of ladders, up to six metres in the air, holding the opposite ends of the drum balancing it horizontally on your arms while you try and fit it into its position.

I was a lot stronger then, than I am now, and didn't have a problem carrying the drums, but I had so many other things going on in my life with music and two infant kids. I was self-employed so one slip off the ladder and that was it, you could either be in hospital or worse. I could get insurance but let's put it politely they will always try and wriggle out of paying out. Insurance is not a risk game anymore.

Never drive when on your mobile phone

Ian was driving the van back home on the M62. I was asleep. Along the stretch from Leeds over Saddleworth Moor, the brakes came on hard and woke me up. We were hurtling towards a brand new A8 Audi that was stationary in a traffic jam ahead. Ian put the handbrake on in addition to the pushing down hard on the foot brake. We stopped about two feet away from it. The Nissan Bluebird behind us didn't. It was moving at 80mph (we found out later) and through the wing mirrors we could see it wasn't slowing down. We braced ourselves for the impact.

'BANG!' I don't think I've heard a noise like that since. All the tools and cases, nuts and bolts on the shelves in the back of the van flew into the air and smashed down all over the floor. There was no panel between the cab and the van, and a Hilti drill hit me in the shoulder. We were shunted straight into the Audi. After the initial shock we got out. There was wreckage over all the three lanes on our side of the motorway. All that was left of the front of the Nissan was the inner wings, engine, wheels that was it!

THE DRIVER CLIMBED OUT OF THE CAR! I stood with my mouth gaping amazed that he actually got out of the car. I noticed the ignition was still on in his car and I turned it off just in case of fire.

'What happened? Did you stall?' I couldn't believe this question from the person who had just smashed into the back of us. The woman driving behind the Nissan, who had stopped in time, confirmed the speed it was travelling as she braked. She said his brake lights never went on and that's how we all knew what speed he'd hit us. The Police turned up pretty quick.

'Ok let's get the car onto the hard shoulder.' says one of the Officers.

HE GETS IN THE CAR, STARTS IT UP AND HE DRIVES IT ONTO THE HARD SHOULDER! WTF!

'I want one of those!' I think to myself.

We all clear the wreckage as best we can and move our van onto the hard shoulder. By this time, the Nissan driver has gone all wobbly with the adrenaline of the crash wearing off and an ambulance is called for him. Apparently, he was a taxi driver from Manchester, who was on the phone at the time of the crash.

There was a sixteen-mile tailback, and we were there for quite a while waiting for the breakdown truck. It caused just under £4,000 worth of damage. The van was three years old, but Ian had done 144,000 miles in it from new, which shows you how much travelling we did. He was hoping it would get written off and get a new one, but he was £200 short of the write off value. We just had to wait to get it repaired and use a hire van. It took a day to clear everything out of the van after the crash.

How to waste money

One contract we had was at Manchester Airport and we witnessed the waste and cost of inept engineers and the problems they caused. While forced to sit around waiting for fire permits, we worked out the waiting time over the four months we were there, and it came to 14 days! We saw a marble floor being laid in duty free that was 60% completed before it was smashed up and re-laid with new marble slabs costing £20 a square foot. Turns out the engineer gave the company the wrong line to start. We put up three very expensive roller shutters that we fitted into a void above the ceiling in one of the duty-free shops. However, they will never be used because they moved the walkways and told us to leave them there and get new ones made!

Sheep and Fire Engines

One of the biggest laughs we had was on the M6 in Cumbria in a blizzard. We were on our way to Cockermouth to fit a door. Unfortunately, a lorry drivers cab caught fire while he was transporting a load of sheep. As you may or may not know if you have live animals on a vehicle and you have a fire you have to release them immediately and so the motorway was closed. We were forced to sit in a traffic jam for three hours and would have helped but we had been told to stay in the van by the Police. They entertained us by their attempts to round up a herd of white sheep in a snow storm. It was hilarious!

We went back up to the part time Fire Station in Cockermouth, Cumbria the following week, to fit what's called a Sectional Overhead

Door. These are panels built up on hinges so that when they lift, they can sit on rails near as damn it horizontally in the roof once opened. It's the most common loading dock door on industrial units these days. They had an old folding door and needed a new one. As we were taking the old door down, we noticed that there wasn't enough room in the framework above, for the door to fit when open.

Ian phones the door company to tell them it won't fit.

'We don't believe you!'

Bear in mind that Ian has worked in this business for nearly twenty years and for the same company before he went freelance, and they are doubting his judgement?

They send for the surveyor who took two hours to drive from Newcastle only for him to say, 'Oh, it doesn't fit.'

'Who the fuck surveyed this?' We ask him.

'I did.' He says and adds, 'it's a part time fire station and no one was there so I just looked in through the window and guessed. I didn't have a lot of time'. What a cock!

Ian reckons we can cut the door down by six inches and it will fit in the void when open.

'That's fine,' I say, 'but is the fire engine going to fit? I saw it come out this morning before we started stripping the old door and it looked pretty tight to the top of the door opening.'

So, the surveyor gets the Fire Engine back from where it was being stored together with the fire officers. We cut the facia that will go above the door, climb a set of ladders each holding the facia where it would be positioned, and they drive the engine in and out. It just fits and I mean just.

We put the old door back on and go back two weeks later to fit the new one once the newly cut panels were manufactured. Luckily when we went back there were no more delays on the M6 with sheep.

***

As I mentioned earlier, Doreen was getting me a lot of work including the radio talent show that was on Magic FM, an off shoot of Radio City in Liverpool. Billy Butler and Wally Scott were the presenters, and they showcased a singer each week and had three members of the public phoning in to give points out of ten. In addition, a booking agent was at the studio who gave marks too. The prize was a TV slot on a cable station. There had been a contestant on 38 points for about four weeks. So, all I needed to do was to beat that score!

I had been to Orange Studio's in Preston, Lancashire to record three songs that used to get sent out as a promo to potential clients by Doreen. I took the backing tracks in for the songs, so it was just one session at the studio. The songs were *Circle of Life, Memories* and *Sunshine of my Life*. All the backing tracks I'd recorded myself. By now, I had a little studio at home with a **Tascam 8 track tape recorder**, a **Roland R5** drum machine and **U220 Keyboard**. It was nearly the same set up as the one I had in Brighton some eight years before. I had to rebuy everything, as I had sold the lot at some stage to raise money for the move to Somerset. We chose to send in *Sunshine of my Life* as the song.

I went to the radio station that day, casually thinking it would just be a bit of promo. All three members of the public who phoned in gave me 10 out of 10 and the agent in the studio gave me 9 out of 10 only because (and I quote) 'no-one's perfect.'

I then had to wait four weeks until the competition closed. I waited and waited but I never got a phone call, neither did Doreen. Billy Butler and Wally Scott left Magic due to some form of disagreement. So, my score of 39 was the leader, but I was not declared the winner and the prize never materialised.

One of those points in my life which could have changed everything, and I could have taken another path.

I spoke to Doreen about cancelling the sole management contract. I needed to start branching out further afield, nothing to do with what she was doing for me, I just needed to try and start getting more higher paid gigs. I'd started working with another solo artist (**Big AL**) doing the odd duo show and I watched how he worked the audience, going into the crowd with a radio mic (something I ended up buying). I learnt a lot about the club circuit from watching him.

He also introduced me to **Artist Showcases** for the club circuit. Now that's an experience and I've done quite a few. Basically, they are all the same format and unfortunately all the same acts most of the time. The art of doing Showcases is not to bother setting your equipment up until everyone else has finished. They all rush in trying get the exact space for their speakers, everyone strutting around most with egos much bigger than what they are actually capable of. That might sound a bit harsh but, unfortunately, that is the case.

You only sing or play three songs: a fifteen-minute slot at the very most. Tell a joke or two and that's it.

The concert secretaries in those days weren't arsed about where you've put your speakers as long as they are not too loud. You're dressed in your stage gear and you've got a good stage presence, and if you're female – you were good looking.

So, they all get setup and then you go in and set your speakers up on the outside of everyone else, just put your mixer and minidisc (yes, we had **minidiscs** now) where you can. You had everything recorded on the minidisc player that you needed. Press the button and do your slot. You then go into a room and haggle with which ever Concert Secretaries come into the room who want to book you. It's a bit like an auction or cattle market but without the auctioneer. When everything was over all your gear was so easy to strip down while everyone else was tripping over themselves packing up.

It's very similar to watching people waiting to board and leave aeroplanes.

Everyone rushes to get on the plane as quickly as possible and will stand in the queue rather than just sit in a chair until the queue goes down. The plane's not going to leave without you. You're at the gate and not going to miss the plane. Likewise leaving the plane, everyone's stood up desperate to get off only to find that we are all getting on a bus. Get on the bus last and you get off the bus first.

I was at a showcase at **Farrington Conservative Club** near Leyland. There was this guy and a beautiful blonde as a duo doing a slot. He was singing and playing guitar, was okay but I wasn't that impressed, she was playing the keyboards. One of the concert secretaries says to me 'Hey aren't they good and she's amazing.'

I say, 'The keyboard isn't plugged in, it's not even on.'

They got booked by every Concert Sec there.

Say no more.

It was at this particular showcase that I met a guy called Derek, who became a good friend and singing partner as a duo for a few years after that. I will come back to that a little later on.

Big AL gave me quite a few contacts of agents and I thanked him for that. I started to get work at Caravan Holiday Parks, Larger Social Clubs, Weddings and other family celebrations. Geographically, they ranged from Scotland down to the Midlands. **Clubland Entertainments** based in Carnforth (who are a great agency and are still in business now) gave me most of my work, mainly in Cumbria and Scotland.

Some of the drives could be nearly three hours long but it paid good money, and I was out at gigs most days a week if not seven at some stages.

I was also performing at Elderly homes in the day which were really good but sad in some ways. I never want to be like that.

I also did two small tours of Scotland, a few stories of which are below.

But before I get to that, on the band side of things, Out of the Blue now had a Keyboard player called **Neil Gordon** (aka **Flash from Bolton**) and Tony (a bassist), who lived in Chorley too. We performed songs by bands like **Go West, Duran Duran, Simple Minds**, you get the idea. We used to rehearse at The Gillibrand Arms in the back room. People used to come in from the pub and have a listen. We didn't mind, both Peter and I had sung there on several occasions as solo artists and most of the punters in the pub knew us.

Peter and I also used to get up on the Karaoke night as a duo if we weren't working. To be honest that was good practice for the solo side of things as I'd choose songs, I didn't normally sing, to see how well I could sing them before recording a backing track back at home for it.

One of the first gigs we did as Out of the Blue was at a night club in Cumbria which turned into a disaster.

Now I know 1980's music is really popular, but we were not a 1980's disco band, we were a 1980's rock and pop band. We lasted the first set, and the owner of the club paid us off. That was a lesson learnt. The other lesson I learnt was after playing so long to backing tracks, it took quite a while getting used to playing with a live group again. I'm glad I'd started doing this as some of the solo gigs I was getting booked for were at clubs that had a backing band rather than using tracks. You had to supply sheet music for the band and am I glad I still had all my knowledge of music theory, albeit a little shaky in places, but I got back into writing out songs.

The backing bands were mainly on the Scotland runs but there were a few clubs in and around Manchester that still had these bands and other places around the UK too.

Although I haven't done the circuit for nearly 15 years, a lot of the clubs are long gone now, but for any that are left, what seems to have happened is that a lot of glorified Karaoke singers with no stage presence make up quite a lot of the acts these days and jumping on the band wagon, do it cheaper as they have jobs through the week.

It's nothing like it used to be, but it was good training for anything thrown at you in the future.

I did mention that I would put down a few funny stories so off we go up the M74 to Scotland.

As a solo artist, three gigs, in particular, stand out from all the other funny ones.

Status Quo Annie Lennox and the Drummer

I was doing a gig in Wishaw (pronounced 'Wishee' or they will kill you), which is just outside Motherwell.

I had a transit van and used to sleep in the van with the gear, get up in the morning, go to the local swimming baths for a swim and a wash, then find a café for a good old English or Scottish Breakfast.

Anyway, there was a backing band at this club, I met the Concert Sec, I set up, gave the music or dots we should call them, and went to get changed in the dressing room. The Concert Sec kept knocking on the door when he wanted to come in, even though it was ajar most of the time.

'You don't have to knock.' I tell him.

'I always knock, and I'll tell you why later.' He says.

I do the gig with the backing band, get back up with the band at the end for a jam with songs by Status Quo and Rolling Stones, the usual thing. A great night had by all.

With my van parked in the car park and being able to stay there overnight, I have a beer with the Concert Sec.

'So, tell me then, why do you always knock?' I ask.

He then goes on to tell me that one night a guy comes to do a show, and his mate comes with him. The Artist is supposed to have come out on stage at 8.30pm but hasn't so the Concert Sec walks straight into the dressing room only to find that the Artist's mate was actually his boyfriend, and they were having sex over the dressing room table.

'So, I always knock!'

At the same gig there's a guy who had been sat on one of the front tables of the audience all evening with his wife who looked the spit of Annie Lennox. He comes up and asks me if I would like to come back to theirs for a drink and that his wife makes a great breakfast. I thank him but all the gear is now in the van and I don't want to leave the van overnight by itself. He goes on and on for about ten minutes trying to persuade me and eventually they leave, and he's quite put out that I haven't agreed to go with them. The drummer of the band comes up to me and says, 'Are you going to their house then?'

'No.' I say, 'why?'

'He only wants you to go and shag his Missus!'

'How do you know?'

'Because I've been there myself.'

I stayed in the van that night. Apart from being with Kim at the time, I don't fancy Annie Lennox anyway. Her hair was too short.

Bingo & Open the Box

I was doing a gig in a Miners Club north of Dundee. I arrive, set up, the Concert Sec says to me,

'Three thirty-minute sets, first set at 8pm sharp and you must finish at

8.25pm as the bingo MUST start at 8.30pm!'

Now, anyone who doesn't know the Social Clubs of the UK, Bingo is the most important part of the night.

You could have Elton John standing on the stage but if he looks like he'll be going over the allotted time and delay the Bingo he'll be off.

Also, most clubs won't let the artists play bingo with them in case they win. I won once, I gave the money back or I would never have played there again believe me! So, I'm surprised that at 7.59pm the concert sec hasn't called me out of the dressing room. It gets to 8.15pm and he runs in, 'You're On'.

'Am I doing 30 minutes?' I ask

'No, you must finish at 8.25 as we said earlier.'

I go on stage, I sing a song, say hello to the audience, tell a joke, sing another song and I'm off. As I come off the stage, he says to me 'That was a great set' …WTF! That was shorter than any bloody showcase I'd ever done let alone a professional gig. The rest of the night went really well, but I ask him at the end why the delay?

All social clubs used to do 'Open the Box'. You draw a raffle ticket and whoever has the ticket, picks a key out of a hat and hopes it's going to open the box. The money builds up every week. If the key, they choose, opens the box they take the money and then the officials then show that the key was the right one and shut the box. If the key doesn't open the box, the ticket money goes into the box to be added to the rest and so it builds up over the weeks. Apparently, there was nearly £1000 in this box, it was nearly Xmas and the guy who had won the ticket picked a key opened the box and took the money. The problem was he was so strong and although he had the wrong key, he opened the box with it anyway and walked off with the money. The officials couldn't get the key out, everyone was complaining, but the guy was so big no one was going to ask for the money back and let him have it as far as I know. I think they were still arguing about it when I left.

A Ladies Night with a Difference

When you do these tours, you are given all the dates beforehand so that you can work out your routes and where to stop over. This particular show at **Livingston Rugby Club**, I had been asked by the agent if I could supply my lights, which I had with me, for the three acts rather than just myself. I agreed but wasn't told what type of gig it was until I got there. So, I arrive and set my gear up including the lights that the agent had asked me to supply.

I then find out from the organiser, a 25-year-old lady, that it's a ladies night, five sets and I'm the warmup act. Next on is a male stripper, another act in the middle set, the stripper comes back on and then I finish the night off. I walk into the dressing room where I meet the Stripper. He's sat down, shakes my hand and has a towel over his legs and is doing something underneath the towel. He explains that all strippers before a show knead and pull back and forth their penis with oils, to make them much longer than they normally are. He spent nearly 45 minutes doing this. 'It must be very small' I thought. It was quite surreal having a chat with a male Stripper while he 'PREPARED himself' for the show. Then he asks, 'The guy who normally operates my CD Player can't come tonight, could you do it?'

'What, out there at the side of the stage, with all the women watching?' Bearing in mind that this stage is just a temporary two-foot-high stage in a hall of the club.

One hour later after my first set, I'm sat at the side of the stage ready to play the CDs for the Stripper with 300 women, mostly in their twenties and thirties and they are already pissed.

I've never watched a male stripper, although I had been one as you know but only as a Stripper gram, it was enlightening.

The women were like animals, but he handled it well, finished the set and we went back to the dressing room.

The next act was amazing, he basically did fifteen impersonations of Artists with full costume changes that his wife helped him with. The whole show lasted an hour.

Then it was the Stripper's return, and I went back to my seat at the side of the stage. I thought the women were pissed enough in the first half; how wrong I was. I was getting girls coming up to me giving me their telephone numbers, not for me but to give to him at the end. The audience in the first set were Nuns compared to what they were trying to do in the second half. He finished his show, and I put some music on and went backstage.

The middle act had gone by now, the stripper got dressed and left and I went back on stage by myself with 300 pissed/rampant women stood there in front of me.

"GET EM OFF, GET EM OFF" They screamed. I had never been afraid of women before, even Kaz was a piece of cake compared to this. I just got the songs going, luckily, I had a guitar on and prayed for the set to finish. I ended the show intact. I had packed the gear away and the girl who had organised it all, came up to thank me after everyone had gone.

'You can come and stop with me tonight if you want to,' she said invitingly.

In different circumstances I would have, but Kim was at home and that was something I had to think about.

Did I have the X Factor?

And last, but not least which I nearly forgot to mention, one evening I think early 2005 having a drink with a few friends I was told I should have a go on the TV show 'The X Factor' as according to my friends I was better than the first winner of the show (Steve Brookstein).

I apply, and a few months later I'm at The Lowry Hotel in Manchester in a massive queue awaiting an Audition.

I end up in a room with 600 other budding TV Stars and asked by the part of the production crew to let my hair down (which I did) and sing my audition song, 'Don't Let The Sun Go Down On Me' by Elton John, which I performed to perfection and had most of the 600 people in the room cheering and clapping. I say most of the 600, because there were certain mothers with their daughters who complained to the crew why their child hadn't been chosen. People become very bitter in situations like this.

I perform my audition in front of 3 of the Production Crew in a room (not Simon Cowell) to be told I'm through to the next round. I return a few weeks later for my second audition. I think I had to sing the same song and again it went down well in front of the Production Crew again.

However, I am then asked what I did for a living, and I told them I worked in the music industry as a musician and ran an Audio Company.

Their faces dropped and I knew I was out of the competition.

I am sure the reason was because I was already in the industry. If I'd said I worked as a checkout guy in a Supermarket, nothing wrong with that job, but I reckon I would have got through because it all hinges on the publics sympathy when they vote. Stars in their Eyes had a contestant who was a professional singer, but this was omitted in the show and was filmed as a checkout girl at a supermarket. She won.

More of that in the next Chapter.

I was on tv albeit only when the trailers for X Factor were aired, there was always a few side shots of me drinking a cup of coffee in the holding area where we all waited to go into our auditions.

Something a youngster in the crowd of one of the Xmas light switch On's I did the following year must have remembered somehow and said to me 'You were on X Factor I saw you.'

It just goes to show how much influence the television set has on people who constantly watch it.

Did I have the X Factor? Well, if I did, I never found out.

CHAPTER 14

Tribute Bands and Community Centres

Things at home in 1999 were not good. Kim was struggling more and more with my work as a musician. Away a lot in the evening, and on tours of Scotland now and then, trying to save my dignity sometimes! Mum and my sister used to come around to help Kim with the kids when I was working. She eventually went to the doctors to be told that she was suffering from M.E. This is a sort of sleeping sickness, but depression comes with it unfortunately and lots of sleep. More of an explanation in Chapter 18.

There were times when she'd sleep for fourteen hours solid, get up, spend a few hours on the couch and then go back to bed again. I think I could have handled this a lot better, if I hadn't had the episode of Kaz in my life, but it was like 'Not Again!' A different situation but at the same time worrying. 'What ifs' went through my head and to the extremes of imagining 'what if', I came home from a gig and found her dead, or worse, she'd killed the kids! That's how depressed she was, and how worried I was. My work/life imbalance wasn't helping.

I'd spent all my life trying to get back into music properly from the late seventies. After the musical and turning down the Rock Show audition, it seemed every time I tried to get up and running, something would happen; like a recession, a heroin addict, or now, a partner who was severely depressed. For a while, I was coming home from a gig sometimes at 2am and, as the kids started growing up, getting up with the kids at 7am and sending them to preschool. Luckily, their preschool and primary were next door to the house, and I could literally throw them over the wall, and they were there. Obviously, I didn't do that. Jonathan was three years old and off he went to preschool in the September. I was looking after Elea while doing some repairs to the odd motorbike or changing an engine in a car for someone. It was a bit of extra income that we needed especially while Kim was too ill to work.

Elea the Escapologist

I remember one day I'd taken Jon to school, and Elea and I went shopping at the local supermarket. It was winter and she had a big one-piece coat on, all wrapped up and cosy. We did the shopping, and I had to go to customer services about something. I'm talking to the lady behind the counter when she looks past me open mouthed and I turn to see Elea flat on the floor on her face, not crying, not in distress just lying there. We laugh about it now. I don't know how the bloody hell she got out of the trolley.

I've had a run in with doctors at the surgery with both kids. When Jon was only a few months old we found that babies powdered milk was bunging him up. I knew what was in it as we made it at Glaxo. We put him on cow's milk, and he was fine. The grief I got from the Doctors saying you can't give a child that young, cow's milk. He's 29 yrs old now, strong as an ox and a very intelligent young man and taking a Neuroscience master's degree. It didn't do him any harm did it?

I used to take Elea for weighing at the surgery. The nurse would say, 'She's underweight' looking at a very large, three-month-old bouncing baby.

'Does she look underweight?' I would say.

'No, but my chart says she's underweight.'

'But you're going off the fact she was over 10lbs when she was born but that was two weeks overdue. Babies put on a pound a week!'

If Elea had been born on time, she would have been within the parameters of the chart! That's my argument anyway. Even the Doctor said that due to her being born at home was the reason she had two very small varicose veins that appeared on her side when she got hot. She's now a beautiful 27-year-old Veterinary Nurse, isn't thin, isn't fat and again, an extremely intelligent young lady. I'm very proud of them both.

Engine oil & Cream Carpets don't mix

Our neighbour across the road had a taxi business in Preston. He had a **Peugeot 504 Estate** that had done 500,000 miles and needed a new engine. He asked me if I would change the engine for him. We went and got a good quality second-hand engine from a car breaker. I went to fit it one day after the engine had been taken out a few days before. I remember it was a hot day, and the car was sat on his drive. He had his patio windows open to the right of the car with a brand-new cream carpet. After fitting the engine, I turned it over and it locked up.

'There's still water in one of the pots when the breakers have cleaned it. I need to take the glow plugs out and turn it over. Close the patio doors please.' I tell the bloke, but he leaves the patio doors open.

It's a diesel engine, I put a cloth over the glow plug holes, turn the car over and a jet of dirty oily water fires straight out of one of the pots (the bonnet's still not on yet) and travels about six metres and lands on the new cream carpet. It couldn't have been a better shot. He wasn't impressed but the fact that I'd asked him to close the doors and had put a rag over the engine, he couldn't blame me. We did have a laugh about it, but he had to get the carpet replaced, I think he claimed it on his home insurance. That car went for another two years before he sold the business and moved to Australia. I bet the car's still going now.

Apart from the solo gigs, the tribute band had a few gigs but not that many. Peter and I worked as professional musicians and the rest of the band were working during the day, apart from Neil who was still on long term sick. Derek (who I mentioned earlier) did a David Bowie Tribute show and I had got to know him quite well. I recorded all his backing tracks for him and for other people too which brought another form of income in. We did an off shoot of the band with Derek as the singer and called the band **Platforms and Trash**.

I was dressed as **Roy Wood** with a very itchy wig. We did a lot of gigs with that band and got paid reasonable money for it too. As another avenue, I went out with Derek as a Bowie duo, with me dressed up as Mick Ronson. Sorry I do not have any photos of me dressed up as Mick! We also had a cabaret duo that we did on and off for a couple of years doing the club circuit all around the Northwest.

Chestnuts Roasting

There was a club in Runcorn, Cheshire, that Derek and I used to do a gig at least once a year and normally it was always around Xmas. I'm not homophobic, but the Compere was as gay as could be, which is fine, but he would always invite young men up to pull the tickets out for the raffle and have his arm around them, you get what I'm saying. We'd be stood on stage, and it was most probably totally innocent, however it was when we were sat in the dressing room, and we can hear him singing 'Chestnut's roasting on an open fire.' and the images that were appearing in our heads of what was happening on the stage outside of our dressing room -

I'm sorry, but with everything else about him, we pissed ourselves laughing, with various images of him on stage that you just couldn't imagine. You could laugh about things like that twenty years ago. You'd be slated now and to be honest it's a shame because it was just innocent banter. Not like now.

The night I became Lewis Hamilton

The other thing that sticks in my grey matter about that time with Derek was finishing a gig in **Egremont** in Cumbria. Now if you've ever been at the top end of the west coast of Cumbria there are only two ways to get back down to Lancashire. Head east on the A66 to Penrith then turn right down the M6, at least two and half hours, or drive down the coast road and get back on the M6 just south of Kendal at Junction 35. Around the same amount of time but less miles. I have done both so many times over the years and know the coast road like the back of my hand. We were starving and everywhere was shut, so I said to Derek, 'What time does The Godfather Kebab House shut in Chorley?'

'3am' says Derek

We look at each other and smile.

'I'll give it ago.' I say, bearing in mind it's 1am so I have under two hours to get there. At the time, I had an **Astra Belmont Estate** which was quick, so off we went. Roads were dry and clear of traffic. At 2.40am we're coming up to junction 8 on the M61 for Chorley. Derek phones The Godfather and orders the Kebab's and at 2.50am I'm parked up outside the takeaway with Derek inside paying for the food. That's all I'm saying, I shaved 40 minutes off the journey, but hey that's rock n roll. You need to eat.

One thing I'll add at this part which relates back to Chapter 13 with the X Factor. Derek was always being invited to go on *Stars in their Eyes* in the 1990's. They would phone him up and invite him on the show and he would get down to the final 48 for the series, then he would be asked to sign a contract to say he wouldn't do his Bowie Tribute show until the series had been aired, so they could say they'd 'FOUND HIM'. This meant that Derek would have to wait up to six months and loose his main income show. He used to earn anything between £300-£400 per gig. He always turned the series down but hoped next time it would be different. There was a Diana Ross lookalike that Derek knew, who won one year. He told me, she was a professional singer but for the makers of the show told the public/audience that she was a Supermarket checkout girl, and they filmed her at the till in a supermarket. But, before turning professional five years before, her job was a checkout girl, they just conveniently forgot to mention the five years in between. Manipulation of the public for voting I believe it's called, and it still goes on today. Allegedly!

***

The 1980's band and Platforms and Trash, we were getting gigs, but they were just a sideline, I was plodding on with the club circuit and my other various money-making ideas, like doing a bit of courier work. I even tried to be an agent for other artists which was a nonstarter. A few years later I was invited by Max Peters and Neil to join a Billy Joel Tribute band that had members from Pulse in too. The band was successful for a couple of years as well but ended up fading away. Again, it was a shame because the standard of musicianship from everyone was outstanding.

I am going to divert one more time in this chapter up the M6 to a funny story from the Billy Joel rehearsals.

Is that my guitar your playing?

One of the last Audio rental gigs I had equipment at, one of the local band members had left a guitar on the stage and never collected it. I took it home, informed the promoters that I had it, but no one contacted me to say it was theirs. The Billy Joel band were playing a semitone down to save the singers voice, something a lot of bands do these days.

I got this guitar setup a semitone down to use with the Billy Joel Band save having to mess around with the guitar I normally used. 6 months have passed since this guitar came into my possession.

So, first rehearsal, I explain to the band that I need to leave my phone on as I'm expecting an important call.

Just as we're about to start the first song my phone rings. I think it's the important call.

'I believe you've got my guitar' says the guy on the other end of the phone.

It's only the guy who owns the guitar I have hanging around my neck that had been left at a venue 6 months before.

I can only say 'Yes I have' again lost for words.

He collects the guitar that weekend and I have to sort another guitar out for the Billy Joel band. Uncanny.

Back to the story

The year 1999, I was in the pub with Neil and I had an idea. As I've mentioned many moons ago, in my teens I had a short stint in a three-piece band and all we played was the whole of *Dark Side of the Moon* at the local youth club and the Remand Home in Garston, Liverpool. **Pink Floyd** have always been one of my favourite bands and since **Roger Waters** had left and **Dave Gilmour** had brought out *Momentary Lapse* and *Division Bell*, I'd always thought about doing something Floyd. I read in the local paper that **Chorley Little Theatre** were struggling for cash and trying to renovate the theatre, which was originally a cinema. The theatre was run by an amateur dramatic society called CADOS or lovingly called CHAOS.

'Neil, why don't we do a full Pink Floyd Tribute show, perform it at Chorley Little Theatre and it will raise a bit of money for the theatre. We have a band. We can base it on the PULSE video of Floyd at Earls Court in 1994?' And that is how the band **PULSE-ECHOES of FLOYD** started, and I still resurrect every now and then for reunion gigs to this day.

I think Peter was a little put out, as he wasn't really a Floyd fan and didn't want to do it. He was concerned about it taking too much time up for the band, but in all fairness, when I had the original idea, I was only looking at the band doing the two 'Charity Fund Raising Gigs'. How wrong I was.

***

I wasn't sure, while writing this book, how I was going to split and present all the different things that were going on my life at the same time without confusing you. I decided to separate them, at least up to around 2006 from this 1999 landmark, as so many things started to emerge. Looking back, I don't know how I dealt with them all, but I did and survived to tell the tale. So, let's continue.

CHAPTER 15

PULSE – Echoes of Floyd

We started rehearsing in the Autumn of 1999 at Chorley Community Centre, somewhere I'd started to get involved with, as the Trustees that looked after the place were all in their eighties except for one guy who was struggling to keep the place going. We did rehearse at a couple of pubs too but sometimes it was very distracting if punters from the pub came into the rehearsal and started having a chat. We were trying to rehearse a two-and-a-half-hour show, full lights, click track, video screen, you get the gist: not easy.

I remember the first rehearsal in a pub in Longton that we'd performed at in the past as Out of the Blue. I knew after the first few songs that we had something special developing and so did the rest of the band.

But we needed extra Musicians and Vocalists.

After the initial rehearsal, we got a sax player in (Paul, a Taxi driver from Preston) and a couple of girls for the backing vocals. I also got an extra drummer who was the boyfriend of one of the backing vocalists. He had an electronic kit and if you've ever watched the PULSE video there are two drummers in the show. **Gary Wallace** and **Nick Mason**.

Now that the rehearsals had started, I was researching a lot about the two mammoth tours that Pink Floyd had done in 1987 and 1994. I needed a circular screen, lights, a PA and a projector. This was one of those turning points in my timeline that was the beginning of the next seven years of my life. I really went over the top with this project. Too much if I am honest. I got bank loans, as I didn't have a lot of money and started buying amps, speakers, a few lights to add to the lights that **John Spicer** owned. He was from Widnes and had joined the team with **Paul Carr,** who worked voluntarily at Chorley Little Theatre. The bass player worked for a plumbing wholesaler and so I purchased a load of copper pipe with connectors, and we made a circular screen using a pipe bender and cross bracing to give it some support. I then got a large bed sheet John Spicer's wife stitched button clips into the edges once it had been made circular. Pull the sheet around the outside of the frame and clip it tight. and, hey presto, we had a screen. Pink Floyd had spent ages researching what type of paint to use on their cardboard boxes on **The Wall** tour and ended up just using bog standard emulsion. We set the screen up in my large garage and sprayed the circular sheet with a thin mixture of water and white emulsion. The projections looked fantastic for what it was, but once you got the smoke or haze on the stage, they were sometimes difficult to see but we made do, and it was great for the initial shows. I still have the VHS of the two shows we did at the theatre.

I now had the bug and before the two initial shows at CLT, I'd got us radio interviews, local press including Lancashire Evening News and, more importantly, I secured another couple of gigs after these shows. One at **The British Legion, Barrow-in-Furness** promoted by a guy called Andy who I will come back to later and one at **The Limelight** in Crewe which was the hometown of **Australian Pink Floyd**.

If that sounds confusing, then I will explain. So, the story goes, as far as I know, **Glen Povey**, a promoter in London, brought Aussie Floyd over in 1988 from (you guessed it), Australia. But most of the guy's, apart from two I believe, went back after a while and so he recruited UK musicians but kept the name and they based themselves in Crewe. They performed at Dave Gilmour's 50th Birthday party in 1996 I think it was. What an honour.

Pulse vs Aussie Floyd

We did the show at The Limelight, and they came along to watch. All these people were saying to me 'Aussie Floyd are here, Aussie Floyd are here' and certain people, well, the expression; 'headless chicken' springs to mind. A tip for the younger musicians; to be anxious or apprehensive before you go on stage is a good thing, you are aware, and it keeps you focused. The day you go on stage and your cock sure is when things can go wrong. I tried to just shrug it off, yes, they were the most famous Floyd Tribute band in the world even then, especially performing at Gilmour's 50th birthday party FFS but you don't show it to anyone else, especially the other band members who think you are unflappable. Inside, I was crapping my pants, mainly because this was only our fourth gig. We had some lights, but nothing compared to what Aussie Floyd used, but I thought 'Fuck Em!'

Now I've never said that we sounded exactly like Pink Floyd, but we were pretty close to the live band and have only ever had one or two adverse comments. We did the show, and the Aussie Floyd guys came up to me at the end and said 'That was pretty good. How long have you been doing the show?'

'This is our fourth.' I said.

I noticed a jaw dropping moment in front of me. That was then. Now, Aussie Floyd and the off-shoot Brit Floyd are selling out arena's all over the world. Even then, with the promotion they had behind them, I couldn't compete. I will say though that up to that point they didn't have a circular screen. I was told the next tour they did, they had one. I'd like to think, wrongly maybe, that I may have been the catalyst that made them get one, although after a while our makeshift screen sometimes looked like a dented peanut with it getting pulled apart every gig!

Anyway, back to the story seeming I've gone off down the M6 to Crewe

I had my small recording studio at home so did the click tracks for **High Hopes, Learning to Fly** etc, I sorted out a website. But, in those days, loading a CD Rom of any form of video, took about fifteen years or the 2mb speed broadband would drop out and you had to start again. Some of the background work I did was painful especially with everything else that was happening at home on a personal level. But the machine had started, and I was determined to get it running properly and make some money. I had to learn fast about contracts for theatres, promotional costs, logistics and on and on. For anyone who doesn't know, normally you are looking at booking gigs a minimum six months or even a year ahead, so that the whole promotional band wagon can do its work to sell the tickets for your show and you have to pay the deposits that far in advance too.

Andy who promoted the Barrow-in-Furness gig and I got together and decided to set up an Irish tour. About eight dates in both the North and South of Ireland. We agreed that he would do most of the promotion and I'd sort out logistics and help in dealing with the venues. But I seem to remember sorting the venues out mostly by myself which should have started alarm bells ringing straight away. Anyway, the gigs where; **Queens University – Belfast, Europa Hotel – Drogheda** (Aussie Floyd had played there), **Jury's Inn – Waterford, University Concert Hall – Limerick**, and **Port Rush Hotel in Port Rush.**

The others fell through. To be honest though, by the time I'd done the last gig, I was knackered. I was driving the truck, setting up the gear, playing, stripping down and driving the truck to the next gig too.

The hotels worked, you hire the room and promote the gig yourself and you take all the money. Andy was doing the doors and taking the ticket money, except for Limerick which was a proper theatre. Before the tour I bought a 6.5 tonne Mercedes Van, huge thing, but it did the job. I had to do a bit of work on it for its MOT, and no power steering. It was handy I could work on the truck myself and believe me that was a learning curve too. I'd never worked on anything that big before. The band travelled in three large cars, there were seven of them plus Andy and I had four crew too, three of which travelled in the cars and one with me driving the truck. Neil (Flash) and Paul had never seen eye to eye for some reason and it all came to a head in Belfast over a stupid argument about a car park. The outcome being I got hold of the two of them by the collar and I said, 'Sort your shit out or I'll knock the two of you out!'

I'd spent a lot of time, effort and money on this tour, and I wasn't going to let a stupid head strong argument ruin it.

They were best of friends after that.

The gigs went well considering no one had heard of us, however there always seemed to be a discrepancy of ticket sales compared to how many people we thought were in the audience. This came to a head in Limerick, I think it was. Russ (one of the crew) and I drove through the night to Port

Rush as it was an eight-hour drive, and we let the band and the rest of the crew sleep and drive up early the next day. We left at 2am from Limerick and arrived in Port Rush about 10am. We got up at 2pm and started tipping the truck by ourselves and setting up. Everyone else arrived about 4pm. It was panic stations to get everything ready, but we did it. However, while all this was happening, I had been told that one of the crew had walked into Andy's room in the hotel. He was counting out money and other tickets that all should have been given to me after each gig. He was on a split of the door, but I was struggling to tally everything up and with driving, setting up etc I wasn't really taking as much notice as I should have been. The crew did an independent count of the audience that night in Port Rush while we were playing. After the gig Andy gave me the total. It was obvious that he had been conveniently marking down ticket sales and pocketing some of the cash from them for himself.

The guys who were working for me had a lot of respect for myself and knew the amount of effort that had been going into this project. After everyone had gone to bed, the crew and I had a meeting. They were all for throwing Andy overboard on the ferry on the way back the following day, something that, although would have been well deserved, I didn't think would be a good idea.

So, I text him to say we were leaving at 2pm the following day, when we were actually leaving at 12 noon. We got the ferry and left him in Port Rush which meant he would have had to somehow get back to Belfast and pay for another ticket to get to Liverpool and then try and get some form of transport back to Cumbria. It would have cost him most of the money he stole. I never heard from him again except for one text saying he was disappointed in the fact that we left him there, but I knew at Port Rush that he was aware that I'd been told of his dealings, so I'm sure it wasn't a surprise to him. After that tour everyone was so tired, but they all did so well and to this day that was both a great experience and an eye opener in many ways.

Anything Explosive?

It was just me driving the truck back via **Larne** to Fleetwood which was the truck ferry. Everyone else was in the cars. I got pulled over by the customs/security going into the terminal. The terrorism situation in Ireland was still not good at the time and vehicles were always getting checked before embarking. I explained where I had been, the guy said to me, 'Okay open the back doors.'

'Are you sure?' I reply.

We go to the back of the truck; well, we used every inch of this van. I open the rear doors, and he looks at the extremely packed truck. Knowing that he would have to empty the goods himself which would take a few hours, he had the dilemma of that, as there was no way just the two of us would be able to unpack and repack this without causing some serious injury to ourselves. He looks at me and says 'Have you got anything explosive in there?'

'No.'

'Okay. Just shut the doors and bugger off.'

I could have had anything in there, but no way was he going to empty it all out onto the dock and I was relieved myself as I would have missed the ferry.

***

While I was sorting out the infamous Irish tour, I'd been in touch with Glen Povey and another promoter called **Mark Shaw,** both of whom were well established promoters and dealt with most of the good mid-size theatres in the UK. They advertised in **Classic Rock** magazine for example and took the hit on costs rather than someone like me having to worry about it. Bearing in mind, apart from me, all the members of the band, had daytime jobs, I asked them would they be interested in doing a 30-day tour if I could get a deal? Everyone said yes and would take holidays or time off. I struck a deal with Glen and Mark. If I remember rightly, it was a £1000 per gig, 30-day tour, we supplied the whole show. In those days a lot of theatres didn't have in house audio that could cope with bands. Also, their lights, normally would only compliment what you were bringing in on the tour. I paid for logistics for the band, but they covered the hotels. This all seemed like a great deal. Glen and Mark did question if the band would do it as they were all semipro. I said yes, as that was what they had said to me. I went back to the band and told them the offer. That's when I started getting the urms and aarhs and 'well I won't get enough time off'. I could see this wasn't going to work.

In hindsight, and as a businessman, I should have just said right I'll get a load of professional musicians to do it but a £1000 per night would have never covered all their costs, we had also been through so much with the first few gigs. I had to go back to Glen and Mark and say that it wasn't going to happen. I suppose apart from the fact that I'd told them that everything was in order and a deal would be made, I looked like a dick in their eyes. Even later on, when I approached them again with a more pro band they never replied, and to be honest, I didn't blame them. They are the guys who are putting their money on the line. Again, that was a big turning point in my life because what would have happened if we did tour for these guys we could have ended up like Aussie and Brit Floyd now.

This decision from the band members set me back a bit. I had put so much time and money, bearing in mind most of it was bank loans, and I was the only one paying it all back. I took it upon myself to start painstakingly trolling through all the venues in the UK and setting up a string of gigs, mainly at weekends so that it wasn't affecting the daytime work for the guys in the band. Trying to do this, still work on the club circuit, which was my main income at this time, and look after the kids when Kim wasn't well, was bloody hard to put it mildly.

My efforts started to produce results. I had gigs at **The Royal Court** in Liverpool, **King Georges Hall** in Blackburn various gigs around the north of England for various small promoters a couple of Scottish mini tours and PULSE now renamed PULSE- Echoes of Floyd was becoming an established Pink Floyd Tribute band. However, it was still myself or **Stardrivemusic** (the name of this part of my business), that would bear the brunt should anything go wrong. In hindsight, I should have set up a limited company, but sometimes you don't think of these things and my accountant at the time, wasn't exactly the best. I set up some gigs down south too, for example **Trowbridge,** it was a disaster, I lost about £800 after I'd paid the crew and band. In 2003 I had HMRC on my back accusing me of earning more than I had declared on the band side of things. They said I'd earnt £18,000 more than I'd declared and were pushing for me to go bankrupt. By this time, I'd sacked my accountant who had put in the same accounts for two years by mistake but had denied that it was his problem. However, I pointed out to HMRC after they had taken my diaries and pulled them apart literally that they were classing the rehearsals as gigs. Contracts signed in say March for a gig in August was two gigs (WTF) and by the time I had gone through this mess I'd reduced the £18k to £400.

'I can most probably find that too.' I said.

'If you carry on, we will want all the names and addresses of all the musicians and crew who have ever worked for you since the band started, and we'll go after them too' they said.

I stopped looking.

At one stage the lady behind the desk said to me, 'Just sign all these bankruptcy forms as I'm moving offices on Monday and want this case closed.' Nothing to do with what was right. After I'd taken overdrafts out to stop the bailiffs knocking on the door from the revenue, I ended up with a £700 rebate as the whole accusation was total shit. HMRC do have a shit job, I don't envy them, but come on guys, let's go for the proper fraudsters. For example, those people who claim disability when they aren't and don't say it doesn't happen because its rife and I'm sure there are many others who know someone who is conning the system.

By 2002, the line-up had changed, **Sam James** had replaced the original backing vocalists but had left due to work commitments which is when I brought **Fiona Ford** in. With Neil not being too good still, I'd gone through another couple of drummers only for Neil to come back into the fold in 2003. Neil (Keys) had left, and **Joe Orban** (Keys) had come in and **Gerard MacDonald** had come into play Sax after Paul had left due to commitments with work too.

Before the first Royal Court gigs, I took out another loan and bought a circular screen taken out of a night club in **Oldham**. I bought a proper rear projection screen made by **J&C Joel**. Bought an Argon Laser from a guy in Oxford which upped the show 1000%. My favourite memory of the laser stood on the stage at The Royal Court Liverpool with 900 odd audience playing the intro to *Sorrow* off **Momentary Lapse** and seeing this laser going over my head as a horizontal fan filling the whole of the theatre below the balcony. The only problem with the laser was that because of secondary reflection you could only have the audience downstairs in case you zapped anyone. To put it in perspective, if it was on single beam full power you could light a cigarette off it. A serious bit of kit. I also had a much better audio system, tales of which will be further down.

Again, strange things can happen when you make a momentous decision of getting a band together like PULSE. You will never know where it will take you. I was asked by **Chorley Borough Council** if I would like the band to play at a festival, they were setting up at **Botany Bay**. This was a large, revamped factory mill on the outskirts of the town with a huge carpark. A massive Marquee would be erected on it. There would be a seven-day festival, and we would perform on one of the nights. We would be paid a fee, and I said 'yes' straight away.

On the day of our gig, we arrived that morning with all the gear, I noticed that the Marquee was not pinned to the ground and that the high winds that day could cause problems. 'Rubbish' said the Health & Safety

Officer on the phone. I explained exactly what was wrong and said that if the Marquee took off and damaged the £80k of equipment we had there, they would be responsible. They sent one of the marquee guys down who basically phoned his depot for chemical bolts and the like, to pin this huge structure down.

Just from that one phone call I got all the event work for the next five years from the Council which I will elaborate on in the next chapter.

Councils like people who know what they are doing because with all due respect, in the early 2000's there were some employed in H&S on various boards, who didn't have a clue about live events. They were going by their little black books with no understanding of what it meant in real life terms. After the Botany Bay show, PULSE was offered a gig on the main 'Flat Iron' car park in Chorley town centre, for the summer of 2001. As I had demonstrated to the council that I knew what I was doing, they asked me to run this four-day event including all the infrastructure.

Early 2002, I get an email from a promoter in Switzerland who wants me to bring the band over for two shows; one in **Bern**, the other in **Zurich**. By now the crew had changed and I had four great guys who had worked with me on the four-day event too. One of the guy's Stev is now a project manager for a big production company in the UK, another, Mike is Pyro Tech for a world-famous female singer and one of the other two (Loz) has their own Lighting Company in Israel where he had come from originally. Well, he did have a few years ago but we haven't been in touch for a long time now. The other crew member at the time ended up in the Army and I'm not sure where Ben is now, but we co-hosted one of the breakfast shows on a temporary licence for Chorley FM. More of that later.

Switzerland was a logistical nightmare as two of the crew were working right up to the day before the first show and spent six hours travelling via **Geneva** to Bern just so they were there for the load in the following morning. I had to drive the equipment over land via **Dover** and the only cheap flights where from Luton, so I had to pay for all the band to drive to Luton for the flights. The other two crew came with me in the truck.

I still had the big Mercedes truck which looked like an overgrown van. Twice as long and twice as tall.

As well as all the gear for the show, I had all the backline. I still can't believe how we got everything in that truck. Driving over was a breeze, it took about two days turning left at **Calais** then a right in **Belgium** just before **Brussels**, and then into **Germany**. On the third day we arrived at the Swiss border. I had never driven through a border before. Ireland and Europe are different. If you haven't been to the border of Germany to Switzerland, the check point is huge as you can imagine the number of trucks that go that way.

Switzerland charge you per ton and per kilometre. You have to get weighed and mileage checked so that when you leave Switzerland, they take a lot of money off you. The guard comes out to see me. I explain I'm private HGV, in a band doing two gigs and I am directed to one of the fifteen private HGV booths at the border with my weighing ticket. I come back out and ask the guard if I can drive on Sunday coming back out as HGV's are not allowed to drive on a Sunday in Switzerland except coaches. (This has now changed to most of Europe I believe). He assures me that with it being private HGV all is good and in we go.

How wrong I was to believe him.

Switzerland is a great country and I've been there a number of times now while performing. The only drawback is the decibel limit in the venues. The rules now might be more complex than they were in 2002, but I think average level over a one-hour period then was 96db. Bear in mind, the acoustic drums are around 100db and a crowd cheering can be up into the hundreds too, you can see what you're up against.

We arrive at the first venue. It's a Thursday morning and one of the crew who's riding with me, asks the in-house technician for some green. He didn't have any vices other than smoking skunk. He only had a small amount with him and with it being legal in Switzerland he asked the question. The technician led us to a small room and after money exchanges hands (£20 I think) he promptly fills what I can only describe as a large see through supermarket shopping bag. I thought my crew members eyes were going to pop out of his head. What I was more concerned about was how was he going to get all this home as he certainly wouldn't smoke all of it in three days!

Anyway, the first gig goes really well, even with a member of the local council monitoring the sound levels all night. I'm assured by the Swiss promoter that the gig on the Saturday will be a lot louder as it's in a disused warehouse.

See the photos at the end of the chapter.

The second gig goes great apart from me forgetting that they are Swiss and I'm jabbering on in English. 'Just shut up Phil and play the music.' I tell myself.

We pack down, the band say their goodbyes.

I set off early on Sunday morning as the ferry leaves Tuesday morning at 9am from Calais. My only concern I have is if we get stopped at the border, as I now have a large amount of cash from the promoter and one of my crew in the truck has about 3kg of green in a bag under the seat in the cab. We get to the border about 11.30am and I should have just driven down the car lane, but no, I drive down one of the HGV lanes and the gates are shut. I walk the 250 metres over to the other side and show an armed guard my weighbridge ticket. He starts waving his gun about shouting out in Swiss. I thought he was going to shoot me. Then the guard, who pulled us over the previous Wednesday, comes out and says, 'Ah, you're the guys from the band. You pay big fine now.'

I'm still not sure if the money went into their pocket or the Swiss government's but I'm glad I only had to hand over £200 (380 Swiss francs at the time). I would have argued the toss, but there were the two issues mentioned above, that I did not want trouble over.

By the time I got home on the Tuesday night, any profit I had made for those two gigs was wiped out by the fine. Incidentally, we got back to Blighty and were not searched. The UK border was more interested in X-raying the trucks for illegal immigrants. My crew member with the green enjoyed the following few months very much.

There are so many stories I could tell about these six years or so, when I ran the band, and maybe there's another book there or a film, but these are but a few.

We had a gig in Scotland and the only desk I had to use at the time was an old MTR desk. This was more of a studio desk but worked fine for what we needed, and our sound engineer was happy with it. I'd had a couple of problems with it in the months running up to this show but, we thought we'd fixed it. Every now and then it would lose power. Nowadays, you have a backup for everything, those days, especially when I was trying to run this band on a shoestring budget, you just got on with it. We had just started the second half of the show, which was always *One of These Days* and then into a full rendition of *Dark Side of the Moon*. We began to play *Time* and as I went to sing, the whole PA stopped working. Unbeknown to me, a very drunk Scotsman had fallen backwards off his chair and landed on the edge of the front of house (F.O.H.) sound desk and the power went off on the desk. Please bear in mind that our monitors in those days were coming from FOH too. I could see the crew frantically trying to get the desk going again. There was only one thing for it.

The band stopped and I shouted out at the top of my voice to the 300 or so audience, 'Ok, this is your chance for a sing-along,' sort of Pink Floyd Karaoke but with 300 people. We turned the amps up on stage and off we went, with the audience in great voice. Well, we were in Scotland. We were getting to the end of *Time*, the audience is still singing, I'm getting worried now as *Great Gig* is next and, although I'm sure all the audience would have tried to sing it, I'm not sure how well that would have gone. A friend of mine **John Charleson** had the answer. The crew had tried everything to get this desk up and running again but to no avail.

John walked up to the desk and gave the underneath of it a large boot with his foot. PING! The desk came back to life (pardon the pun), the crowd cheering, and we finished the show off with no other problems. That was a nail biter. I know things like that happen, but normally you have a promoter who will apologise to the punters and hand the money back. I was the one who would have had to give the money back but, I was running on a really tight budget with most of these gigs, absorbing all the costs if they went wrong. Which leads to the next story;

The first tour of Ireland which, apart from the dodgy promoter, went well and so did the second tour performing at some great venues. These included a different hotel in Drogheda, and it was rammed. Watching 450 odd people holding lighters up in front of you while performing

Comfortably Numb with all the light show too was incredible. I just wish I had photos of that night. The other memorable one was **The Quays in Galway**, an old Church. The band were positioned at different heights from where the choir stalls used to be. I was performing from where the Pulpit had been.

I'm only mentioning all this to set the mood, as the third tour we did was a different kettle of fish. We had to split this one into two halves due to some of the crew being booked for other things. We did the first half, over three shows, Waterford being one of them and I actually made a decent amount of money on top of paying the band and covering all the logistics. We had a show in **Workington** just before the second part of the third tour which wasn't a great show. There were problems with the lasers, I had been so tired trying to promote the shows; contacting the media, radio stations, blanket emails, extra posters etc, I went blank in the middle of *High Hopes* from sheer exhaustion. I didn't know where I was in the track, especially as it was on a click track too. Luckily, I got myself back into it and finished the song, but we didn't have very good reviews from that gig.

Straight after that gig, I drove the truck to **Stranraer** to get the ferry the following morning while the rest of the band set off the following day and sailed from Liverpool. We had a spare day, but I wanted to make sure I was there with the gear and two of the crew for the load in at The Hotel in Drogheda. We had had such a great show last time, but it was quite a difficult set up with it being a conference suite. I arrived at the Hotel only to see no posters up anywhere. I went to reception only to find out that not only were there no posters, but they had also forgotten we were coming, and no tickets had been sold either. Apparently, the Manageress, due to personal circumstances, had, over a period of time, stolen the money in the till and vanished.

On top of this, all my emails that I had sent to all the media, not just for this show, but also for the other gigs had all disappeared down an internet black hole and no one knew we were performing. In those five minutes of realising what had happened, any money I had made a few weeks before from the first half of the tour, vanished in a flash.

The guys set up, while I frantically went around phoning radio stations to see if I could get any announcements but to no avail. Due to where the venue was, we were not in the centre of Drogheda, people had to drive or get taxi's so word of mouth wasn't going to work either. We played to ten people. For the band and crew, it was a paid rehearsal, for me it was a financial disaster and an expensive lesson. I should have been following up my emails with phone calls, faxes etc. The last time I spoke to this hotel was about six weeks before the gig and, as far as I was concerned, everything was good. The other two tours I had paid for radio adverts around Southern Ireland, but for this tour I just couldn't afford it and that was the start of me thinking if I should carry on with this project.

Cutting to the chase, I set up a bar tab for myself and the band, we all got absolutely pissed and after packing the gear up the following morning, we left without paying the tab. I think the hotel just didn't bother trying to ask for the bill to be paid due to what had happened. I lost £1500 that day, as the second gig covered costs for its own show but nothing more and I drove back to the UK, with more problems than I'd started with before I went over there.

On a lighter note

We performed at The Windsor Suite, King Georges Hall in Blackburn quite a few times. It was always a great gig playing to around 400-500 people. We did the show and, while the crew started stripping down, I went to the back of the room to sign autographs on the posters people had taken off the walls as fans do. Kim was at the gig and was stood about ten feet away when this woman came over and handed me a ball point pen. 'What do you want me to sign?' I said, as she pulls down one side of her t-shirt and points to her breast. Kim is glaring at me, but I was more concerned on how much pain I am going to inflict on this woman's breast with a ball point pen!

'The ink will wash off.' I say.

'I'm never going to wash again,' she replies.

Well, there we go.

The first time we played the Royal Court, Liverpool, we had an audience of around 700. It would have had more except we couldn't open the balcony due to using the laser. But, for the second time we played there, we had over 900 in the crowd. The theatre has an orchestra pit and a set of stairs each side of the stage from the auditorium. Once our speaker system is stacked on each side there is no way you can access the stage from the auditorium apart from jumping into the orchestra pit and then trying to climb up onto the stage, which you could most probably do but not very quickly. Apart from that there was security at the front of the stage so there was no way anyone could get onto the stage in the space of a few seconds even minutes.

So, we finish *Comfortably Numb*, the lights go down for the start of *Run Like Hell*. I'm just about to start the song, the lights come up and there's a guy around 30 years of age, stood in front of me with his hand outstretched.

'Great Solo Lah.' He says to me in a scouse accent. He shakes my hand; the lights go down and back up within a few seconds and HE'S GONE.

Two issues with this;

1. He couldn't have disappeared that quickly, even off to the side of the stage and
2. I turn to the band members behind me, and I say, 'Did you see that?' and they say, 'See What?'

I wasn't on drugs, no one else in the auditorium said anything or cheered as you'd think they would if they saw someone on the stage, it was really weird. The previous gig there we had a guy get up on stage dancing, but everyone saw him and cheered. To this day I'm convinced that guy was not real, or should I say not real in our reality, but he shook my hand, although thinking about it there was no cold or heat in his hand, it was just a hand that touched mine. I just carried on into *Run Like Hell* and we finished the show. It was pointless discussing that incident with anyone else, because as far as I was aware no one else saw him.

We performed a gig in **Cardiff** *at a place called* **The Point** *and the following day we had a private show at a guy's house (yes, a house) near* **St Albans**. *He'd got in contact with me, it was his birthday and wanted us to* *play in his garden. No stage just set up and off we go. Minimal lights, more to do with the sound so wasn't going to take too long to set up. We went through St Albans and as we came to this village and driving under an amazing tunnel of trees, it was like we had entered into a fairy tale setting. In this village all the houses were owned by Stockbrokers or the like, I'd never seen so many houses that big. We pulled up outside his house and he had a few friends help get all the gear in the back garden which did take a while. We had to run cable everywhere as it was all running off 13amp plugs While all this was going on he let the backing singers go and have a swim in his indoor swimming pool and led me to his garage.*

'I bought myself a birthday present' He says to me, 'would you like to see it?'

I nod and he opens the garage to see a brand-new **Ferrari**, I can't remember what model. It might have been a **Testarossa**.

'I wish I'd charged more for this gig now.' I thought to myself.

He was a really nice guy, paid for us to stay at a local Travel Lodge in St Albans, covered the taxis. We didn't have to pack any gear down until the following day and so I left the truck at the guy's house. It was free drinks all evening and he even gave the band a crate of wine which we took back to the hotel.

We nearly got kicked out of the hotel as we were still all drinking at 4am in one room. 'It got very messy' as the saying goes.

Anyway, back up the M1

I carried on with Pulse – Echoes of Floyd until 2005 and our last gig (apart from the reunion stuff which I'll come to later) was at **The Leyland Eagles** MCC Rally were my Sax player and one of the Backing Singers became an item and are still together now and I don't get to visit them enough. My other memory of that gig was Elea stood next to me dancing on the stage all the way through the show. She was seven years old. Both my kids loved Floyd while they were growing up and still do. I wonder why? The reason I called it a day was that I just couldn't afford to take any more losses with gigs. Money at home wasn't great due to various reasons and there were other avenues that had opened up over the years while the band were playing which I needed to concentrate on. There's more Floyd stuff later but for now I need to go back to around the year 2000 and enlighten you on other parts and paths of my life I was going down at the same time as this. But first enjoy some photo's.

The initial lineup 1999; Switzerland 2002; Another lineup at a gig in Blackpool.

Pulse at a reunion gig in 2014; Pic of me circa 2001.

Gerard and myself 2013; The Royal Court L'Pool 2001.

Zurich 2002; Burnley Mechanics 2002.

CHAPTER 16

Stardrivemusic and Event Management

Stardrivemusic started from Mike Still's studio shed while I was in Brighton back in the early 1990's. It was always my business name under which I recorded and produced backing tracks etc. Once Pulse was born, and I had all the equipment, I was slowly drawn into hiring the kit out with myself and some of the crew who were working for me. It was a similar way to how Pink Floyd setup **Britannia Row Productions**, in 1975. When Floyd's gear wasn't being used on tour, they used to hire it out with their crew of engineers, riggers and other technicians. They are still one of the larger rental companies of audio equipment today, with a large unit in Twickenham (Southwest of London). Although my business was miniscule compared to theirs, **Stardrivemusic Event and Rental** began just after those first two charity shows. I can see now that one event led to other opportunities, for which I am grateful. I could have been sat in a bloody nine to five job somewhere, which I could never have done.

My work for Chorley County Council expanded rapidly. Stardrivemusic became a full-on event management set up, involved in the Christmas lights switch on's, a wide range of events in the park and firework displays. It operated as a Sole Trader business with my small crew, and I hired in subcontractors as and when I needed to for bigger contracts. You get the picture.

The four-day event on the Flat Iron Car Park (Chorley)

This attracted daily audiences of up to a thousand people. Thursday was for original local bands; Friday and Saturday featured cover bands, both lots were from around the local area including Pulse who headlined on the Saturday night. Sunday was an all-day Dance Festival Headlined by **Altern-8** – the **Techno Rave** duo from Stafford noted for wearing gas masks on stage.

Prior to the event, the Arts Development Officer (**Chris Mellor**) had asked me to apply for the **Entertainments Licence**. Due to local legislation and funding rules, although the council paid for the staging of the event and the bands etc, this licence had to be held by the person (i.e. me) running/managing the whole show. I put my application in and received a phone call from Chris. He told me that the police had registered an objection on the grounds that I was '…of an unsavoury character'. Now, I hadn't told anyone about my conviction in 1995 because it was community service and should have been cleared after five years. But, as some of you may know, the police keep all records of everything and so my name is on their computers, even though there is no information under it. That's a fact as I've been told by the police that that's the case.

I came clean to Chris and explained the whole saga and he's fine with it, but the council set up an emergency meeting in council chambers with all the councillors, the Police and myself. We needed to get this sorted as soon as because everything is booked and promoted under my name and the council's. Talk about not doing things in halves, I will try and explain this whole afternoon/evening process as briefly as possible, but it needs to be told.

Picture the scene; after the formal preliminaries of the chamber, the council's solicitor stands up and says to the Police Licensing Officer, 'Without telling the chamber what the actual convictions that Mr Baker has, can you tell us why he is of unsavoury character?'

Now in fairness, I'm not sure how I would go about answering that question. The Officer says, 'These Drug Convictions!!!' and stops in his tracks. He's just broke the **Data Protection Act.**

All the councillors look at me at once, including **Catherine Hoyle** (now officially Lady Hoyle) who is the wife of **Lyndsay Hoyle** (currently, **Speaker of the House of Commons**). I had done a lot of work running events for Cathy as she was Chairman of the **Disability Trust** (now Home-Start Central Lancashire, a registered charity based in Chorley).

A Councillor to my left stands up and asks, 'I'd like to know if what we are talking about here is Class A or Class B drugs? I'm sure some of us, at some stage in our lives, have had a dabble at Class B.'

I can't believe what I'm hearing, but a lot of the chamber nod in unison. I interrupt and explain the whole story; of Kaz, her attack on Kim, the raid and why it was taken to Crown Court. After my speech to the Chamber, myself and the Licensing Officer are asked to leave while the councillors debate what has occurred, but not before the Council's Solicitor asks the Police Officer why my community service conviction was still on my record.

'Because he has other criminal convictions.' He states.

This is a surprise to me.

'What are they?' The solicitor asks.

'For Speeding.' He responds.

'They are not criminal convictions.' The Solicitor states firmly.

By now, if you'd given the Police Licensing Officer a spade, he couldn't have dug himself in any deeper.

We leave the chambers, to get called back in 40 minutes later, although the Police Licensing Officer didn't bother and had left already: I am granted the License. I think being honest was the best thing I could have done, because, for the next few years I was always invited to tender for their events, installs, shows etc and even consulted sometimes for advice on aspects of the industry too. Anyway, a few days later I get a call from Lyndsay. Cathy had told him what had happened and, he asked me if I wanted to take the matter further with the Data Protection thing, or the fact that my convictions where still there. He said he would support me, which I thought was a really nice thing to do. I thanked him but said I didn't want to rock the boat too much. However, in hindsight, it was not until 2016 when I got a full five-year US visa that the convictions disappeared and, to this day, I'm still not sure why.

The 'Highs' and 'Lows' of the Event

I got one of the local bike clubs (Leyland Eagles MCC) to do the security for the four-day event. I borrowed a caravan for them to have a twenty four hour presence. I put all the infrastructure in place too. The stage was built by a scaffolding company: a mobile stage was going to cost a lot of money. I was having to learn fast on my feet. It was the first big event I ran, and the experience helped me in so many ways with all the other events I was involved with or managed over the next fifteen years.

We had a few incidents with the usual dickheads. You always get these types at any free event paid for by the local council for the public's enjoyment. Unfortunately, some of the 'public' are a pain in the arse and ruin it for everyone else.

A large, disposable cup, full of cola was thrown at the circular screen on the Friday night, which had been set up for the Pulse show the following night. I had to wash it down to remove the stain after the event. Security got the guy who had an 'accident' later on, falling down the steps on the local underpass. Such a shame!

A large fight broke out on the Sunday evening, what a surprise! I'd never really been interested in dance music, apart from the song I mentioned earlier that I composed with Mike Still called *613 Express*. Aside from it being used for the BT phone line for the UK Top 40, I believe it got played at some of the dance clubs around at that time. But that was over ten years in the past which went along with all the business with Kaz and the addicts. So, the public getting completely off their heads while I'm trying to run an event, meant that dance music just didn't appeal to me although I started to like **Drum and Bass** after that Sunday.

A minority of the troublemaking public don't even have to get off their heads; they are just very angry at society and have such a grudge (which maybe not their fault). However, it's people like that, I wish couldn't go to such events as it would be so much easier to stage and run them, but then that defeats the object.

The deal with the caravan was that I would try and sell it for the people who owned it while I was using it on site. It was the only way I could get something for security overnight and a production office for me during the day. Once we had finished with the caravan, the people who owned it didn't want it back and I said I'd try and get rid of it. I was still working from home and had nowhere to put it. So, I parked it up on my mate's parent's driveway who were happy to help. I was wary about leaving it there but had no choice and intuition proved me right as the following day from dropping it off, I went round to clean it out. It had six days of being lived in and the toilet could not be emptied because we didn't have anywhere to dispose of the waste. But it wasn't on the drive. Yes, it had been nicked, and I spent about nine months having to find around £150 a month to pay the owners the money that they wanted for it. They lent it to me in good faith, but it was an expensive lesson. I should have just got a proper cabin for the event, but I was trying to cut costs. When doing quotes from then on, I made sure all costs were covered apart from things like having to pay the Swiss Border Patrol the fine for driving on a Sunday!

You Can't Enter

When Altern-8 were performing, **Spike**, *one of the Leyland Eagles, (who also worked for me now and then), was on the backstage gate. I had told him not to allow anyone backstage who didn't have a pass. All of a sudden, I heard this commotion going on at the gate and I was radioed down to sort it out. When I arrived, Spike was stood firm and refused entry to some guy as he didn't have a pass.*

'In all my time as Manager of this band I've been able to get in anywhere.' He says to me. Spike had told him that he could be the Queen for all he cared but his boss (me) had told him no one was allowed in without a pass. It turns out he was actually the manager of Altern-8, but neither Spike nor I knew him. Next thing he asks me,

'Would you do security for our gig in Manchester next month?'

I declined. I was reminded by one of my stage crew that, this duo is a Garage band and, usually, at those type of gigs then (and most probably now too), the security has to sort out the trouble that comes with Drug Dealers, Gangsters etc. Which is what happened at The **Academy** *in Manchester around that time when the underworld came into the venue after overpowering the security (or bribing them), locked all the venue staff in the office and after stealing all the money, told all the audience drinks were on the house. Apparently after that gig, security from Liverpool took over, looking after venues in Manchester and security from Manchester looked after venues in Liverpool basically so no one could get bribed, so I was told.*

Back on the A6

As you can see just as things are starting to go well for me and I get a brick smashed in my face to knock me back down again. It has happened so many times in my life as you have read that it wasn't <u>if</u> I thought it was going to happen, it was a case of <u>when</u> I thought it was going to happen again.

Over the next few years Stardrivemusic (SDM) started expanding, while Pulse was losing money most of the time and my personal life was slowly disintegrating (more of that later).

SDM was mainly active in and around the northwest of England but it did start working for a great guy **Steve Stanley** from **Solid Entertainments** (who is still a friend). I used to do a lot of the smaller bands/gigs for him but also some of the bands from the 1970s and 1980s that had been revamped hoping to achieve the same accolade that they had decades earlier. I did quite a few of these gigs for various promoters or venues. However, some of them were just one hit wonders. They couldn't understand why they only got 50 people in a 300-capacity venue. Some kicked off blaming the sound engineer (a.k.a. me), or one of my crew because they realised that no one cared who they were any more. That was something I paid close attention to as you'll see later on.

A rant about three (not) outstanding musicians

Karl Palmer. Although a great drummer, Karl sends a tech spec on a piece of paper and expects his fourteen piece, gold plated, drum kit to be 'mic'd (up and bottom), on a £250 gig: He only attracted 80 people. I didn't get paid for that one. I told his sound engineer I'd played at the venue myself a few months before and had an audience of 400. Fuck you!

The Rezillos. This Scottish pop-punk band had minor success with their single *Top of the Pop* (UK chart position 17 in 1977). They blamed all my sound equipment for a buzz on the PA when it was their own microphone. This became obvious as it fell to bits in one of the male singer's hands as he started to sing. As none of their crew had a spare, I gave him, and the female singer, my own radio microphones, but they started swapping the mics around while performing so I couldn't tell who had which microphone (a sound engineer's nightmare). What a pair of tosspots.

A bass player (in a band I choose not to remember), couldn't hear anything from his monitor during a sound check. It happens, despite all the care to avoid it during the sound check before the main gig itself.

I know a lot of you know what a sound check is but for the readers who don't

The sound check is done after all the equipment is set up. It is usually the role of the roadies but, for small bands, that don't have them, they have to do a lot of that themselves or with some of their mates. They are used to this as they will have to load in and out of rehearsal spaces while practicing. However, these practice places are usually too small for a full PA. Furthermore, some hire conditions for such places have a clause about noise level volumes. Hence, at a gig, the sound check (as the name indicates), is an opportunity for all the musicians to check that all the equipment they bring, ensure it works and, for any of the kit the venue or hire company (i.e. me), provides is working too. This is usually; the PA speakers, microphones and their stands, and stage monitors (the floor speakers/monitors that amplify the sound back to the musicians).

While the band is running through a song, all the house lighting is up so the sound engineer/technician and musicians on stage have a clear view of each other. Any sensible experienced musician would indicate a problem to the sound engineer by sign language. A simple case of pointing to the equipment; using hand gestures e.g. pointing 'up' or 'down' to ask for higher or lower sound levels. Back then all the sound equipment was hard wired into a mixing desk. This desk controls the level of each instrument or microphone (vocals) by way of sliding nobs on a desk board. Each one is labelled accordingly 'Bass', 'Lead Guitar', Lead Vocals etc. But, in the case of no sound, it requires detective work to find the cause which is usually a loose lead or faulty cable somewhere.

If you are lucky enough to have a dedicated Monitor desk at the side of the stage purely looking after the sound on stage things are always easier.

So, this particular gig, Monitors are from F.O.H and during this particular band's sound check for a multi-line up gig, is the bass player a polite, sensible musician?

No!

This Dickhead decided to scream down the microphone that '...the sound engineer is shit!' This is in the presence of the other bands sat around awaiting their turn, causing unnecessary panic. So, I pull all the volume levels down, the rest of the band stops. Silence! My Stage tech walks all the way over to the stage, calmly climbs to face this bass player and, politely says (so everyone hears) 'Switch your amp on mate!'

As I'm sure, as many people in this business have, there are so many stories on all aspects of the event industry. But mine are about things that affected my life along with the odd funny or amusing incidents, although there is an element of sadness in some of them.

I could write a whole book on just those type of incidents. Ok that's enough of the rant.

Chorley Community Centre (CCC)

It was 2003/4 and things were getting very busy. I'd got involved with CCC after I'd used it for one of the Pulse rehearsals when our other place wasn't available. The original building on Railway Street, was a United Methodist Church dating back to 1900. The railway station faced opposite. The site it stood on is now part of the **Inspire, Chorley Youth Zone** structure. But at the start of the noughties, it was so run down. With all due respect to all the Trustees, most of them were literally *Knock'in On Heaven's* door apart from Colin Evans who wasn't very well, and you could tell he needed help running the place. I decided to set up a local bands' night every Saturday, to get the teenagers off the streets. I suppose it was a bit like a youth club when I was a kid. Some of my friends and work colleagues now, used to go to those gigs when they were teenagers and one of them still has his membership card. Fantastic!

Matt Cogley at Chorley Community Centre with Let's Not Lose Mars to The Commies with kind permission from matthewjamescogley.com 2001.

A few friends of mine helped every week as I was sometimes working elsewhere with gigs if I didn't have an engineer available. It became quite a respected venue, and bands came from all over the country. **'Let's Not Lose Mars to The Commies'** has to be one of the best names for a band ever. Two of its members (**Matthew James Cogley** and **Robert Catlow**) were also members of Duck Hunt, who changed their name to **Failsafe** when they got signed to major record labels.

Unfortunately, New Years Day, 2015, in Belfast Northern Ireland, Matt Cogley, who co-founded both bands and was on the brink of stardom as a solo artist, died suddenly at the age of 30. A very talented musician, and he brought so much to CCC at the time, and I was shocked to hear of his death.

Forward a year or so once the bands had started and I had got **South Lancashire Arts Partnership** involved (or **SLAP** as I will call them from now on). **Michelle Graham** who ran SLAP, convinced the Trustees of SLAP to take the centre over. They applied for funding to put some life back into the building and I think around 2004/05 SLAP took it over just before I built the studio in one of upstairs rooms for **Chorley FM**. More about that episode later.

I still had Pulse out on the road although not as much and I was still doing solo/duo work.

However, going back to the gigs I was doing on the hire side of the business, I was now getting recognised as a trusted Audio Rental Supplier as well as an Event Manager.

I used to sub hire in, any infrastructure I needed, and I had a fair few freelancers working for me, some who are still good friends to this day. On of these is Nick Hansen. Today he is a world re-known Lighting Programmer in both Live and TV work. But back when he started, he used to work for me when he was a teenager and came on a Pulse Tour to Ireland at one stage as one of the LX techs.

There used to be a converted cinema on Church St, Preston, called **Aqualenium.** It had band nights on every Thursday. The main function area was two flights of stairs up. For about a year, we had to load in and out all the gear for this venue every week and Nick used to help with these. This particular night, sound checking **Birdman**, a very bass orientated band, I'm trying to sound check the drummer, but the bass player won't stop playing. Nick walks up and says, 'Listen here ya knob, my boss is trying to sound check the drums so shut the fuck up!'

Nick walks back to the FOH desk. I explain to Nick that he could do with being a bit more diplomatic or he could end up getting punched, as he'd only recently turned fifteen and was a bit on the small side. The bass player did stop playing though! Yeah, total knob!

The Xmas Light Switch Ons

Whether in Chorley or Preston these were always 'enlightening'(!-sorry couldn't resist it) for both good and bad reasons. One year, we had put fencing up for the Preston Xmas Light Switch On outside the Harris Museum. Afterwards, I watched the public trying to squeeze down the side of it only to find they couldn't get out the other end. I thought to myself, 'It's there for a reason dimwits!'

Walking down Chapel Street in Chorley

Picture this; me at the front of a parade that consisted of a Police Van, open top double decker bus with the VIP's and about a thousand children. The kids all in Xmas fancy dress and of course Santa is there in his sleigh. My two kids were his Elves …as the real ones were too busy, of course!

I'm halfway down the street and a member of the public comes out of the crowd, stands in front of me, with his hands raised to stop me in my tracks and the parade grinds to a halt.

'I'm reporting you to the Police for bringing a Double Decker Bus down a one-way street the wrong way.' Honest to god's truth that's what he said to me.

There's about 3000 people lined up on the parade route waiting to cheer us to the stage I'd built in Market Street for the finale, and I've got this dickhead trying to get me prosecuted. The fact that there was a police van in the parade too, didn't seem to sink into his one brain cell that must have been bouncing about in his head with all that air.

'Sir, I would go and report me to that community officer, over there.' I point to her as she was on the pavement opposite and off he goes.

Later, I asked her what she said to him, and she said, 'I told him to fuck off, politely!'

On another occasion one year, our small generator (aka Gennie) was in use at the top of market street. It powered the small PA for interviewing the VIP's on the double decker bus, which was where I was too. However, it runs out of fuel. Kim runs up the stairs to inform me, 'It's the Gennie'. Some of the VIP's and Councillors look at each other and asked, 'Who's Jenny?'

Problems with Double Decker buses or their drivers

I was running a Disability Awareness Day on the Flat Iron again. There are the usual things like cars left on the car park from the night before. There are signs up for the past 4 million years telling everyone to not leave the cars there or they'd get towed or blocked in!

I had a small arena in the middle of the car park that I ran cables from the tops of the lamp posts to the arena. I had warning tape on them and at fifteen-foot high there was just enough for the bus to drive in. However, I told him on no account to leave the event without my permission. I would be taking him out via a different exit. Fast forward and the event was winding up, when I hear shouting on the other side of the arena.

'STOP STOP!' I see the bloody double decker bus moving towards the entrance he had come in earlier that day but had caught the nylon rope that I had attached across the car park which had all the audio and signal cables on. I run over and tell him to reverse back. I look up to see that the rope is only about ten foot off the ground, but nothing is broken.

I then look at the lamp posts the rope was attached to. They were bent about 45 degrees from the vertical.

'LOOK WHAT YOU'VE DONE!' I shout, and his reply, his unbelievable reply was;

'**What do you expect with 11 tons behind it**!' I'm lost for words which was a first.

'You were told to stay were you where, I was taking you out a different route as the rope was always going to droop a little through the day.'

This is when your public liability insurance comes into its own. There ensued a battle between myself, **Stagecoach** (the bus franchise) and Chorley County Council as to who was paying Lancashire County Council for the Sunday call out, damage and repair.

Public Liability is about negligence, and if you can prove you weren't negligent, then you're in the clear and your insurance will pay out, if required. I had checked everything including height of double decker buses, and the driver had been told not to move, so he didn't have an excuse as to why he did. After lengthy reports, Stagecoach paid out eventually. What I thought was funny was I spoke to the Bus Station manager a few weeks later to be told that the driver was still getting the piss taken out of him. His 'little' accident was nothing compared to the bus a few weeks earlier full of kids, heading towards a low bridge and in the last few seconds the driver realised his mistake. He turned around on a petrol station forecourt only to take the stations roof out with the bus instead. Fortunately, no one injured but hilarious.

Jabez Clegg in Manchester was one of those great venues but a pain in the arse to load in and out of. I was doing these gigs just at the right era to see many of the bands who have become famous over the last 20 years, pass through this venue. There was insufficient power in the venue, and I had to supply a generator for one gig, a **Starsailor** intimate gig. The generator is sat outside on a trailer, and it was fun watching the traffic wardens trying to see if they could put a ticket on it even though I'd taken the registration plate off. That was pay back for all the tickets they gave me when we were loading in even though we were allowed to load in!

Anyway, I digress again. The main reason I mentioned this venue is that this story is about the pain in the arse **Pete Doherty** from **Babyshambles/Libertines**. Pete Doherty's gigs are renowned for the public going ballistic, and normally all off their heads but not as much as him. I met him once and he breathed on me, and I nearly fell over with how much alcohol was on his breath. I did a New Year's Eve gig with him at a different venue, and he borrowed a guitar off one of the bands and nicked it. He was well known for taking the microphone he was using off the stand at the end of a gig and going home with it too. I know he's sorted himself out now, he's even been on **Desert Island Discs** FFS! But that does not excuse some of the things he did that I witnessed at the time.

The other pain in the arse was the promoter who I had to deal with at every gig at Jabez Clegg and if he cut the costs of any gig to zero to line his pockets he would. **Vuz Kapur** was his name, of **V Man Events.** He was actually a nice guy but had no idea about health and safety. Imagine the calamity if he and Doherty got together! …Imagine no more! I mention to Vuz that we need a crowd barrier for this Babyshambles gig, and I can supply it if need be but he wouldn't pay the cost and got pedestrian barriers instead. The difference between the two is like using a Fiat 500 instead of a 26ton truck to do the job that you wanted the truck to do. I warn him. "any damage and you're paying mate". I had another show that night, so I get back to Jabez Clegg around 11.30pm just as the encores had started and had to rub my eyes with what I was watching. Security guards behind each stack of speakers trying to keep them from falling over. The lightweight barriers had fallen over due to the 600-capacity crowd even though it should only have held 500. But to be honest, it wouldn't had mattered.

One of my crew was stood on top of one of the stacks holding the multicore up, with another crew member holding the end up at FOH because someone had pulled it down from the ceiling. Blood all over the monitors because when the barriers fell forward a couple of the public had head butted the wedges. Pete Doherty then shouts, 'Everyone on stage,' and about 60 of the audience pile onto the stage. It was a total *Baby*

Shambles. Sorry for the pun.

Vuz got a big bill off me that night and yes Mr Doherty nicked the SM58 microphone he had been using, AGAIN!

Due to my experience with Kaz in Somerset, I have no time for him. I'm saying no more.

I'm coming up to a very important conversation that I mentioned much earlier, another one of those strange events in my life, but before that I just want to go via the M74 or I should say the A1M.

Does anyone have a spare gearbox?

Two of my crew were travelling to the Northeast of England to do two Xmas gigs for Steve at Solid Entertainments. I get a phone call that the gear box had gone on the Luton Van fifteen minutes from the first venue. They get towed to the gig but have another show 50 miles away the following day. This is where my experience at Blue Circle kicked in and the saying 'Just do it' saved me a shit load of money and a good example of the saying 'The Show Must Go On'. I have a spare gearbox in the unit. I have some nine hours to get to **Middlesborough**, change the gearbox before they will have loaded out and on their way to the hotel they were staying at. I arrived about 4.30pm bearing in mind it's the middle of December, very cold and dark. Luckily, the pavement outside the town hall is huge and I have loads of room, I run power out from the venue for a light and off I go just hoping I've brought all the tools I need.

I have the gear box out by the time the first band is on. The guys at the taxi rank across the road think this is highly amusing, watching me working on the truck as they drop off and pick up punters from the rank. I get one of my crew to come out and just help me lift the replacement gear box onto the flywheel and then leaves me to it. I'm still tightening the last few bolts up as they are loading the truck after the gig and at 11pm they jump in the truck and off they go to the hotel, and I drive back home absolutely knackered, but the sense of satisfaction was fantastic.

Wearing an invisible gold necklace

With being part of the motorcycle community, I ended up getting involved running a lot of motorcycle rallies for various MCC bike clubs. One of the rallies that I was still organising the infrastructure for up to Lock Down, was **Mobile Chaos MCC** up in Cumbria. Before moving from the original site a few years ago due to red tape, this particular year (I think, 2005), it was a Saturday night the bands were starting to play. All the crew were on it. It's a time when I can relax a bit just keeping an eye on the generator and catch up with a few old friends who I only see there once a year. This night was different. A girl came up to me. She was about twenty years old.

'I've seen many people with silver necklaces around their neck but not a gold one. Why have you got a gold necklace?' She says.

Now the fact I don't wear a gold necklace made this comment very weird at first and I thought she must have been on drugs or something.

'I'd like to have a chat with you if you don't mind?' She says.

This was not a chat up line, although she was very beautiful, she was deadly serious. She told me she was the daughter of a friend of mine's new girlfriend. I had only just met his girlfriend that day, but I never saw the daughter with them, she just told me that when she started talking to me. I say he was a friend, but I only knew him from one of the bike clubs that came to the rallies I worked at. I went and checked the generator, and we went and sat in my pickup, put the engine on to warm the cab up. The conversation then lasted for around three hours and one that I will remember for the rest of my life. She wasn't a psychic but had been able to see everyone's aura's that all human beings have, ever since she was a child. As well as aura's, she told me that there were certain people who had silver necklaces around their necks and she said she had seen a few over the years, but never had she ever seen anyone with a gold one. She asked me about my life, and I explained some of the things I'd done including people I'd helped to get on in life. I told her that I felt I helped many people, but I never seemed to be able to get on myself and there was always something that would stop me in my path. (Little did I know what was going to happen to me in two years' time but that comes later).

She told me that the reason why that is. There are three levels of reality in this world. She could see it. There is a lower or first level where human beings are just bobbing along. The third level there are people with silver necklaces. Those on the third level pluck people from the lower level, subconsciously, and place them on the second level. It all sounded a bit like they are a catalyst for the person they have pulled from the lower level, and it helps them, sometimes without realising it. In this way it leads to that person having a better life or making something of themselves. She was adamant that I must be someone on a higher level than the silver as she couldn't see where I was in the levels.

Now, I know what you're thinking already, 'Phil's off his head and so is she!' And maybe I would have doubted all of what she was explaining to me.

But, considering all the strange things that happened when I was younger, the episodes like that one at the Royal Court, and other events later on in this book and the fact that she was completely serious, no drugs and only a couple of glasses of wine while we sat talking in the cab…? We finished our conversation, and she got out of the pickup, and I never saw her again, not even back in the marquee that night or the next day. I didn't see the guy or his girlfriend either after that and I got the feeling that it should be left at that. This happened to me in Somerset with a guy at The Castle, remember the bodyguard episode. He appeared in the pub one night, spoke to me for an hour or two about my life at the time and then left. Old guy, big white beard, white hair. No one had ever seen him in the pub before or after. That was a weird one too as he only spoke to me, no one else and then left. Kathy, the landlady, Chapter Nine) made a comment later after he'd gone, I think she knew there was something strange about him too.

Over the years I've spent supplying Staging/Lighting/Audio and Generators to the many motorbike rally's I have been involved with, three people who have been an anchor to doing this are -

Mike Stone, Rob Crossland and **Spen** who unfortunately passed away a couple of months ago while I was finishing the book off in August 2025. R.I.P. mate.

CHAPTER 17

Chorley FM

I was asked by Michelle from SLAP to come to a meeting at 37 Steeley Lane, Chorley, their premises before they moved into Chorley Community Centre which I mentioned in the last chapter. It involved setting up the second temporary Radio Station licence (known as a Restrictive Service Licence) which Ofcom* issue to community radio stations that are trying to apply for a full licence. The idea being that you are allowed to apply, and run, three temporary licences to see if you would be suitable for a full five-year licence. The rules from Ofcom are very strict and must be adhered to by the letter or you can't apply for the full one. For example, you must cover; a wide range of listening age groups, use minimal advertising, be community based, to validate the 'Community Radio Station' tag etc. You will be restricted to broadcast in a limited radius (approximately five miles) from the source location of the transmitter you use. The first temporary licence was 2000 which I wasn't involved in, it was only when the second licence in 2001 in conjunction with the Midsummer Festival at Botany Bay where Pulse played (See previous Chapters) and I had started to get my name banded about Chorley to do with my knowledge and work in the music industry that I got involved. Paul Kay (No relation to Peter Kay) was the main technical guy and supplied all the equipment for that licence and the third which followed the following year 2003 as far as I remember. Initially I was involved helping Paul and the Station out with the studio itself as there weren't many volunteers who had a lot of technical knowledge. I didn't know that much about radio but understood generally how it worked. This was so beneficial in the coming years for what I was about to undertake in late 2005. I'm heading off down the M61, getting carried away, I'm back now.

The title of 'Chorley FM' is now part of England's comedy legends. So, I'll explain how it originated and why it received this accolade compared to many other community radio stations past and present. 'Chorley FM' wasn't owned by Peter Kay (the comedian from Bolton). The first temporary licence had already been aired before the name of the station came up on the TV series (*Phoenix Nights* – broadcasted from Jan 2001-Sept 2002). In fairness to Kay (who co-wrote the series), although ours was a small community station, people all over the world tuned in, thanks to the title being banded about on British TV. Peter Kay did ask to buy the brand name at one stage, as he owned the Patent, but we the directors of the station and after consultation with the local council's Cultural Services Manager refused, mainly because it was the station's name, but also because he only offered to do a charity gig for the station and that was it! Don't get me wrong, I love anything Peter Kay has done, but the Chorley FM name was us and was based in the centre of Chorley as it would not have been authentic, calling it 'Coppull FM', 'Euxton FM' or 'Whittle-le-Woods FM.' Those adjacent villages were free to use their name for their own station if they had wanted to, but it wouldn't have meant what Chorley FM stood for.

As I said. Michelle had brought me in initially to help with the technical side of things, however I ended up neck deep in something that, to be honest, after what happened to me in 2006 (which is in the next chapter), contributed to keeping me alive and somehow solvent too.

I was very interested in all the Station's activities. The technical side (both on and off air), was a given. But what I did not appreciate, was the tremendous amount of organisation that goes on behind the scenes of any community radio station. It is heavily dependent, in the main, on volunteers at every stage and I was in the thick of it! For example, there are people who make the shows and present them, the support staff who see to hospitality for guests, others handling the telephone calls and emails, the advertising/publicity and sponsorship/fund raising teams and more: it is all quite staggering. Hence, as the process developed during the second and third temporary licence stages, I end up on air! It's hard to describe the feeling of talking to X-amount of people you can't see, but know they are enjoying your show from the texts and emails. The buzz was as good as performing on stage and I can see why some presenters (not DJ's) do it all their lives. There is an art to it though, and I wouldn't (as they say) pack my daytime job in, or apply to be a presenter on Radio 2. I could talk without a problem, but I have this habit of saying "Errrr" in my sentences quite a lot, and I was conscious of this and still am with my Vlog's on the motorbike restorations which I started in 2020 and are freely available on You Tube under 'Wreckedem Motorcycles' channel.

When you're on stage, if you make a mistake talking, it doesn't matter. I never had a problem with telling jokes live on stage, but you try and do it behind a microphone staring at a wall rather than an audience and it's a completely different kettle of fish. I hosted the 'Breakfast Show' on the second temporary licence and hosted a 'Rock Show', on the third. The licences only lasted three weeks so you were normally on quite a lot even if it was a specialist show.

The second licence was broadcast from a vacant floor space above the Iceland store on New Market Street. It was a glass fronted building in the shopping precinct and everyone walking past could see you and would be putting the thumbs up looking up at you.

I was busy with SDM and as a musician playing whenever and wherever I could. Once the temp licences had finished, I didn't really give the station much thought after we had applied for a full licence. However, all that changed when we received notification from Ofcom, in September 2005, granting us a full five year licence starting on 24th November 2006. YES! By now Michelle and SLAP, had moved into Chorley Community Centre, having also been one of the main contributors to getting the main licence application approved and it was also their job to obtain funding for community projects like the radio station. It was obvious that having the Chorley FM's studio in the same building was the ideal place. By mid-2006, as I always do with life, I went into a full learning curve of becoming Radio Studio builder, Technician, and later Station Manager too. We did have a Station Manager at the start, but due to certain grievances between various volunteers they ended up resigning before the station even went on air and I ended up as Station Manager aswell. I will not bring names into this there is no reason to drag up the dirt and the person in question has passed away too and so I thank them for all their effort at the time and R.I.P.

It must be mentioned that even though I'd never done this kind of thing before, well not on this scale, I had a lot of support. As I mentioned earlier Paul Kay had been involved, much more than me, on the temporary licences, lending broadcast equipment etc. But, with funding, we were buying all our own equipment for Chorley FM to own, and I was the main guy for this side, although Paul did lend the Station a broadcast desk until we could buy our own. Don't get me wrong, I couldn't have done it all by myself, but it was a great feeling knowing that you were building something that was going to be part of history, even if my input was only in a small way.

While we were getting the station ready there were many other people/volunteers involved, who left and joined and left again and who had been involved with the temporary licences, a list I would like to write down here but feel that if I missed someone out because I've forgotten their names, they may feel left out which is not the case and some may get upset which is the last thing I want to do and so maybe it's better that at some stage I and/or other people write a full book on the story of Chorley FM with everyone involved but it will take a fair bit of research.

Anyway, the last three months before the launch were manic. The kitting out of the studio and all the internal logistics were complicated and varied. Externally, to have the maximum signal strength, we had to get the radio masts installed on the spire of the local church (St Georges Church) as the Community Centre didn't have the height, however this was around 250metres away from the Community Centre and so a link transmitter had to be installed from the top of the community centre to the church to receive what we would send out from the main mast which obviously incurred another licence to transmit those 250metres, a licence that we had to renew every year for quite a large fee. Satellite dishes were installed on the side of the community centre to receive the news from Sky every hour, which included all the football commentary and results, every Saturday for the sports show. This satellite would also include emergency transmissions for example if a member of Royalty passed away a special recording is beamed via satellite to every station in the country and must be played. No Songs, no adverts, no news, no presenters just the recording.

We had to supply equipment required to be able to record every show, a rule that all community radio stations had to adhere to and keep the recordings for approximately a month in case there were complaints something that is still done to this day. All Broadcast organisations, TV or Radio must do this, one of OFCOM's conditions.

Aswell as the usual breakfast, midmorning and drivetime shows, we had specialist shows aimed at the specific age groups or community shows.

The station was designed mainly for the 15 -25-year-old age group and the LGBT community.

Sunday Nights and then a repeat in the week of 'Breakout' the LGBT Community show and The Flat Iron Show that went out on a Thursday, repeated in the week, aimed at young up and coming bands, were the Flagship shows of the station and how we got the main licence in the first place.

The Flat Iron Show became a technical nightmare because as it became more and more popular, bands wanted to play live in a studio and if you tried to fit a drumkit in the studio itself, the presenters and the rest of the band would be sat outside!

So, most of the live sessions were Un-plugged or of that ilk.

With the LGBT content that was really important to the station, in late 2007, CFM 102.8, won a Community Service award for 'Breakout' at the National LGBT Health Summit and I had the honour to accept the award on behalf of the station at Manchester Town Hall and it was an insight meeting and talking to senior managers of Ofcom who were in attendance and listening to their bugbears battling against the private providers of broadband, transmitters, phone lines and the reluctance in making sure everyone in the UK had even minimal internet connections, something that 10 years later was still the same problem Ofcom had, no fault of theirs. I think the communications companies had too much clout with the government departments of the time and personally I feel that's still the case now.

There were so many good things that came out of the first five years of the full licence; watching under privileged kids learn a skill, severely disabled people becoming presenters co-hosting sometimes with myself as the main presenter. There are a few people who are now quite a way up in the radio business because of what Chorley FM gave to the up and coming. It is a proud feeling to be part of that and maybe the girl at the rally was right, in some ways, when I get a phone call from someone who thanks me because (and I quote). 'If it wasn't for you Phil, I wouldn't be where I am now.' That makes it all worthwhile.

I was mainly technical manager, but when, as I mentioned earlier the original station manager left, and I took over that role as well, it was full on. Oh, and I also became chairman in 2008.

I presented some shows but more of a stand in if someone was ill or on holiday.

I do remember having to stand in for the sports show one Saturday afternoon and being amazed how you had to deal with talking to the listeners, while trying to listen in one ear what is coming in from the satellite feed about a particular update be it Football, Cricket or Rugby that's arriving live in 30 seconds with a count down, and at the same time sometimes interviewing a guest and trying to keep the show running with the Adverts/Community sections/ News on the hour and not having a producer sat in another room who would normally be assisting the presenter.

As a small station like ours we didn't have that luxury. I take my hat off to all presenters on TV and Radio who have to deal with situations like this. It is a special skill believe me.

We even bought an Outside Broadcast system which worked off a mobile Sim card and we had presenters commentating at Chorley FC matches amongst other things.

It was the cheapest system that we could find and although it worked well, it didn't work well all the time and would drop out at the worst possible places leaving you in the studio trying to find something to fill the gap. Silent radio is bad radio.

However, with all the shit that was going on in my life outside the station, it kept me sane, and the floor of the studio was my bed for many nights through 2007 working late into the night making sure that we had 24hr content loaded up onto **Myriad** (the playout system). Even if the station was running on auto with no presenters present, the content had to be adhering to the conditions of Ofcom and quite rightly too.

I was genuinely, knee deep in anything radio and loved every minute of it. The local band nights we had on in the community centre were still going in 2006/2007 and we used to stream live, Saturday night. Straight after that, the local DJ's would take over with their dance music through to 4am mixing; House, Drum & Bass, Scouse Donk, etc you get the idea. It's all in Wikipedia under Chorley FM now. (which many others and I have co-wrote over the years)

Once we had the station streaming online, we had listeners from all over the world including Europe, the USA, Australia, the Far East: it was amazing.

There are so many memories of that period, and I will share just two that I remember on a personal level.

Red Nose Day. Me presenting mid-morning show.

Firstly, Red Nose Day March 2007 (see picture) and getting my legs waxed live in the studio and the sounds that I was making trying to show it didn't hurt and secondly –

I used to help out on the Breakfast show now and then with STEVIE DEE and for a while I used to do a section called Club Singer similar to what Reeves and Mortimer did on Shooting Stars and watching Steve collapse in his chair laughing at the noises that were coming out of my mouth and trying to figure out what the hell I was singing.

One day, Janet (who looked after some of the Community outside broadcast interviews), had the chance to interview Mia Dolan. She is from the Isle of Sheppey and is one of the United Kingdom's top Clairvoyants. I had the chance to tag along to the interview as a technician for the recording. We did the recording and while Janet had gone to get a cup of tea Mia said to me 'I can see what you've been going through but don't worry it will all work out fine' and mentioned to me 'Germany' and then Janet came back into the room and the conversation stopped. You will see in the next chapter what she meant as the interview took place in 2007, and certain things happened in 2006 which will become apparent.

Anyway, leading on from the interview, the station then decided to bring in a couple of mediums to the centre. This was mainly because of strange things that had been happening there. For example, the breakfast show presenter thought he heard me coming up the stairs into the studio at 6.15am, only to find that there wasn't anyone there and I didn't arrive until fifteen minutes later. You get the idea.

The station decided to have a sort of fright night, and two mediums were recommended by one of Janets friends and they had been on Most Haunted a Paranormal Reality TV series or if not that particular show, another very similar possibly 'Haunted Homes.'

While venturing around the Chorley Community Centre (hoping maybe to tap into the people who used it as a church and Sunday school in the past) we hoped they could find out what was going on.

We would have it all recorded too as part of a special show on the radio the night after. We went into the cellars and the open drains which hadn't been touched for about 70 odd years. It was disgusting down there and the hairs on the back of my neck stood to attention every time I went down there. I didn't like it. We were just turning around to walk back into the cellars from the drains, I was stood next to one of the mediums and a hand was placed on our adjacent shoulders. We looked at each other and the medium said to me 'I don't like this I want to get back upstairs.' To me that's like a dog cowering underneath a table when you can hear footsteps coming up the stairs but there's no one there (which happened to me when I ran The Admiral).

If she's frightened, then it's time to get the fuck out of there. We all hastily scurry back upstairs. I am then told by the Mediums that there are three 'Watchers' on the balcony, there's a guy with a white overall on, covered in blood in the cellar and he's not very happy and a suited gentleman in the next room in the cellar recording details in a book of some sort. But on top of all this, and the reason why the hairs on the back of my neck used to go ballistic whenever I entered the building was that there was a woman who attaches herself to me as I come in through the door and walks around with me all the time, until I leave the centre.

We then had a séance and John and Andy (our IT guys) recorded it all with infrared camera's while everyone sat at a table. There was noise, there were glasses flying about, it was pretty impressive I can tell you. I must admit I didn't feel worried at all. Now I know a lot of you are going to say,'What a load of old bollocks!' (or gentleman's balloons). I may have said the same thing many years before but not anymore. After all the strangeness that has followed me through my life it seemed quite normal, and we had everything on film. Three things happened, that shocked us all. First, something happened to the video footage after we had watched it. What we all saw did not get recorded on it.

Secondly, After 6 months of research it was found that the cellars of the centre had been used as the rooms for autopsy's and recording deaths of people who had been killed on the main railway line opposite the centre, hence the vision of the guy in the white coat covered in blood and the suited guy with the record books that the mediums had seen. There was no way they could have researched that in advance.

Thirdly, two weeks after that séance, Andy Bonner (our IT guy who had been filming it all) died in his sleep. He was only in his late 20's. Apparently, he was a diabetic but didn't know. RIP Andy.

The station was going well but we struggled with finance, you were only allowed to receive 50% of your funding from advertising and although our two marketing guys were great we were limited to what we were allowed to absorb financially so it was a constant battle to apply for funding from various places and SLAP again were fantastic in finding the money for the station.

With a volunteer organisation like this you are always going to get people at logger heads now and then and it was apparent that certain members of the board wanted to move away from the Community Centre and set up elsewhere, something which I suggested to the board would be a logistical nightmare and cost a lot of money too. I'm not sure if it was certain people getting too big for their boots or some of the board having delusions of Grandeur but as chairman and under pressure I agreed to the move but on some very strict conditions one of the main ones being that the move would not affect SLAP's day to day running of their objectives to the community and fund raising for various projects.

One of my main concerns was that Chorley FM wanted to keep the telephone number of the station which was on all the Idents or Jingles that went out on the station. Since we started the main licence, we used to pay a retainer each month to a voice over artist who when asked would record and produce new jingles or idents for presenters for example 'The Rock Show with Phil Baker on 102.8 Chorley FM.' A lot of these jingles had the telephone number in, and you can imagine to redo all the jingles and all the leaflets with a new number would cost a lot of money. I only agreed to the station taking the number and not setting up a new phone line, was because certain members of the board had told me that SLAP would still have a phone line and internet connection from the day Chorley FM switched to the new building and that SLAP's phone line/ Broadband which we shared with the Stations number in the Community Centre would not be disconnected.

This didn't happen and SLAP had to wait 6 weeks to get a new phone line and internet connected which caused so many problems for their work and I felt responsible even though I had been assured that it wouldn't happen. I knew they were wrong before they did it and again which I'd done so many times in the past, I should have heeded intuition and stood firm.

Apart from letting SLAP down, Michelle was a close and dear friend who I had known for nearly 9 years and I took this personally too.

I stayed with the station up to around 2010 but felt that although Chairman, if people weren't going to listen to me why was I there.

The new building they moved to in Railway Road, Chorley was in fairness a lot better for disabled access with it being on ground level something which was difficult to achieve at the Community Centre with the station being up a small flight of stairs above SLAP's offices.

I used to go back to the station for interviews on the weekly Rock show with **Terry Birnie** and even did a few assists on some of his shows but I felt it had lost its character with all the love, time and effort spent by so many people in those first 3 or 4 years, I felt Chorley FM's soul stayed in Chorley Community Centre when the station moved and the Radio Station as a whole lost something.

As I mentioned briefly in the last chapter, the community centre is now knocked down and 6 years ago made way for an amazing building called 'Inspire Chorley Youth Zone' which took 2 years to build and is an amazing place for kids of all ages and disabilities to go to, which Michelle ran once it was built until she moved on in 2024 to pastures new. It's good to think that although there's a completely new building there the soul of the old building maybe living on trying to help the kids.

Chorley Community Centre 2010.

Inspire Chorley Youth Zone 2022 sited on the centre.

If you look at the left-hand side of the Inspire building the brickwork is where Chorley Community Centre stood.

I could do a full book about Chorley FM and maybe I will at some stage but for now we need to move on as there's so much more to go through.

*Source: The **Office of Communications**, commonly known as **Ofcom**, is the government-approved regulatory and competition authority for the broadcasting, telecommunications and postal industries of the United Kingdom. (source Wikipedia)

CHAPTER 18

Beyond The Dark Side beckons and then it got even darker

This is one of the hardest chapters of my life both financially, and mentally. Certain parts of my professional activities were rigidly interlocked with my personal circumstances and continue to disturb me ever since, due to the hurt inflicted upon me by others and my own failures.

I disbanded Pulse – Echoes of Floyd after the Leyland Eagles gig in 2005. Some of the band had applied to an advert from **Beyond the Dark Side** (**BTDS**) who were a Pink Floyd Tribute Band from Australia. The founding member, guitarist and lead singer of the band was **Kevin ******. Kevin was British and, had decided to relocate back to the UK and set up the band for touring in Europe. BTDS, as far as I am aware of then (and now), were not connected to any other famous Pink Floyd tribute band from Australia. If I met the founding members of BTDS in hell it won't be a day too soon: one of them, **Athol Sargood**, died in August 2020 and beat me to dragging him there.

BTDS were looking for an audio company and Front of House (FOH) sound engineer to look after that side of the show. They had transported all their lighting equipment (LX) from Australia in a 40ft shipping container. Before this arrived in the Midlands, where Kevin lived at the time, I had a meeting with him. Mistakenly, he seemed pretty genuine as he explained that he was looking to rent premises where all the LX equipment could be stored, serviced and prepared for future shows. In late 2005, I decided to share the costs with Kevin for renting a small, brand-new warehouse in Cowling Business Park, Chorley. Kevin relocated to Chorley with his wife and redirected the shipping container to this new unit before it landed in the UK. My share of the overall costs of the unit, was a struggle to cover, but I could see the possibility of us both making a lot of money from the tour he had secured in Germany the following year.

BTDS was a limited company, registered in the UK as **BTDS** The Act Ltd and **** (…rhymes with ?) secured a £100k loan from his bank to finance the tour costs for BTDS and by now the Lighting Director (LD) Athol Sargood had flown in and was living at Kevin's house with the sheepish Michael (dogsbody to the other three) who I'll get to later.

The promoter was called **Axel *******, who set up **BTDS** Europe Limited and arranged concert dates all over Germany for the nine-month period of the tour. The costs of venues were reduced by the hire of a large circus tent, and all the infrastructure Axel subcontracted in, fencing, toilets, generators and the like.

2006 was also the year that the FIFA World Cup was held in Germany, so the summer part of the tour coincided with that too. Everyone would make a shit load of money. My share would be around £70k from supplying services to BTDS The Act Ltd and to BTDS Europe Limited to yield me a £45k profit. I felt that a successful tour would put me in a strong position with the promoter too. It would place my audio rental company (SDM) on a trajectory to the next level as well.

It was a 'We'll be singing when we're winning…' moment for us all.

My only concern was that I would be needed to do FOH engineering for the tour and drive a truck. This meant I had to have someone in the UK to run my business while I was abroad. I was very twitchy about this. After seven years SDM was trading successfully, and my bank were happy to support me too. I proceeded to buy a new trailer to transport their container, a tractor unit to tow it and a 7.5t truck to cover the overspill of other equipment. To cover that lot, and ensure I had enough audio equipment to fulfil my commitments to gigs in the UK, I took out a new business loan and negotiated a larger overdraft. I also needed a Goods Vehicle Operator's Licence for the trucks (more cost) and pay for a lot of the upfront logistics. These included all the channel ferry costs and organising credit cards for fuel etc as I was tasked with finding all the crew for the tour until they arrived in Germany, where the (so-called) promoter would take over. At this time, I didn't have a Heavy Goods Vehicle Driving license either and needed to take both tests to give me a full Articulated Lorry Licence (artic). With this, I could drive the 44ft truck while another member of the crew would drive the 7.5t truck on a car license.

To obtain the full HGV (Heavy Goods Vehicle) licence in the UK, there are a number of vehicle tests you have to take. The Articulated Licence (which is called C+E now) was the Class 1 then. You have to take the Class 2 first (rigid) before you can take your Artic test (Class 1). I passed my Rigid Licence but failed my artic test something that didn't go down well with BTDS, quote: 'We don't like failure!' That set the standard they expected, and I should have picked up on the unease I felt. While all this was happening, a rehearsal room was set up in the warehouse, being used by the band. BTDS, now included various musicians from Pulse who had passed their auditions while I focused on the production & logistics of the tour. On reflection now, I should have converted SDM into a limited company, but it was way down on a long list of priorities.

Would you trust your business to be run by someone else?

There was a guy named Charlie who worked for various audio companies in the northwest who had said he was happy to run my business while I was away touring. Great I thought, he'd been working freelance for me for a couple of years, and this would solve the problem. But, three weeks before the tour, he told me that he didn't feel he could do it. Personally, I think he wanted to be the FOH engineer on the BTDS tour all along, which, as it turned out, he ended up doing. At such short notice, I couldn't find anyone else that I trusted to run SDM to avoid potentially destroying the whole business in a matter of months. I was conflicted, weighing up the pros if I went on tour and been (literally) in the driving seat, against the cons of risk: the biggest being the state of SDM when I returned. With what did happen, I now know that it all hinged on this dilemma and the fact that I hadn't passed my artic licence and was, therefore a burden that BTDS didn't need. In making my decision, to stay, I sealed my own fate in more ways than one. But first I had to tell Kim the 'good' news.

The stench has never gone away

In parallel to my busy, but theoretically, brilliant business prospects, my home life was in steep decline. My relationship with Kim was broken and we could not fix it. This crisis was something that I never wanted to happen. I was not able to handle home life with Kim and the impact of her chronic illness that is Myalgic Encephalomyelitis (ME). It was my failure to understand and adapt my life to help her that was at fault, and I entirely accept that now. My way of (not) coping was to pour myself into everything I was doing outside of our home life. I can now see how I was protecting myself at the expense of those I loved. Not to excuse my actions but to help me contextualise it, I did it deliberately to avoid the fall out I had experienced in my past relationships. These included; Jane trying to end her life, Dawn and the problems she had with my music, Sharron who only married me 'to make a good father for her daughter' and Kaz with her drug addiction. Our family life was unravelling before me and, if I could turn back time, I should have concentrated a lot more on making sure everything was as best as it could be at home, before dedicating so much of my time on my business ventures. I didn't and cannot reverse that now.

It all came to a head one day. Before I had decided to not go on a tour that would keep me on the road for three quarters of the year, Kim and I had a massive argument. During this I knew I had fallen out of love with her, and I told her. There were other problems which didn't help the situation. For example, meeting someone else and having a relationship with her, as a civil partner and father of two, wasn't an affair I was proud about. In my defence, I was isolated and when I had any down time, I was consumed with thoughts of previous relationships that had created problems. I was not in a good place at all and needed someone who was sympathetic and understood my problems. She presented a way out or something else. I'm not sure. All I know is that as much as I loved the kids, I tried to stay away from the house as much as I could because of the problems I had with Kim. However, when I told Kim the good news that I was not going to be away from home for those nine months, she asked me, 'So when are you leaving?' Quite rightly so, as I said I didn't love her anymore.

Like any parent, I had never ever thought about what it would be like to tell my eight- and ten-year-old children that I was leaving their home for good. It is something that I will never ever forget. To anyone else, I always say that if you can solve your problems with the mother (or father), please do it. Watching the children you love; crying their hearts out because of something you have caused and the prospect of not being in their lives as much as you have been, rips at parts of your soul that you can never repair. Until you have experienced that, nothing compares – even when someone close to you dies. As a result, a couple of weeks before BTDS left for Germany, I moved out of the house and rented a bedroom from a close friend of mine. I then lived five minutes away and I made sure I saw the kids a couple of times a week. These included taking them swimming, climbing and sword fencing at the local leisure centres in Chorley and Preston. It was the best I could do during a very difficult time for all of them…it was a shit show of mostly all my own making, and I did my best to mop it up, but the stench has never gone away for me anyway.

Throughout this crisis, I ensured that all the BTDS logistics and audio equipment (mainly racks, stacks, speakers and amps), was in place for the tour to start at the end of February 2006. Part of the total chaos that ensued has been captured by Simon Ash (who was the drummer) in his book: *The Chapters in the Life of Rex Roman*. It is a tongue in cheek account, and I ended up getting involved with him when it was made into a Pink Floyd comedy musical (see chapter 19). But, rumour control, here are all the facts I know: so, this is my truth!

I'll start at the end: bottom line I ended up with a debt of £65k. £40k was required to pay back various finance/leasehold companies, including the purchase of an articulated trailer. A load of credit cards were maxed out, the huge bank loan repayments were crippling, and my overdraft was up to its limit too. The original cash flow solution was that credits came in from the monthly tour revenues (i.e. tickets and merchandise sales) which would repay all the debts way before the final gig. So, I assumed the best and carried on with my work in the UK and left the European side to the others. How wrong I was! On top of the fact that the tour collapsed, I had to pay for the ferries and fuel on the return journey in order to (hopefully) salvage some funds when they returned to the UK!

Once the trucks left for Germany, I dealt with the aftermath of my personal circumstances. This, unfortunately, was jack-knifed by what quickly unfolded abroad. I was chasing the expected income from both the band and the promoter when it didn't arrive at the end of the first month. Money from them, under our agreements, were to pay a large chunk of both my business and personal overheads. I was receiving messages from musicians and crew members raising their concerns that all was not satisfactory. The promoter kicked off when the tractor unit (towing the trailer that held the container) arrived in Germany. It wasn't that the type of tractor unit I had indicated was coming over, but it was more than adequate to do the job. He sent it back only for it to break down ten miles from my unit and I ended up with a £600 recovery bill. The truck had had a full service before it left the UK, so I assume someone had tinkered with it in Germany. This became apparent as a piece of rag was found in the fuel tank which blocked the fuel pipe. Axel refused to pay me any rental for the tractor unit but said he would still pay for the trailer and the 7.5t truck which was £3k a month. I then had to try and sell the tractor unit at a reduced price to help the finances.

In the years since this fiasco, I discovered that if I had sent for example, a top of the range Scania Tractor Unit, which would have cost me another £40k, I would have never seen it again as that was part of the con/plan which was unfolding. The promoter hired another unit to tow the trailer in Germany, but by mid-March, I hadn't been paid any money at all from either the band (for the equipment they had hired off me) or promoter, even though the agreements had a set fee income to me of about £5k per month in total. Increasingly frustrated, I jumped on a flight to Berlin and drove in a hire car the rest of the way to **Dresden** (where the show was set up for another gig). I forced a meeting with all concerned. There were a lot of heated words exchanged, but I stated my case clearly: expenses for February, March and part payment for April which came to around £12k. I desperately needed this to settle my financial commitments as I had not had a penny. I was begrudgingly handed a cheque for £6.5k. After that: I received nothing. I could have demanded a return of all the trucks and gear back to the UK but, I had been offered verbal assurances that all would be fine. I should have gone with my gut feeling and backed out there and then, but wanting to believe in the good nature of these people, who looked me in the eye, I didn't. By May, allegedly the Promoter had embezzled 500k euros into a Luxemburg bank account and he hadn't paid anyone, including the crew (which was part of the agreement too). Hence, I arrived at that £65,000 loss.

While this is a part of my life that I cannot change, it also impacted certain members of the crew and musicians who were my friends. This could fill another book and would include how most of the touring party (apart from BTDS themselves) had to escape overnight from the rest of the band, the Tent Master and his crew (who owned the Circus tent) in fear of being beaten up or worse. In Germany the rule of law at the time was that if a Tour in a Circus Tent 'collapses' the Tent Master is liable to continue whatever that show is contracted to and is also liable for all the costs incurred.

The BTDS guys came back a different route and made up some excuse as to why they didn't leave with the rest of the band and crew. I never believed them. They expected me to collect them from the airport. I didn't.

Everything returned from Germany to our warehouse in the UK by end of May. BTDS had not paid all their half of the UK expenses while they were in Germany or settled any of the other associated running costs (i.e. heating, lighting, insurances etc) which had been agreed to before the tour started. Something else I had equally liability to pay. Then, as if to break me with the final straw, while I was working away for a few days, BTDS took all their gear and fled back to Australia. They had waited and dumped me right in it! I tried every way I could to get back what I was owed and got nowhere. They were impossible to trace, and no one helped me who did know them. Meanwhile, I was left with a massive drain on whatever income I could scrape together from any work I could put my hands to.

A literal dead end of which ever highway to hell I was on!

In times of desperation, I was plagued by some of the darkest thoughts imaginable over many sleepless nights. Eventually, I found out exactly where those BTDS shits lived in Australia. I sent demands for what they owed me, and they still refused to pay. In one of my moments of a mad delirious state, I imagined myself being introduced to a professional hitman (contract killer). We met and I could see in his eyes that he meant every word he said to me face to face.

'Mr Baker, I will fly to Australia and take out the main guys of BTDS for £5,000!'

I was shocked to my core! The whole sentence was delivered in a calm, matter of fact tone – like a business-to-business statement. It was like I was talking to someone from pest control who was detailing how they would remove vermin. I half expected him to add: 'it's all in a day's work and no trouble at all, Sir'.

Now, don't forget I'd met a few of these type of people over the years, but I'll never forget those eyes; ocean floor dark pupils in a glacier cold white oval frame, way beyond something you'd expect in a **Netflix** blockbusting thriller! Then, as I am processing this moment, two things stopped me. I didn't have that kind of money, and I doubted that the drop-down menu for the; 'purpose of loan?' question from a bank would include 'contract killing' alongside 'holiday', 'new car' or 'school fees!' No, the only condition I could not agree to was that he would have to take out everyone in the vicinity of the hit. There could be no one left alive who could recognise him or who could raise the alarm. 'No collateral damage,' is how he phrased it – told you he was some mean mother fucker!

Besides, there was one guy entangled up in this who has sadly passed away not long ago. He was just a mixed-up kid, and I couldn't let him take a hit for something that wasn't his fault.

"I get knocked down..."

That whole sequence is how my anger had manifested. To be so low in my misery, and have such thoughts stabbed into my head, I knew was the wrong outlook. But, until you go through something like that, do not judge how you would feel when there seems like no other option available to make it stop. Luckily, I came out the other side even stronger which is what I do, so to AXEL & BTDS: FUCK YOU!

In a nutshell: it took me over five years to try and pay back all that I owed as I was determined not to declare myself bankrupt. When you are insolvent, some people say that taking the legal process of bankruptcy is a sensible measure. But there are so many repercussions if you do: including trying to get Visas to the USA. I'm glad I never went down that path.

Axel *******, with his ill-gotten gains safely hidden away, declared himself bankrupt with BTDS Europe in his wife's name. I found this out after making enquiries through a German solicitor for a set fee. However, his costs for taking on my case to completion would be 200 euros an hour. Furthermore, he didn't know exactly how much time it would involve recovering the £26k debt, but he wanted a considerable sum in advance and offered no guarantees of any success in the matter. I could not afford to pursue this both financially or mentally. I could not put myself through the stress. The satisfaction of winning would come at the cost of any gains being stripped away to possibly zero by the privilege of his work for me! Unfortunately, this was definitely not one of those, 'No win no fee' deals and the old adage of *throwing good money after bad*, stuck in my head too.

The final nail in the coffin from the whole Germany fiasco was a visit from Customs & Excise. This department of our British taxation system covers Value Added Tax (VAT). Most western countries have some form of VAT equivalent which is a burden when the income your business turns over or exceeds a certain limit. I had been VAT registered since 2003 and had always paid what I owed on time. But, with everything going on with Germany and my personal life, I had neglected my quarterly returns. This came to a head when the inspector told me that the equipment I had bought for BTDS, had not been declared properly and I owed Her Majesty's Government a considerable sum. Day to day living became increasingly difficult due to the amount of money I had to pay back after sorting out agreements with the various financial companies and the Inland Revenue. At one stage I was paying around £700 a month to various creditors. If I hadn't been so determined to get through this unbelievable mess, I may have considered the easy way out and it wasn't bankruptcy!

...But I get up again..." Even when pissing the night away hits a dead end!

Part of my income came from running Chorley FM. During this time, Michelle Graham asked me to do some maintenance work at Chorley Community Centre. I have always been able to adapt to my situation and this included getting into building maintenance which I had done before. To make a significant dint in my debts I had to sell all my assets; mainly my audio hire equipment, the trucks from the tour and by early 2008, although not cash rich, at least I was covering my costs. While I was still renting a tiny tidy room from my friend, mentally I was in a mess. Not living with the kids was literally doing my head in. I was constantly in the pub in the evenings and feeling sorry for myself.

Things came to a head one night when I was leaving **The Crown** in Chorley. There was a lady who had a load of shopping she was having to carry home, and she said she lived off Pall Mall. I said I was getting a taxi and offered her a lift. She accepted. Maybe I was looking for company or a chat but how wrong I was. We got out of the taxi and off she walked towards her street. Then this guy appears, who (I found out afterwards) was the main drug dealer in the area. He was her boyfriend and put 2 and 2 together and made 5. He shouted to her aggressively and then walked towards me. I was more concerned with how he was treating her more than anything else, when, 'BANG!' He hit me in the face which felt like a brick being smashed into my nose. At the time I didn't know how much damage he had done. I stood my ground and said, 'What did you do that for?'

He was astonished that I was still upright. He walked away only for his mate to decide to have a go instead. I said to him, 'Come on then.' He saw the state of my face and ran off. Apparently, this dealer's party piece was to smash you in the face with a knuckle duster and when you fell to the ground, he robbed you.

I had offers from various Back Patch Clubs to help out for revenge. I could have taken out my own retribution for the damage he caused to my face, but to be honest, I'd had enough, with all the shit going on. I decided to put it down to experience but, since that punch, I have never been the same mentally. I cannot put my finger on what it is. It's gradually dissipated into the grey matter, but I still think briefly about that episode in my life at least a couple of times every week.

I was not going to put any photos in this chapter because of the shit I went through but thought I'd add these onto the end of the chapter which are the drawing BTDS gave me to get the Hogs made and the diagram of the tent that went around Europe with them too.

And just in case BTDS want to put a complaint in about this chapter or sue me, Kevin, I still have all the emails and paperwork from 20 years ago just in case. Considering we were supposed to be close business associates he has never once been in contact with me since June 2006, apart from telling me that he wasn't going to pay the VAT that he owed to Stardrivemusic.

Axel even asked to be my friend on Facebook 3 years ago!
What the Fuck!

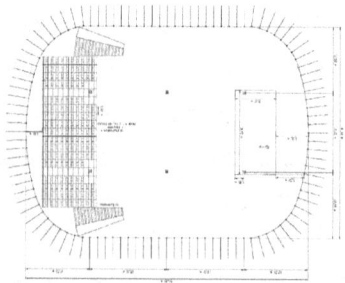

CHAPTER 19

The Aftermath of BTDS and Rex Roman

Late in 2007, I had started going back to my former home for the odd evening meal with Kim and the kids. Eventually, in early 2008 I ended up moving back in. This wasn't ideal for Kim or me, but it was good for the kids. Kim had a job now and was covering her costs for the house, but I couldn't help that much due to the amount of debt I was in. We gave it a go but, it was inevitable that at some stage in the future our paths would part.

By mid-2008, I had got rid of the warehouse, sold most of my equipment at the best prices I could (but well short of their true value) and I was freelancing for an events crewing company. This work paid a reasonable income, and I was still Station Manager and Technical Director of Chorley FM on a voluntary basis (picking the odd bit of paid work for building maintenance when I could). Finally, although not having any infrastructure, I was still running the odd event for the local councils: I subcontracted what was required rather than supplying it myself. With having my HGV class 2, I did some work for a marquee company too, so some good had come out of the BTDS fiasco.

There was a much better thing that came out of all the shit. A couple of years after all the other band members had recovered from the crap that they had experienced with BTDS, Simon Ash contacted me about *Wish You Were Here The Chapters in the Life of Rex Roman*. (*Chapters* for short).

By 2009 we had done a few music rehearsals come impromptu auditions in front of music moguls for the feedback. *Chapters* ended up as a Pink Floyd comedy musical which eventually took us to **Edinburgh Festival** performing nineteen gigs over twenty-one days. We also performed the show at theatres around the UK including Henley-on-Thames were Dave Gilmour's manager and **Phil Taylor** (Dave's Guitar Tech) came to watch.

I met Phil Taylor and his wife after the show at Henley and he asked me why I didn't use a Fender Strat as Dave Gilmour does. I explained that, due to my short fingers, I found it difficult playing a Strat. Phil's wife says, 'maybe we could give him one of David's guitars?'

It was a pleasure meeting such a great Guitar Tech as Phil Taylor but, deep down, I would have loved to have met Dave Gilmour. Maybe one day.

I was of the opinion that Simon was trying to get Floyd to finance *Chapters* the way **Queen** had financed *We Will Rock You.* Unfortunately, it didn't happen. We performed at Chorley Theatre too where my daughter was dressed as a hot dog on stage, as was I too at a few of the venues. Hot Dogs feature a lot in *Chapters* but in a funny way.

Simon Ash is still a great friend as are all the members of the cast & crew.

We try and get together even if it's only to recall fond memories. One of these was when a local actor (who was supposed to wear a hot dog costume in the foyer) called in sick. I volunteered to be said hot dog before I went on stage.

I did it so well I think I ended up being the hot dog in a few other venues too, when no one else (mysteriously) was available. Don't even ask how I ended up in this position. It's something I'll never forget.

A general run down of the show was:

The Synopsis (which you'll find on the web).

'Meet Rex Roman. British actor, fading star. When Rex hears that Pink Floyd are reforming for the Live 8 concert, his life is plunged into a free fall of indecision. In order to attend, he must end his self-imposed exile from Britain and confront the pain of his past...This is a tale of love, tears, laughter and a large chicken. A journey through time that reveals a tomato ketchup conspiracy, the identity of a government assassin, and the best-kept secret in rock history. We wonder if the entire acting industry is obsessed with poultry as we follow the story of one man's life, influenced by his favourite band of all-time...Pink Floyd.'

Throughout his life, Rex also plays air guitar to Dave Gilmour's amazing solos using either a Stratohoover or a Les Brush, you get the idea. That, and more, is all in Simon's book and I won't spoil it for you. In preparation for live shows, we would go to the local supermarkets close to the theatre we were performing in. We bought lots of sweeping brushes to sell at the gig and invite everyone who bought one to come up on stage in the final song *Comfortably Numb* when I start playing the main guitar solo.

Again, if Pink Floyd had come up with financing the *Chapters*, my life may have taken another completely different path and might not have performed with the bands I have worked with since 2010 which will all come clear in the next few chapters of my book not of Simon's *Chapters*. Confused? Join the club.

Some of the cast including myself promoting our show at the Edinburgh Fringe on one of the Royal Mile stages with some of the audience with Les Brushes or are they Stratohoovers? They look so similar ha ha.

Air Guitars (well Les Brushes) at the end of Comfortably Numb at Edinburgh Fringe.
[Reproduced by kind permission of Simon Ash].

Around the same time as *Chapters*, I had started working for a local crewing company called '**Local Crew**' based in Wimbledon, London that was trying to setup a northern branch (not to be confused by the company Local Crew that now exists in 2025).

I applied to work as a crew member at the northern branch. However, more good fortune came my way, as I got the job of running the northern branch itself. It came with an office rented out at a lighting rental company called **HSL** in **Blackburn**, Lancashire. They are now called 4Wall. I also had work on various events down in London: two of which stand out a mile. Off down the M1 now.

1. **How to Rig a show in 2 hours.**

I was part of the crew hired to setup a meal, a stage for a band, a full sound system and lights at the **Natural History Museum.** This event was for 300 people to be sat around the dinosaur that was on display there at the time. The main problem was that the Museum didn't close to the public until 5.30pm and the guests arrived at 7.45pm! So, 125 – that's One Hundred and Twenty-Five – crew/technicians had just over two and a quarter hour's to make everything ready. We did it! As the last guest left at 1pm, we had less urgency but still had everything packed back into the trucks by 4am. It cost the client half a million pounds for five hours of wining and dining! It is not my place to say who the client was.

2. You Didn't Hit Anything.

I was asked to take a 26t truck down to **Henley-on-Thames** music festival which is normally held a week after the **Henley Royal Regatta**. All the marquees were still up, and I had to try and manoeuvre this truck through all of them without damaging anything. Then I had to; complete a three-point turn on a penny to back the truck up to the stage, unload the truck onto the stage (which is half built in the Thames River!), turn around and drive back through all the marquees again. The production guy, who is sat with me in the truck says, 'that was really well done, you didn't hit anything.'

I say, 'isn't that the idea?'

'Well normally they always hit one Marquee or another!'

I'd like to think that that was good driving on my part which I have been known to do over the years. Not trying to blow my own trumpet, well fuck it yes, I am!

Back off the motorway

End of 2008, the northern office of Local Crew wasn't working due to logistics, lack of employees up north and politics from certain people in HSL and the office closed down. With me knowing most of the staff at HSL, they asked me if I could come in and help out in their Rigging Dept due to sickness of various employees. Rigging was something that I had been involved with in various guises over the years. This included the cement works in the 1980s, events I had run through SDM, building stages and with Pulse-Echoes of Floyd too, but nothing on this scale.

I started in Nov 2008 and, by early 2009, I was running their rental rigging dept with full responsibility of everything that holds equipment in the roof of Theatres and Arena's while on a tour. Something which to this day I am still involved with but with a different company. This freelance job carried on until December 2012. I learnt so much more about rigging in those years including training in a form of automation (Kinesys), inspection of rigging equipment, training in repairing, stripping and rebuilding electric hoists/chain motors and so much more. I also took my National Forklift and Telehandler licences which became invaluable later on. I had worked with plant machinery over the years but had never had to take the exams. I was on site a lot too, including rigging Audio Delay Towers at stadium concerts and full setups of shows. For example, pantomimes at the SEC Armadillo (Glasgow) for over 6 years, as well as many large inside (10000 capacity) and outside music festivals etc. I also did a lot of driving so the HGV Class 2 licence came in handy once more.

By the end of 2012, I decide to leave HSL due to my workload with other projects that I had on the go. Although I had had a shit time in 2006, most of my clients I had worked for, still knew I would come up with the goods when it came to making an event happen. The event side of my business had started to accelerate again, and I was also supplying a Portable Appliance Testing (PAT) service for various clients including Theatres. In making industry safe, legislation came into effect on 1st April 1990 (in response to the Electricity at Work Regulations 1989). This was a step towards making sure that all portable appliances were safe i.e. anything with a plug on it and could be moved around. Although not a legal requirement it was something that most industries were having to get tested due to insurance and the like. I started getting involved with PAT contracts in the 2000s with checking all of my own equipment that I used but, gradually, I was being asked by other companies if I could test their equipment too. I had taken the exams that you were required to pass to be certified in electrical safety and so another feather to my cap.

I veered off down some motorway then – back to 2009

Any days off during the three weeks in Edinburgh performing *Chapters*, I spent riding back from Edinburgh to Blackburn on my motorbike to work at HSL and then back to Edinburgh the following morning. Finances were tight and I was still paying off these huge sums of money I owed, so I worked as much as I could. August of that year, Kim took the kids and moved back to Swansea. I couldn't blame her but the way it was done upset me. I knew they were going but it was just a shock when I returned from Edinburgh only to find most of the furniture, bed, fridge, etc. had been taken too. I'm sure it was easier for them to leave without me being there, but it was still a hard pill to swallow. For the first time in over 25 years, I was without a partner in my life. The reality hit me like a car crash; you don't build a family to get to your midlife thinking you will be totally on your own! Its water under the bridge now and all in the past for us all.

I had to get lodgers in to help with the rent, which was a disaster. The first were an unemployed couple. I knew the son's parents who were neighbours when I lived in Warton Place. They needed a place of their own and so I agreed to rent a bedroom, they said they would pay me out of their benefits. However, it soon became apparent that they were spending all their money on clothes, weekly visits by the girl to hair salons and a new car (FFS). I didn't get any rent at all, so after a few months I kicked them out. I soon got visits from the Bailiffs to seize their car amongst other things, as all the debts they had racked up had been registered at my address! Another lesson learnt.

I travelled to Swansea a couple of times that autumn of 2009 to see the kids.

Kim was happy for me to visit and stay over and it was good to see Jon and Elea. After that the kids would come and stay with me over the years meeting Kim halfway on the M50 in Gloucester, to collect them and the same on their return to Swansea. This carried on until they were old enough to travel by themselves to see me in Preston via train or on the National Express coach service. I missed the kids so much then, but we spoke every week on the phone too.

September 2009 – I performed my last gig with a band called **Rubian** (from Preston). At the end of the gig, I had the guitarist (JK) up the wall by his neck due to the band being ripped off from a previous big paying gig. I only found out because I had a friend who knew the organiser. JK got paid £1500 and there were five in the band but he told us it was a £300 gig. In short, he was pocketing £1200!

I only mention this as I sang for a band whose vocalist was ill at the same venue a month later (**Grasshoppers Rugby Club**. Preston). It was here that I met my partner Angela for the next five years. She was in the audience, and she was a drummer from a band I'd seen in the past. She had just gone through a horrendous break up of her own. I had known her for a while but only to just say 'hello' to and I suppose we were both very vulnerable due to our circumstances and became an item.

Meanwhile, my sister's partner had been offered a job in Quatar, and she was going with him. She had asked me to move into her house to look after it with my nephew/her son as I was finally leaving Warton Place where Kim, the kids and I had lived since late 1996. All my bike spares I gave to Leyland Eagles MCC and the rest of the shit still in the large garage took three days for it all to be removed by a scrap man including two cars. I can't believe how much crap I accumulated, well actually I can.

I recall many outstanding times with Angela, including four weeks in New Zealand over Xmas 2010. I handed over the keys to Warton Place the day before I left for the other side of the world. Amongst some of the brilliant times there; swimming with seals and visiting **Fox Glacier** and then sitting at a bar just before midnight New Years Eve overlooking the Glacier with Dark Side of the Moon playing in the background. And, although that trip involved surviving a flood in the camper van, 2011 started a change in my life for the better.

When we returned, however, I discovered that my sister's partner's job had been cancelled and that they didn't go to Quatar after all. So, for the first half of 2011, I lived with my sister, wondering where to go to from here especially when I still had so much money to pay back. Angela, while happy for us to be a couple, didn't really want me to move in. I didn't have a place I could call my own but then, as fate would have it, the house next to Angela came up for rent. She suggested I take it on, and I became the boyfriend next door, something which was fine for both of us for the next few years.

Her independence was very important to her, which I respected, and I was actually getting used to living by myself and not having to be responsible for someone else – which was closer to the truth.

I settled into my new accommodation, and I had a reasonable income that covered all the finance I still owed from the BTDS mess and my living expenses. The kids were in their teens, and we saw each other as much as we could. Angela had cats and so it was only a matter of time that I ended up with one. His name was Gypsy and there is a cute photo on my first album cover which we'll come to soon.

Off down the M6 again: The Gypsy King

Gypsy was a character and deserves a special mention as he made me laugh and was an unexpected comfort to me. He used to like being my car companion on short journeys. I arrived home one morning after picking some groceries up from the local shop, to find HMRC officers outside my place. They had come with regards to my accounts but, as I opened my car door, Gypsy jumps out of the passenger seat to greet them. They had very quizzical frowns on their dour faces – so I did explain that he doesn't always travel with me and when he does its only locally. Afterall, it's not like I claim him as a deductible expense! No, they didn't laugh either!

I returned home one day to find feathers all over the house and a poor little Wood Pigeon (that Gypsy must have dragged in through the cat flap somehow), was shivering in a corner by the front door with no feathers and a broken leg. Gypsy sat there looking at me as if to say, 'Hey look what I dragged in!'

I picked the poor bird up, placed it in a box with a small bowl of water and put the poor thing in the shed to pass away with dignity.

Unfortunately, Gypsy had to be put to sleep when he was only six years old due to a blood clot in the capillary tube along his back moving to his heart and the vets couldn't save him. I still have his ashes wondering where to scatter them. Maybe I should throw them in the garden so the birds can get their own back, with the amount of grief he used to cause them back in Preston some ten years ago.

Angela and I formed a band with some other local musicians and did a few gigs in and around Preston. We were called **Urchins**. I think that came from a term of endearment that Angela used to call me. 'My little urchin' springs to mind but maybe I'm just making that up, I can't remember. Anyway, we did some motorbike rallies as well and it lasted for a while until she got offered a place in a local blues band (**After Hours**), that she'd always wanted to play in, and we disbanded. To be honest, the band wouldn't have lasted as I was that busy with HSL, my own SDM events I was doing for local councils, and the shows I had now started to play in with some famous musicians from certain groups.

This is such a beautiful photo of Gypsy asleep with his paws around my Mandolin. The photo is at the beginning of this book and on the back cover of my first album.

You wouldn't have thought looking at him, he was such a little shit to the birds in my back yard at the time!

I think Gypsy just liked music and my little recording studio.

Part of the Power supply(400amps 3 phase) and motor controllers including the Kinesys we used to use for the panto's at the Armadillo in Glasgow and the rig nearly built.

CHAPTER 20

Uriah Heep Legends

I have said it many times, that certain decisions I have made and the directions I have chosen to take, have had a profound effect on me both short and long term. This chapter documents one more of them and, it is probably one of the most prolific experiences I may ever have as it is still shaping my future now.

You will recall that I listened to Uriah Heep while learning to play electric guitar.

The 1973 *Uriah Heep Live* album was released at a turning point in my life. I wore out my copy of it and many of their others, as well as Ken Hensley's first two solo LPs. Collectively, they were a massive influence on my song writing. If this is the first time you've heard of the band then I hope my short introduction will help you understand my passion for them.

Uriah Heep

Formed in 1969, the band released 25 studio albums, 20 live albums, 41 compilation albums and God knows how many bootleg albums are out there too. I watched them many times in the 70's with both the original singer **David Byron** and his replacement: **John Lawton**. **Paul Newton**, the original bass player on the first three albums, was briefly replaced by **Mark Clarke**, before **Gary Thain** took over. The drummers: **Alex Napier, Nigel Olsson, Keith Baker** and **Iain Clarke** were eventually replaced from the fourth LP onwards, by **Lee Kerslake**. Lee took his place in 1971 and, after a few years departure (1979-1981) was the permanent drummer until 2007. He did two guest appearances in 2015 and 2018 but died in 2020. **Mick Box** (Guitar & Backing Vocals), and **Ken Hensley** (Keys, Guitar & Vocals) were the other members back at the start and

Mick still tours with Uriah Heep. Most of all of those who played in the band were songwriters at some stage, however Ken was the main writer over the years while with the band. I only mention their names because some of them appear later on as they became an integral part of seven years of my life. Finally, in early 2025, Uriah Heep announced their last ever tour as ***The Magician's Farewell.*** I went to one of their shows in March and it was the first time for many years that I saw them live, after watching them in Liverpool five decades ago.

The Legends

In 2008, I didn't have a lot of money, as you can imagine, but I needed somewhere to go; a breakaway, to off load everything that had occurred over the previous two years. I found a website one day that was advertising a **Uriah Heep** fans' convention in Spain. There had been a few of these types of events for other bands in the past, but I had never seen an advert for a Uriah Heep one before. Once I had scraped the money together for the flight, and purchased my ticket for the convention, I noticed on the website that there was an option to apply to play in the 'Jam Bands'. This is an event for the fans of the band as part of the main itinerary. It is a chance to get up on stage with other fans/musicians and sing/play your favourite song of the band in question. A guy (nicknamed 'Muzzy USA') had setup this convention's Jam session and I put my name down for a lot of the gaps in each song he had listed. A bass player on one song, a singer and/or guitarist on another – you get the idea – so I had several options to be considered for.

These very complicated sessions required careful management. There was one on the Friday and two on Saturday before the band started a full concert that evening. Muzzy was originally going to stage manage the Jam sessions. However, after long conversations across the pond, Muzzy asked me if I would do it instead. 'You've got the experience,' he said confidently and I was both flattered and delighted.

There are many videos on You Tube of that convention. While writing and researching for this book, they brought back many memories of that week. On Wednesday 17th September 2008, I flew to Granada, Spain. At the airport were John Lawton and his very close friend Alan Keetley. They greeted me along with other **Heepvention 2008** ticket holders who had arrived early. Some 300 people came over the next two or three days and made their way to the venue called **Huétor-Tájar** which is 43km west of the Andalusia city of Granada.

Once I arrived at the hotel and had checked in, I went down to the bar where I saw Lee Kerslake. I had met Lee a few times in the past at gigs, but this was a full-on face to face meet with one of the most famous drummers in the world. For fucks sake, this guy apart from playing with **Uriah Heep**, was the drummer with **Bob Daisley (Bass)** and **Randy**

Rhoads (Guitar) who wrote all the songs for the first **Ozzy Osbourne** solo album, and I think most of the second album too. Some people may deny this but, personally, I think people can make up their own minds amongst all the controversy.

Anyway, I diverse

I started chatting to Lee as if we had known each other for many years and, maybe in some subconscious way, we had. That night, after many bottles of wine and singing many Uriah Heep songs with other Heepvention fans, Lee (The Bear) Kerslake and I forged a bond that took us on a journey for the next twelve years. Consequently, he will remain in my heart until the day I die.

Thursday was the 'meet and greet' with Lee, Paul Newton and John Lawton, the latter two, being the first time, I had met them in person. Ken didn't arrive until the following day. More wine was drunk on the Thursday night with many Heep fans who have become friends for life. Having offered to help set up the sound system, by the Friday morning I became aware of a few issues that were troubling the engineers who were supplying the PA (audio). With all my experience of these things I offered to help and quickly became an integral assistant in more ways that I had anticipated before I arrived. I had also now met Muzzy in person, and he had given me all the breakdowns/paperwork of the Jam sessions the first being that afternoon. Talk about being thrown in the deep end!

To be honest, I cannot remember which songs were performed on the Friday or on the Saturday, but I helped as much as I could in both singing, playing guitar, bass, the odd keyboards too and everyone had a great time. On the Friday night **Dieggi** a Uriah Heep tribute band from the **Faroe Islands** played and we all became close friends and still are. It was great to see them at the Heepvention, Belgium in 2015. That was the last time we met.

Stealin my place in the band

From what Lee had told me after the convention, he and John had been watching me perform the songs on the Friday afternoon. My relative ease and accuracy impressed them. The Saturday night was to be the main show with John, Ken, Paul, Lee, all ex-members of Uriah Heep and their guitarist **Jan Dumée** (**Focus**) who couldn't arrive until late Saturday afternoon because of commitments. On the Saturday morning John asked me if I would play guitar for them at the sound check in Jan's absence. As I knew all the songs on their set list, I immediately agreed to what was a surreal short gig in a way and unlike any sound check I have or will ever take part in again.   Picture the scene: I'm on stage about to play guitar on *Stealin* with the aforementioned heroes of mine. But to be honest I was crapping my pants whilst simultaneously being in a dream like state; I will never, ever, forget that moment!

We complete the sound check and then the Saturday Jam Session started. After that there was Q&A's with Lee, Ken, John and Paul and then these ex-members or "Legends" of Uriah Heep do a full show for the fans. By the end, I'd lost my voice, due to too much singing, shouting at getting the fans up for the jam sessions and of course too much wine. It was bloody fantastic.

The following day I was invited by John, Paul and Lee to come to Alan Keetley's home to have a buffet and a few drinks (a privilege I felt at the time) before we were all to return home on the Monday. John Lawton (a world class singer in his time) paid me the following compliment, 'You've got an amazing voice'. For that to come from such a great singer was a huge boost for my confidence, especially with all the shit that had been going on for the past few years.

We all returned home to Blighty after Lee and I had exchanged telephone numbers. I'm certain in my exalted state, I flew all the way to and from the airport to my doorstep fuelled by a massive high. Six months later, Lee phoned me to ask if I could play the first show in Finland for the **Uriah Heep Legends** which had been formed with himself, Ken and Paul during the interim. John Lawton wasn't involved, something to do with Ken which was why Ken hadn't been there for the meet and greet at the convention. We'll leave it at that.

I had just signed a contract with Simon Ash for the *Chapters* shows in Edinburgh and they overlapped, so I couldn't do the Heep show. I had to decline :aahhh! For fucks sake!

I thought I'd lost the role forever, only for Lee to phone me the following year and ask me again with a string of shows for the **Legends**, starting in Finland again in 2010. Apparently, they used a Finnish guitarist for the 2009 show and Lee wasn't impressed and wanted me to join them. This time, I said yes. I could spend so much time writing stories about playing with my heroes who became very close friends. I will try and keep it short.

Our first gig as **Uriah Heep Legends** was at Himos, a ski resort in Finland. This was the first Uriah Heep Convention that the Fins had organised. It was a success, gig wise, but the **Uriah Heep Fan Club Finland** lost a lot of money due to attendance as it was, shall we say, a bit out of the way to get to.

Before I went on stage at Himos, I met a guy called **Martti Suhonen** who was Lee's chauffeur for the weekend. A good choice, as he ran a Coach or Bus company in Helsinki. He was a completist Uriah Heep fan as he had every vinyl, tape, bootleg and CD that the band had ever produced. Martti couldn't speak a word of English and just called me 'BAKER BAKER'. A translator told me that he was going to watch me playing for Lee, Ken and Paul and would decide if I was any good. No pressure then.

To be honest, again, I was crapping my pants.

Martti Suhonen showing me how I should be playing Uriah Heep guitar prior to performing at Himos 2010. We have been friends ever since.

It was bad enough having to stand/play on stage with your idols but, now I had to perform to one of the band's all time renowned fans in Finland. He also ran the Finnish Uriah Heep Fan Club too (FFS!) and knowing he would be watching every note I played. Well, you can imagine how I was (not) coping mentally by the time I finished the show. I can handle pressure, but this was something different, more nerves. I came off stage and met up with Martti. He looked at me and put two 'thumbs up' and smiled. I had his approval.

That feeling was so important to me. Not just for making Martti happy but knowing that I had been able to fill the boots of guitarist Mick Box for the Legends: the same Mick Box who was still touring with the original band in 2025! This indeed was an honour. To play with Ken Hensley (a big influence as you know), Lee Kerslake and Paul Newton was (and still is), one of the highlights of my life. We also had two fantastic vocalists who sang with The Legends. **Eirikur Hauksson** (Icelandic) was with us for Himos and Joensuu. Then we had **Roberto Tiranti** (Italian) who took over for all the other gigs we performed. Both singers sang for Ken's band **Live Fire** at various times.

After the Himos gig, Martti set up a **Phil Baker Fan Club** on Facebook and whenever we played in Scandinavia, I had fans asking for autographs, and people making me socks (Finnish socks are fantastic by the way) and gifting me an assortment of other presents. This was something I had never experienced before, autographs, yes, but nothing as amazing as this level of "fan" generosity.

I still have a Christmas hat that Martti gave me with 'Phil Baker' emblazoned on it.

We went on to perform in various places in Finland and Sweden including Salo, **The Rock at Sea** shows on the Viking Line Ships and the **Kokkola Festival**, to name but a few.

There were a few embarrassing times too!

For example, when I broke a string in the middle of a set, and I had to ask Ken to play *Rain* while I restrung my guitar behind the stage. I didn't have a spare guitar with me, because of the ridiculous cost of luggage charged by the airline – the limited tour budget did not stretch to extra baggage or a private jet! Fortunately, Ken saw the funny side and took the piss out of me for the next few days. Again, something that was very surreal to me in certain ways being one of my all-time music heroes.

My gigs with Lee and the Legends lasted until 2015. In between, amongst everything else I was doing, I travelled to Crystal Palace a few times, where Lee: the 'world renowned drummer' lived. You would imagine him to have a twenty bedroomed mansion, set in acres of private land, a Rolls Royce (or three), a swimming pool, tennis courts etc etc. In reality he lived in a small flat with his wife and their dog. They were virtually penniless because other people in the business had ripped him off and couldn't appreciate his talent when he fell on hard times. So sad.

Paul, Lee and I had done all the Heepventions since 2010. There has only been one after lockdown up to now in May 2023 but, sadly, without Lee*. Hence, **Russell Gilbrook** (Uriah Heep's drummer since 2007) came over to Finland with **Iain Clarke** (who was the drummer on the 3rd Album *Look at Yourself*), and both performed with Paul and myself as well as other musicians. Another story for another time.

On the highways of Finland now

I always remember two things that happened at, and on the way to, the Kokkola show:

Be wary of small planes

Lee, Paul and I flew via Helsinki to Kokkola. The plane we boarded in Helsinki was the smallest plane I have ever been on, and you feel very vulnerable in a strange way.

We were joking that we hoped there wouldn't be a problem with such a small aircraft. Halfway to Kokkola the plane has a fault and we have to turn back. Luckily it was only a minor issue with the batteries that start the engines, which weren't charging. If they had not rectified the matter, the pilot wouldn't have been able to return once the plane landed at Kokkola. The airport there was so tiny it didn't have a jump pack to boost the batteries. That's how small and vulnerable this plane was.

Always keep your guitar with you

I'm sure Paul won't mind me mentioning this. We are all sat in the green room at Kokkola which was some 50m from the stage. We get the green light to head over to perform, but Paul had gone off somewhere for some reason and so we went on stage thinking he wouldn't be far behind us. Unbeknown to us, security locked the green room door behind us as we left so all our belongings were safe which was what they had been told to do. However, Paul comes back from wherever he had been, only to find he couldn't get in the green room to get his Bass guitar. We have been introduced over the PA and take to the stage. Ken started playing the **Hammond** B3 Organ as a warm up before the beginning of *Stealin* (from the ***Sweet Freedom*** album). THE BLOODY START OF THIS SONG IS THE BASS GUITAR! Paul finally appears in front of the 5000 strong crowd and introduces himself by saying, "Sorry guys, I was locked out of the room". A roar of applause explodes and huge relief swept over my sweating brow! I think that was the longest five minutes I have stood on stage wondering what the fuck is going on. Paul and I still have a laugh about it now.

Gallery

Below: photos and words on my Facebook page the day Lee passed away Sept 2020

"I spent many evenings, listening to Lee's rock'n'roll tales and one night, singing together so much, we struggled the following day to sing backing vocals at a show, we were so hoarse.

I phoned him during his last week, but unfortunately, he was sleeping and I never got chance to talk to him. If he's reading this upstairs I would like to say "I will always remember you Lee, from the days I used to sit in the front row of Liverpool Empire watching Uriah Heep in the 70's, to the times I was on stage right playing guitar, looking over at you and you smiling back at me. We were having a blast.

My daughter always mentions you, from when we came for a visit and remembers 'The Bear'.

The world has lost an iconic drummer, and you will be missed by so many, and I will always remember you.

Lee Kerslake R.I.P. ♥ "

Paul Newton and myself in Tavastia Helsinki 2015. Not my finest gig. We were that late going on stage (due to the band on before us doing an extra hour), that I got a bit pissed and made quite a few mistakes. I was so embarrassed and apologised.

Photo by permission of **Mimmi Tverin**.

*Ilovaarirock Joensuu July 2012. Looking out over the crowd with Eirikur Hauksson on vocals. We had **Doctor Feelgood** supporting us at this show. 4000 Fins in the pouring rain made it special.*

I miss them all, but I still go and visit Paul, his wife **Joan** and the cats in Herefordshire whenever possible. We frequent the local British Legion for a few beers normally on Paul's birthday and I perform with him and some of his friends who are great musicians in their own right.

I also still keep in touch with **Steve Weltman**, who was Ken and Lee's manager and who used to look after all of us on all the Legends gigs.

My part in Uriah Heep Legends started a roller coaster ride that took me around Scandinavia, Europe, USA and many more places. It was if in 2010, I had been given a second chance after turning down that audition, so many years before when I was eighteen.

I had the music bug's venom back in my veins and, with all the attention playing guitar for the Legends, I started to venture a lot more outside the UK. I now regularly perform abroad and had the enthusiasm to finally record and produce my own album.

*Lee passed away 19th September 2020 from cancer and I had the honour to be one of the 30 people in lockdown to be invited to his funeral in London. A documentary has been made about the last years of Lee's life entitled 'Not on the Heep' by London Bridge Films.

I will always remember Lee for giving me that chance that he saw in myself to perform to my best ability for Uriah Heep Legends and which sent me on a journey that is still on going.

Ken Hensley passed away suddenly on 4th November 2020 following a short illness.

John Lawton died suddenly from an aneurysm 29th June 2021, and, although we only spoke a few times on the phone after Heepvention, I will always remember him.

Back stage Tavastia still waiting for the other band to finish.

Ken, Lee & Paul get the Keys to Salo. I got a woolly hat which I still have.

CHAPTER 21

Songs to the World and a bit of Bakering

In 2011 while playing with the Legends, I was struggling playing guitar with my right hand and was dropping plectrums on the floor without realising. I'd wake up in the morning not being able to feel my right arm and it would take a good 45 minutes for it to come back to life so to speak. At first, I thought it was blood circulation with me abusing my body over the years; drinking, smoking and fry ups every day. I went for tests, and it turned out to be Carpal Tunnel Syndrome. I won't bore you with the details you can look them up, but basically the nerves that run through your wrist are being compressed by the tendons that go through the same carpal tunnel. After years of repetitive motion in your hand, for example, playing guitar for a long time, this condition gradually becomes worse. Typists get it and apparently, these days, the younger generation are prone to it too with gaming and texting on phones putting repetitive stress on their thumbs.

Given the diagnosis, you can imagine my first thoughts were: my guitar playing days are over. However, (and this is for anyone who develops this syndrome) it's an easy fix with a small operation that takes around 15 minutes. Recovery differs for everyone, but I think I was one of the lucky ones. I had the operation in December 2011 and by the following February, I was back playing guitar. I was told there was always an element of risk that something could go wrong but you take the chance hoping it doesn't. Luckily, I didn't have any gigs around that time and most of the Legends gigs were in the spring and summer, when I was back up and running without a problem by then.

Once I had moved into Connaught Road in Preston (next to my girlfriend, Angela), my personal life quickly settled into a more relaxed routine, apart from a few episodes that I will mention further on. I couldn't have got through the Carpal Tunnel Op without her helping, because I wasn't allowed to use my right arm to do anything for a month, I had to keep it up in the air for the first week after the op too. I'm not saying that my personal life was boring, it just became something of the norm that most people's lives are compared to how my life had been up to 2012. But, my professional life, started to accelerate more than I ever thought it would.

After the Carpel Tunnel Op 2011 and having to keep my arm raised for 7 days. But deffo no "high 5's" for me though!

I was still running events for various councils throughout each year, but given the confidence gained from the Legends gigs, I started to think about promoting myself as a musician in other ways. For many years, I had wanted to record and release a collection of my own songs. A one-off album I could be proud of and, if nothing else, I'd always have that to look back on. Up to this point, the songs existed in some format or other, but fate played her hand. In the past it was a case of: I either had the money and not the time, or the time but no money to complete the undertaking. 2013 seemed to solve both dilemmas together.

At that time there was a lot of the PPI (Personal Protection Insurance) compensation claims. These were made against banks and building societies for the way they sold insurance on their loans, and mortgage, as well as the same for a host of other finance and credit card companies. I applied for as much compensation as I was entitled to. In a nutshell, over a period of time, I received quite a bit. This was mainly from loans I had taken out in the 2000's to do with my business and, more specifically, a lot of them from the BTDS period.

I decided to take three months away from freelance work, apart from jobs that couldn't be cancelled. I paid off a few of my debts, bought a studio from a friend of mine that would fit in my bedroom and started to do something that I'd wanted to do for years.

My studio equipment included a computer with Logic Pro 9, microphones, a Midi Keyboard, Electronic Drum kit, and array of musical instruments, studio monitors etc. I had recorded the odd song or two in professional studios in the past and self-produced backing tracks for so many people, but I had never sat down and said to myself: this will be my album. I had a book with lyrics in, I had recordings with only music, and I had loads of riff's that had just stuck in my head over the years. I used most of them, and the leftovers were put to one side should I ever get round to making another album which hopefully I'll have time to complete after I've finished the book.

Working with Logic Pro 9 (Apples version of Pro Tools) was a learning curve. I had only ever used analogue 8 track recorders and a very primitive digital programme called Data Becker which I recorded all the click tracks on for Pulse – Echoes of Floyd a decade earlier.

It was a bit like learning the Myriad playback programme when I was with Chorley FM, so it was only a matter of time that I taught myself the main part of Logic 9.

I started recording in January 2013 and most of the album was complete (in some form or other) by end of March 2013. It took longer to mix the songs than it did to record them, which is something that happens with many bands I have since discovered. I knew and/or played with lots of musicians around Preston on the pub circuit. This was in effect all variations of **The Phil Baker Band** I had assembled around me or recruited while deputising for other bands. I pulled in the talents of **Stan Mansfield** a bassist for *The Whale* song (Track 2) and a drummer **Geoff Haydock** for *Out of the Blue* (track 4). Angela played percussion on *The Whale* song too.

The rest was all me! I used drum loops and rebuilt midi tracks for the drum tracks which took a while. I loved every minute of it and, if I could make a living as a producer for bands, I'd be there like a shot, but I haven't had the chances so far, as you know.

I have heard that a good studio engineer, when mixing a song, will listen to it over 600 times. This could be more than a member of the public who buys the song will listen to it in their lifetime and I can understand why. I'd mix a track, burn it onto a CD then go and sit in the car outside the house and listen to it. I read that it was important to mix a track so that it sounds great in a car. The neighbours (including my Angela) must have thought I was nuts! One moment I was sat in the car for five minutes listening to a song the next I returned inside my house until say twenty minutes later when I'd repeat the process again and again! This went on for days, and, in hindsight, I wished I'd sent the tracks to get them Mastered by someone else. Nevertheless, I wanted to do it all myself and who knows; sometime in the future I'll get it remastered.

August 2025 – I have just sent my remastered album Songs to the World to the duplicators to print the new batch of CD's. Thankyou Martin of Roughgrain.com

Anyway, by June 2013 the album was complete. I then had to design the artwork, which was the disc of a CD and the cover, fitted perfectly. The other learning curve was learning about another learning curve in itself, believe me. It was vital that what was going to be printed on Copyright laws and essential information that I had to upload, especially if the album was to be online too. **PPL – Phonographic Performance Limited. PRS – Performing Rights Society** and **Mechanical Rights**: it's a minefield but well worth doing for any up-and-coming song writers reading this.

After my three months wind down, I was very busy again, combining my day-to-day work with preparation work for the album release and the printing of the CD through to uploading the digital version. It all took a lot longer than expected. Eventually the day came for the album launch, which I did at **St Gerards Club** in **Lostock Hall**. It was a place that Angela and I frequented on a regular basis. Friday 11th October 2013, the date I will never forget.

The Red Lentils at the sound check at St Gerards.

I got a band together and rehearsed through September. The main problem (and a mistake that many musicians make when recording albums) is the more instruments in each song the more musicians you'll need when performing them live. That is if you want them to sound anywhere close to the album rather than using click tracks which a lot of bands do now, and I've only ever used click tracks with Pulse. In the end I had two extra guitarists and could have done with two keyboard players too but only ended up with one. Some musicians, who I really wanted to use from Pulse, were busy from what I can remember but it all turned out okay and they all did a great job. We had **The Red Lentils** as support, a fantastic quintet made up of Angela's nieces and friends and they played the strings live on *I Am a Child* (Track 5) on the night too. I was a bit of a headache for Rob the sound engineer for the gig. It was a great night though and the following month I ended up taking the band over to Helsinki to do an album launch at On the Rocks on 2nd November 2013. This cost me a fortune, but it needed to be done to meet the standards I set for myself and my fans. This included the Fan Club over there and I had visited Finland quite a lot with Heepventions, Uriah Heep Legends, solo gigs, and the fact that I wanted to share this moment with as many of the terrific friends in that wonderful country.

Unfortunately, on reflection I had been my own victim of delusions of grandeur. I thought I was more well known over there than I actually was. The turnout/ticket sales were good but didn't cover anywhere near the costs incurred in taking a full band with me. Initially I had thought about using musicians who I knew in Finland, but it was impossible for that to happen because of the rehearsal side of things. My sound engineer (Rob) and his partner (Tanya) at the time (both who are very good friends of mine even now) got some T Shirts made with 'Bakers on Tour' printed which was a bit of a private joke. I will now travel down the M6.

Serious 'Bakering'

This has nothing to do with bread or cakes. Over the years when I've been doing various complicated events/projects various friends used to say 'We can see some serious Bakering going on here' and it stuck. For example, trying to get 44,000 litres from a temporary swimming pool to the sea that is serious Bakering. I think **Rob Crossland** was the guy who started this, a picture of us below -

(L) Some serious discussion of Bakering going on between Rob and myself at a Mobile Chaos MCC Rally. Most probably to do with generators or fencing. (R) The T Shirt.

Bakering is something I could write a whole book about but not now.

Back on track again

Over the years I've sold a few CDs of the album and quite a few digital downloads but it will never make me rich. The fact that I did it, will always be something that allows me to proudly say "I've done it". One of the royalties from streaming came from a Japanese TV channel who use part of *The Whale Song*. This surprise was detailed on my annual statement from PPL/PRS which was 64 pages long! It lists all the streams or use of my songs worldwide. I thought 'I should get a decent amount of money from this!' How wrong I was.

The bank transfer came through and it was.. cue DRUM ROLL....

£9.73 !! that is Nine English pounds and seventy-three pence for a bloody year!

To rub more salt in the wound, subsequent annual royalties have been a lot less. So, a word of warning to all you budding songwriters: don't ever rely on income from the web unless you've got a global mega star recording your songs. **Song Cast** is the digital music distribution company I use which is based in Akron, Ohio in the USA (…but other digital platform services are available folks!). All my songs are available to listen to from it; be it on Spotify, Apple Music, Pandora and SoundCloud. As at November 2024, for the previous twelve months, I had seven streams (not sales) for one particular song, and I received $0.03 (3 US cents). Someone somewhere is making a shed load of money and it's not the artists or the songwriters. Just on Song Cast, I've had over 10,000 streams over the past few years but only earnt under a $100 from them.

What came from all this effort though was that I ended up performing many solo gigs in Finland over the years and have released other songs with collaborations by Finnish artists including **Maria** Hänninen (*Over the Ledge*) and **Mikaela Mansikkala** (*Better than me*).

Over the Ledge was a memorable journey. I wrote the song and knew it needed a female vocalist. Maria recorded her parts at home in Helsinki but after the release of the song, I travelled to Finland to do some solo shows. We recorded a video when we performed the song at On the Rocks. We asked all the fans in the audience to film it on their phones and send them to me to edit. The video is on www.youtube.com/@philipbaker5928.

On my solo travels in Finland in 2013, I was accompanied at various venues including the musicians named above and a certain **Trevor Hensley,** Ken Hensley's brother who I met from playing with the Legends. Trevor is a great friend, musician and runs an internet radio station **Red Five Radio.** The day after one gig in Helsinki with Trevor, I went off doing an audition for something which is in the next chapter, Trevor went to the airport and had a massive heart attack and was only saved because there were two Paramedics in his queue for the plane. He spent a month or so in a Helsinki hospital and, once back at home in the UK, he wrote a book entitled **Lucky Man.** In his own words, Trevor describes it as; 'this little book is my views, and those of my family, following my heart attack..." and I recommend it to anyone who has been impacted by a similar incident. Off down the runway now...

Cold it's not Cold

When I did a gig in Joensuu in January 2015, the temperature was minus 28 Celsius. I arrived on the train and went to my hotel which was built into the shopping mall where the venue was. I didn't have to venture outside to travel to do the gig which was great. Minus 28 is very cold but it's not as bad as you think it is, because in Finland, it is a dry cold as there is no moisture in the air. The reason we feel the cold in the UK is because we inhale frozen moisture crystals which makes minus 5 feel even colder. Anyway, in Joensuu there were still people out on pushbikes on a Saturday afternoon. Fantastic.

So, as the temperature is so warm in the mall, I leave my jacket behind and walked to the venue. I have a great gig, but I try to return to the hotel and the Mall is closed, and I have to take an outside route back to the hotel. This is about 100 metres; I am in the short sleeve shirt I have been playing in.

'Only 100m, it won't take long,' I think

As I stepped outside, I am stopped by a fan who had been to the gig, absolutely pissed out of his head. He is wrapped up nice and warm but wants to talk to me at one o'clock in the morning. Five minutes later and I had to cut him off in mid-sentence and walk off. If I had continued to talk, I would have got seriously ill from the cold, which that time of night, was even colder than earlier. If he ever reads this book, I apologise for walking off, but needs must. He most probably never remembers it anyway he was that drunk.

Gallery

While playing for the Legends and during all my solo gigs in Finland, certain people had been watching me which leads onto the next chapter.

Trevor and myself playing at a café/bar in Helsinki circa 2014.

Trevor and myself at a Question & Answer Kerubi, Joensuu 2014.

Trevor, Maria, Mikaela and me prior to performing an acoustic show at On the Rocks circa 2014.

CHAPTER 22

Playing God and playing a High Priestess

At the gig at Himos in 2010 with The Legends, I met **Matti Häyry** and **Tuija Takala** for the first time. They are both in the Uriah Heep Fan Club in Finland and we became good friends.

Matti is a Professor of Bioethics and Law and specialises in Moral and Political Philosophy and, of course, Bioethics. Tuija is a Doctor of Philosophy too. Both are, not only highly intelligent, but are amazing people, for reasons below.

Whenever I was in Finland over the next few years I would always meet up with Matti and Tuija. They invited me to stay at their homes and we would often end up talking into the early hours about anything and everything. At the time of Trevor Hensley's heart attack, I had been invited to Matti and Tuija's apartment in Helsinki. It was for an audition of a project they had been working on titled: *Playing God, The Perfect Child* created by Mr C as described further down the page.

The CD had already been recorded by Finnish Musicians and **Corky Laing** (the Canadian rock drummer and member of rock band **Mountain**).

The audition was around the dining room table in the apartment with a Gibson Les Paul, 2 bottles of Jaloviina (Finnish Brandy) and Matti playing the album to me. He was testing me to see if I could play parts on the album as the project was to be performed live in Helsinki later that year. The audition lasted for around eight hours until 15mins before my taxi was due to arrive to take me back to the airport around 6.45am. Tuija had collapsed and gone to bed, Matti was playing extremely loud rock music and, while I put my jacket on to leave, he told me that I had passed the audition, and he went to bed. How Finnair let me on the plane going home with that much Jaloviina in my system I'm not sure.

The whole concept of this project was described on the internet promotion as follows. *"The good people of Happyville, set back in a 1970s version of tomorrow, have enjoyed the advantage of genetic engineering for decades without any thought, but the day of judgement is near. When Luke comes to town, and God has developed an interest in Mr. C's science peddling, the secrets of the townspeople are about to be revealed, and their lives may never be the same again."*

The idea was to produce a live show that could be toured around universities/colleges and attract students of Genetic Engineering. Afterwards, there would be questions and answers with Matti and Tuija. A sort of musical lecture, if you will, so that students could write a thesis or something similar. A fantastic idea. I could write another book about this part of my life/career but, again, I will keep it brief… well as brief as it can be ha ha!

Heavy Rock subdued by Hot Rods

After practising at home over many months it was decided to do a show in Basel, Switzerland August 2013. There was a conference on Philosophy in Basel, and Matti and Tuija set up a venue for professionals to come and watch the show. The event was set up with the purpose of getting feedback from the audience to see if it would work as a tour of universities. We rehearsed at a house of one of Tuija's relatives who lived in Basel. I also got involved with the technical aspects of the show prior to us flying into Switzerland. I continued in this role while we were there too, working with **Clair Global** who were supplying the sound system for the show.

Everything was great except for the decibel limits that Switzerland have, which I had experienced when Pulse went there in 2002. Corky was playing the drums that loud he was tripping the decibel meter all on his own! He is a 'heavy rock' drummer after all, so the only option was for him to switch to using lighter drumsticks known as Hot Rods. The show wasn't the full-blown Rock Opera that it ended up as, rather it was the album in its entirety with a small amount of acting from us. It was challenging to say the least, but we did it and got very good feedback from the audience of Professors, Lecturers, Doctors from the Conference and the general public who had paid to come and watch too. I was in the middle of trying to sort out my album launch at the time aswell, so that summer was full on.

Now that we had the initial gig under our belt, a full show was booked with actors, musicians, costumes etc for 28th March 2014 at Gloria in Helsinki Finland. Rehearsals were intense at Matti and Tuija's country house and the dress rehearsals even more so. This version of the show had a projector back drop explaining each scene too. The list of everyone on stage from the full show is below and, in a photo lower down.

Taken from the Playing God Facebook page

Corky Laing (CAN/US), **Bonnie Parker** (US), **Denny Colt** (US), **Joe Venti** (US), Phil Baker (UK), **Stefan Berggren** (SWE), **Harri Väyrynen** (FIN), **John Vihervä** (FIN), **Maya Korvela** (FIN), **Juho Pitkänen** (FIN), **Matti Korvela** (FIN), **Johanna Ahola-Launonen** (FIN), **Mikaela Mansikkala** (FIN), **Paul Savage** (CAN/FIN), Tuija Takala (FIN), **Ismo Virlander** (FIN), **Jarkko Rantala** (FIN), Matti Häyry (FIN), **Niall Scott** (UK) **Pete Baron** (US)

Corky and I rehearsing for the first live version of Playing God.

The Gods 2014. Including Niall Scott & Mikeala Mansikala.

There were many other people involved too and I'm sorry if I've missed anyone out. In my defence, we did another two shows at Gloria in 2016 and that was an even larger one with all the same crew and a lot more people. The show was a massive success, and we all flew home to our own countries on a high. Shortly after, I got an email from Tuija asking if I would be prepared to do a couple of shows in the USA. Bloody hell yes!

I then sat back for a minute and thought about how I am going to get to the States with having the conviction from 1995 over my head. This culminates in where I started (in the Forward of the book) at the USA Embassy in Northern Ireland. In a nutshell, I get a Visa Waiver through about three weeks before we were due to fly to the states to start rehearsals. Talk about cutting it fine.

*Niall Scott (an Amazing Lecturer on Dark Metal Music including editing the book **Reflections in the Metal Void** who was one of the Gods and he looks like a God too), on our way to the USA.*

So, Niall and I fly to the states via Dublin, so much easier to do as the USA has a state in Dublin airport. You walk in, past the American flags, to be interviewed at the airport as if you are in the US. Everything gets cleared and when you arrive at, say JFK where we landed, you just walk into baggage claim: fantastic! I've been over to the USA a few times since my first visit there in 2015 and all my business entries to the USA have been fine. But the time I flew in for my son's wedding, well we'll get to that in the last chapter. Sorry went off on the M6 again.

How I became a God

So, we arrive in New York and go into intense rehearsals on Long Island for a week. We had a great director, **Kate Mueth** from Long Island and what a difference this made. During the American stint, apart from playing guitar, mandolin, keys and vocals, I became a God (see photos). Well, I'd been Jesus before in a musical, so it was obvious that this was the next step up. They needed another so I was asked. Who am I to say no. I've been a stripper for fucks sake!

Rehearsals went well and we did a very low-key version of the Rock Opera at Yale University, 5 days prior to the main show 23rd April 2015 at Kaye Playhouse in Manhattan.

Poster for the main show in Manhattan.

(L) Me. Matti, Johanna and Maya. (R) Me (as God) before the show with Joanne Jammers (Twisted Radio).

One sad thought at this time. A good friend Paul Callaghan who I visited 4 or 5 days before I went to the states. His wife Maz had phoned me to say the cancer had finally won. I visited on the Friday and by the time I was in the states he had sadly passed away. R.I.P. Paul.

I'm off up the Interstate now ha ha

There are three things that stick in my mind about this adventure, and they had nothing to do with the show even though it was a great success.

Ice Bathing

We stayed on Long Island in a sort of holiday home camp, on the banks of the Hudson River. It was April and at that time of the year, the river is about 3 or 4 degrees Celsius. I had Ice bathed once in Finland prior to this, but to be honest for our Finnish friends who were with us, 4 degrees is a breeze. Off we went first thing in the morning and into the river. I won't go into all the details, but it was the reaction of two American road repair workers, sat in a truck having their breakfast.

'Are you Fucking Crazy!' They shouted. 'No one swims in this river until June, you guys are mad!' Their faces were a picture. I only went in twice.

(L) Kate Mueth & Corky discussing the USA shows. (R) The USA cast.

Rules of loading into a theatre in the USA

Now I'm all for unions looking after workers' rights and all that but this takes the biscuit.

We drop our backline into a yellow square outside the stage door of the Kaye Playhouse. We are not allowed to carry it into the venue. Stage crew carry it in, and it all must be placed within 2ft of where you need it. I am then only allowed to move my equipment within that 2ft area but if I move something, say to the other side of the stage, I could cause an all-out strike! No wonder it takes twice as long in the states to load into venues as it does in Europe and the UK.

We set all the gear up and are about to start having a rehearsal but had to stop because the crew of the theatre went on lunch and locked the theatre up. We had to twiddle our thumbs for an hour outside until they came back. I'm sure you will agree that what I'm saying is, <u>that</u> it's fucked up.

Meeting the real New Yorkers

While we were all stood outside waiting for the theatre crew to return, I was looking at the bin wagon driver. He can't do his job because someone had parked a car across the exit of the street he was in. I spent 30 minutes talking to this guy who told me his whole life story. He was brought up in the Bronx and his kids had amazing jobs because he told them not to be like he was when he was a kid getting into trouble with the Police and not going to school etc you know what I mean. You can be a tourist in New York and see the sites but for me, meeting that guy was the best thing that happened to me on that trip because I got to know the real people of New York. Anyway, back off the interstate.

We had two great shows and flew back home again on a high. Then another email came from Tuija to say we are performing the show again in Helsinki at Gloria on the 8th and 9th April 2016. More people on stage and I'm still God as well as playing various instruments too. It was fantastic and will stay in my memories forever.

The 2016 Poster. (Top R) Me as a God with Mikaela, Denny & Jarkko.

Maya, Denny, Sebastion and myself.

CHARACTERS:

DEATH (Paul Savage)
A dark, sarcastic figure, who cynically – and eventually with some disappointment – follows the deeds of gods and humans.

STATISTICIAN GOD (Denny Colt)
Pedant, prompt and decisive.

EASILY EXCITABLE GOD (Jarkko Rantala)
Absent minded and a little goofy.

SECRETARY GOD (Mikaela Mansikkala)
Flirtatious and kind.

CHAIR GOD (Phil Baker)
Commanding figure.

LUKE (Corky Laing)
A bluesman who took part in experimental immortality treatments decades ago and has not aged since. Kills himself in the beginning, but gods send him back to Earth.

MRS PIGAFETTI (Bonnie Parker)
Mother of the "perfect" designer boys. A caricature of a person who thinks that everything in life is about appearances.

MR PIGAFETTI (Harri Väyrynen)
Father of the "perfect" boys. A caricature of a person who thinks that everything can be bought – and measured in money.

MR C (Matti Häyry)
A genetics salesperson who takes advantage of people's hopes and dreams. In his hybris, he cuts corners. Is he the villain or a scapegoat?

TONY (Stefan Berggren)
First-born of the perfect twins. A troubled rock star admired by the whole town – not least by the girl-next-door, Sophie.

ALEX (Juho Pitkänen)
Tony's quiet and thoughtful twin brother, who has secretly loved Sophie for years. Alex writes poems and both envies and despises his brother.

TINA (Maya Korvela)
Tina was created to be a savior sibling for her ailing brother, Tim. She wasn't a match. Tina struggles to cope with her inability to save him, but eventually triumphs.

TIM (Ismo Virlander)
Tim was born with a rare immune deficiency and, with no matching donor, his option was experimental gene therapy. This gave him leukemia, which leads to his death.

SOPHIE (Johanna Ahola-Launonen)
Sophie works with her single-parent father at the vegetable stand and occasionally assists Mr C. She has always lived in Happyville, but has worldlier dreams.

MR VEGGIE (Joe Venti)
Sophie's over-protective father. He runs the organic vegetable stand that caters all Happyvilleans their greens.

TOWNSPEOPLE (Matti Korvela, and others)
Other habitants of Happyville.

The cast for Gloria 2016.

While all this is going on, Matti came up with the idea of the next Rock Opera **Orkid**.

Matti explained it to me as: 'it's all to do with Orcs and how they are just misunderstood beings and it's the Elves that are the bastards.' Love it, well Matti is a philosopher.

Over the next six months or so I fly to Finland for various Legend gigs and stay in this wonderful country. I lay down vocal and guitar tracks for the next Finnish Rock Opera *Orkid*.

Lasse Väyrynen, who actually played guitar in Switzerland on the first outing of *Playing God*, is the engineer for Orkid (as he was for the *Playing God* recordings too). I will always remember a session when we are double tracking the vocals. I am complimented that, although I've sung two tracks of the same song, he cannot distinguish which track is which because I sang them exactly the same. For me that is something that not many vocalists can do and yes, I am blowing my own trumpet for that.

Once the album is mixed, I receive another email from Matti to say we are to perform it live and it will be filmed for a DVD at Golden Café in Helsinki. As well as singing and playing guitar, I will be the High Priestess – yes, a female High Priest called Philotheos. However, I ended up just a High Priest and avoided the need for any gender operations (just a joke)!

We were called the **Visitors from Bellatrix**, the third-brightest star and a candidate binary star in the constellation of Orion. We also had most of the musicians that were in *Playing God* plus **Maria Hanninen** (Violin), **Jan Rechberger** on drums (amazing Drummer of the band **Amorphis**) and **Natasha Jane Julian** who I will explain more in the last chapter. Meanwhile, the whole show can be found on YouTube and the album is still available online.

What was close to my heart with this project was that Lee Kerslake, before he became ill and knowing Matti and Tuija too, wrote one of the songs **Ceremony of Death** on the album and has him narrating in the middle section of the song. I think he played the drums on this track too.

The album got rave reviews from various Rock magazines. The live/DVD show was the following: -

- Bonnie Parker – Orkid the Queen, Bass
- Phil Baker – Philotheos the High Priest/ess, Guitar
- Denny Colt – Trahaldur the Bard, Guitar
- Harri Väyrynen – Thiamer the Wizard, Guitar
- Johanna Ahola-Launonen – People, Herald, Keyboards
- Mikaela Mansikkala – People, Herald
- Maria Hänninen – People, Violin
- Natasha Jane Julian – People
- Jan Rechberger – Drums, Effects

Story and direction by Matti Häyry, Music and lyrics by Matti Häyry, Tuija Takala, and Lee Kerslake, Musical producer Lasse Väyrynen.

I think this was one of the most complicated live shows I've ever done. But I loved every minute of it, and I thank Matti and Tuija for having the confidence and trust in me to take me on a journey with them through both Rock Operas and an experience I will never forget.

Orkid Rehearsals at the Country House with me, Denny, Harri & Jan.

All the band members after a successful session
John, Me, Matti, Corky, Maya, Tuija, Lasse, Bonnie, Stefan, Natasha & Harri.

CHAPTER 23

Climbing a Mountain with Corky

The band Mountain formed in 1969 on Long Island, New York. It originally consisted of **Lesley West** (guitar and vocals), **Felix Pappalardi** (bass and vocals), **Steve Knight** (keyboards) and a drummer by the name of **N.D. Smart**, who was soon replaced by Corky Laing. You can read their full history online rather than me taking you through the whole history. Corky brought the Cow Bell into its own in rock music, featured in songs like *Mississippi Queen* from the band's debut album, *Climbing*.

Unfortunately, Lesley, Felix and Steve are with us no more as I'm sure most of you know.

I first met Corky in November of 2012. Tuija Takala had been involved with promoting Corky's career (now his manager) and getting him involved with *Playing God*. He had a show entitled *Best Seat in the House* that he had taken to various venues in America and elsewhere. Basically, Corky played a few songs and talked about his life as a drummer since 1961. His opinion was that the drummer had the best seat in the house. He also has a fantastic book out entitled *Letters to Sarah*.

Matti Häyry, and Tuija were involved with the **University of Central Lancashire** (UCLAN) as part of their work as lecturers. Tuija set up Corky's show in UCLAN's lecture theatre but, he needed a guitarist and a bass player to perform a few of Mountain's songs. He preferred to use musicians in the countries he visited. I was living in Preston at the time and Tuija asked if I'd be interested in playing guitar for Corky and sourcing a drum kit and bassist. I immediately said yes, and I asked Angela if I could 'borrow' her drum kit as well as **Doug Long** (her bass player in **After Hours Blues Band** at the time). We rehearsed at After

Hours' rehearsal studio a couple of evenings before the first show on the 12th November 2012: the first gig I ever played with Corky. I believe we only did two numbers *Mississippi Queen* and **Silver Paper.** We may have performed a third but to be honest, again, I was crapping my pants playing with a musician/song writer who had influenced me and so many people over the years.

Corky had a band in the states at the time called **Corky Laing and the Memory Thieves** which featured Bonnie Parker and Denny Colt. Both of them came into the Rock Opera fold too, and also have a great band based in New York called **Tang**. I didn't meet Corky again until I travelled over to rehearsals for *Playing God* all of which you have read about in the last chapter, but we got to know each other, while in Finland, much better than the whirlwind of 2012 when it was two rehearsals in two days, a show and goodbye. It was either in between the *Playing God* shows in Helsinki and the USA or just after the States shows, that Corky asked me if I would be interested in playing guitar/vocals for him with **Joe Venti** (bass/vocals) in a band playing songs by Mountain. Joe if you remember was part of the USA and second shows in Helsinki of *Playing God* as well.

2015 and 2016 were full on performing, bearing in mind I still had my business in between tours/shows. I mentioned to Tuija I knew a few promoters in the UK from when Pulse was going and when I was doing a lot of sound for various bands. With her approval, I got in touch with Solid Entertainments, who set up a tour of the UK for Corky. We rehearsed at **Smokin Beats Rehearsal Rooms,** Lostock Hall, Lancs, and set out in November 2015 for the first tour in the UK as Corky Laing Plays Mountain. For legal reasons Corky couldn't use the name Mountain by itself. Our first European tour came in February 2016 with On Stage Promotions based in Germany. After this we were back at the second lot of shows of *Playing God* in Helsinki in the April. The band returned for more gigs in the UK for Solid throughout May. We had a break until November when we played Rock at Sea, Sweden (which I had done with the Legends two years earlier). That show was playing first with Kofi Baker performing Cream numbers, then Corky with Mountain numbers and then the two drummers got up.

Corky then asked me to come over and do some shows in America. Shit! I only had a one-year visa for the States and that had run out. I re-applied and, after only two months (because they had all my details from the year before), I was approved a full five year USA visa: HOORAY!

After performing at the Giants of Rock at Butlins in Minehead (January 2017), the following month, we flew over to the States to play two gigs and recorded a TV show on **Don Odell**'s Legends. We had a great keyboard player with us for these shows called **Ken Sidotti**. That was when I met **Kofi Baker** for the first time too. Kofi's dad was **Ginger Baker,** the drummer of **Cream**. Cream featured in Corky and Joe's life before. Felix Pappalardi as well as being the bassist for Mountain, produced Cream's albums and also taught Joe how to play bass and Joe used to look after **Eric Clapton** in the early days before he became famous. While I was driving the band around the UK on the first tour with my Jeep and trailer, Joe and Corky would tell me amazing stories of those years.

After the pictures I will be going off down the freeway to tell a few tales. Again, they could all fill a book in their own, but I've just picked a handful.

(L) 1st UK Tour. (R) 1st European Tour.

(L) Corky, Joe & myself, Germany. (R) UK 2018 Tour.

2nd UK Tour 2016.

Rock at Sea with Kofi & Corky, Joe and Myself.

Joe and Myself.

(L) My old faithful Jeep & trailer. (R) Mark & Myself Romania.

Corky, Joe & Myself Rock at Sea.

So here I go, going down as many highways as I can.

B.B. King's Time Square

There are times in your life when you do something; be it a gig or help someone in a predicament and they stick in your mind forever like an indelible stamp. Well, playing B.B. King's is one of those imprints as impressive as a first day cover (if you'll excuse the analogy). Firstly I can't think of a more difficult load in than this for such a small amount of equipment. B.B. King's is in the basement of a building in Times Square, New York. You can imagine what Times Square is like during the rush hour. You cannot park outside on the road, well you can, but just wait for the tow truck to arrive! The front doors of the venue are there in front of you but it's the back door entrance you have to go in, and a guy comes out with a trolley/cage to transport all your equipment around 100 metres down this corridor and into a lift to take you downstairs. Only one trolley/cage and it takes three trips while you juggle with the parking. I'll forgive them for that because this is B.B. KING'S for fucks sake!

Eventually, we get all the gear set up on stage and a friend of Corky's, who I had met at the Rock Opera the year before, came in to say hello. His son is carrying a 1972 Gibson SG, original case, you get the idea.

'Will you play this guitar on one of the songs in tonight's show?' His son asks me.

'Of course I will,' says I, 'let's plug it in and hear how it sounds.'

OH MY GOD! This guitar was so good! A '72 SG through a Marshall Stack is amazing and Corky declares, 'you've got to use that on a song.'

'Can I use it for the whole show?' I ask.

'Sure,' he says to my relief as I will never be able to afford to buy one, let alone, play it through a vintage Marshall Stack, in B.B. King's, with Corky Laing. What else do you need to do to die and go to music heaven!

For all you guitarists, that guitar didn't go out of tune once and the pickups were just unbelieveable. Has anyone got £5k I could borrow to buy that guitar? Says I – in my dreams!

It was a great show and various other people who I'd met when we we performed Playing God in New York turned up to watch the show too.

Don Odell's Legends

The day after B.B.'s we went to Massachuettes without the SG. This was for the recording of a Channel TV show with Corky for Don Odell who I'm sure a lot of you will know. The idea is the star (Corky) gets interviewed and then the star and the band play a 40 minute set in front of a small audience. The cameras are on tracks in front of the audience recording the whole show which is later transmitted on Cable.

We set up and my amp dies and just won't work. SHIT! SHIT! SHIT! was the expression at the time. Cut a long story short, we put the pedal board straight into the desk and recorded it that way. If we had been playing a live show to a big audience, this would not have worked but for a studio it was fine, and there are many clips of songs from that filming on line which sound amazing.

How to improvise when the drummer is caught short

I'm sure Corky won't mind me telling this story. We had a gig at

Rimsting Blues Club Chiemgau, Bavaria, the third time we played there. This is in the premises of a Fire Station and the venue is on the first floor and people from all around come to watch shows there as its a unique venue. Corky had been ill all day on and off the loo, you get the idea. Halfway through the show he says I really need to 'go'. If I was being polite, I'd describe it as an emergency number 2, but I'm not: he had the shits! I have had that awful experience of having to perform on stage when ill and it's the worst thing that can happen to you.

Corky runs off to the loo and I'm stood there with Mark (see further down) wondering what to do with 300 people in front of us. I just launched into a guitar solo with delays, tapping, various repeat delays – you get the idea. Mark joined in wondering what the fuck I was playing. It was like the guitarists such as The Edge (U2) meets Alex Lifeson (Rush) with a bit of bass chucked in.

It lasted for about ten minutes and I reckon it was one of the best impromtu guitar solos I have ever done. Afterwards, I thought to myself – 'fuck me! That was good'. Even **Joe Satriani** would have been impressed. But do you know what, despite all the phones in the room that had taken pictures of Corky and ourselves in the show, NO ONE FILMED IT! I'm gutted to this day because I would have loved to just listen to what I'd played and never will. I've scoured YouTube and cannot find a recording of it, but, if anyone has one, then please get in touch.

Berlin & Midges

We were invited over to Germany to do a one off gig in an Amphitheatre June 2019.

It was when the summer nights in and around Europe were around 30 degrees C, and evenings in Germany were about 5 degrees higher. We decided not to put stage gear on and just played in shorts: it was so hot. Over the years I have given insects a lot of joy, for some reason they seem to love my blood. This night was no different. When we finished the first song, I turned around to change a setting on my amplifier and I had a commune of midges all around my bare legs having a good chew. You should have seen the state of me after we finished the show!

*A photo at the end of the gig in Berlin with the guys from **Ten Years After** too. That was a hot night hence why a lot of us were all in shorts.*

Back on the main highway now…. There were so many other gigs we did over the years up to 2020 and we have done more since. There were times when Corky brought **Richie Scarlett** over as I was busy with other projects, or it was easier to rehearse in the states with Richie before flying over to do shows in Europe.

This happened in October 2019, but Richie had commitments with **Ace Frehley** (**Kiss**) for the last three shows of the tour. I was asked to help out, and I flew in to do the last two shows in Germany and then a Live Recorded show in Brasov, Romania. A full two-hour show of DVD quality exists, featuring **Mark Mikel** on bass who had toured with Corky in 2018, along with guitarist **Chris Shutters** and both these guys had been playing with Kofi at some stage too, but at this recording it was me and Mark accompanying Corky and I'm so glad I was there. What a show.

This whole adventure for five years was amazing and is still carrying on to this day. We have a show at a festival in December 2025, and a tour is scheduled for early 2026 with Corky in the UK but that may be another story in the future.

One thing I will say at this point and again to do with which direction your paths lead. At the Barnoldswick Music Centre gig in May 2024 is where I caught up with **John Winstanley** after not seeing each other for many years, and that meeting lead eventually to this book being printed with John editing the book for me.

For the record – below are the tour dates that I played with Corky, up to the time the book was sent for publication. Some of the dates are month/day/year rather than day/month/year.

CORKY LAING'S MOUNTAIN

   2/5/2024 The Bullingdon, Oxford, UK

   5/5/2024 Wrecking Ball Arts Centre, Hull, UK

   **8/5/2024 Barnoldswick Music and Arts Centre, UK*

Corky Laing's Mountain (with Phil Baker and Bernt Ek)

   9/1/2023 Nene Valley Rock Festival, Peterborough, UK

Tuija & I tour managed this tour and I guested on various songs too.

Corky Laing's Mountain (Richie Scarlet & Bernt Ek)

   11/15/2022 100 Club, London, UK

   11/16/2022 The Bullingdon, Oxford, UK

   11/17/2022 Waterloo Music Bar, Blackpool, UK

   11/18/2022 Bannermans, Edinburgh, UK

   11/19/2022 Parish Hall, Sedgefield, UK

   11/20/2022 Blues, Rhythm & Rock Festival, Whitby, UK

CORKY LAING PLAYS MOUNTAIN (with Mark Mikel & Phil Baker)

   10/30/2019 Legends Lounge, Olching, Germany

   10/31/2019 Blues Club Chiemgau, Rimsting, Germany

   11/2/2019 Brasov Jazz & Blues Festival, Romania

CORKY LAING PLAYS MOUNTAIN (with Mark Mikel & Phil Baker)

   6/29/2019 Berlin, Germany

CORKY LAING

   12/31/2017 Special Guest at Golden, Helsinki, Finland

   5/20/2017 Rockjungfer, Arnstadt, Germany

   5/19/2017 Blues Club Chiemgau, Rimsting, Germany

   5/18/2017 Beavers, Miltenberg, Germany

   5/17/2017 Yard Club, Köln, Germany

5/15/2017 Meisenfrei, Bremen, Germany

5/13/2017 Maria's Ballroom, Hamburg, Germany

5/12/2017 KultBahnhof, Gifhorn, Germany

5/11/2017 De Pul, Uden, Netherlands

5/10/2017 Blue Notez, Dortmund, Germany

5/6/2017 Golden, Helsinki, Finland

CORKY LAING

5/4/2017 Drummers' Evening, Golden, Helsinki, Finland

CORKY LAING & THE PERFECT CHILD

5/5/2017 Golden, Helsinki, Finland

CORKY LAING PLAYS MOUNTAIN

2/24/2017 Sellerville Theater, PA, USA (with Kofi Baker)

2/26/2017 B.B. King, New York, NY, USA (with Kofi Baker)

2/27/2017 Don Odell's Legend Studio, Palmer, MA, USA

1/28/2017 Giants of Rock, Butlin's Minehead, UK

CORKY LAING PLAYS MOUNTAIN

11/17/2016 Golden, Helsinki, Finland (with Kofi Baker & special guests)

11/18/2016 Rock At Sea Cruise, Stockholm, Sweden (with Kofi Baker)

11/19/2016 Rock At Sea Cruise, Stockholm, Sweden (with Kofi Baker)

CORKY LAING

08/11/2016 Golden Special by Virgo Cohesion, Golden, Helsinki, Finland

CORKY LAING PLAYS MOUNTAIN – UK tour 2016

5/6/2016 Talking Heads, Southampton

5/7/2016 Blues Festival, St. Ives

5/8/2016 Blues Festival, Frome
5/9/2016 Robin 2, Bilston
5/10/2016 100 Club, London
5/11/2016 Greystones, Sheffield
5/14/2016 Library Theatre, Darwen
5/15/2016 Blues Festival, Lincoln

CORKY LAING AND THE PERFECT CHILD – PLAYING GOD: THE ROCK OPERA

4/8/2016 Cultural Arena Gloria, Helsinki, Finland
4/9/2016 Cultural Arena Gloria, Helsinki, Finland

CORKY LAING plays MOUNTAIN – German Tour 2016

2/9/2016 Meisenfrei, Bremen
2/10/2016 Markthalle, Hamburg
2/11/2016 Roxy, Flensburg
2/12/2016 Kulturwerkstatt, Melle-Buer
2/13/2016 Beavers, Miltenberg
2/14/2016 Rock Jungfer, Arnstadt
2/15/2016 Kofferfabrik, Fürth
2/16/2016 Blues Club Chiemgau, Rimsting
2/17/2016 Harmonie, Bonn

CORKY LAING plays MOUNTAIN – UK Tour

11/8/2015 The Roadhouse, Birmingham
11/9/2015 Fibbers, York
11/10/2015 Think Tank, Newcastle
11/11/2015 Yardbirds Club, Grimsby
11/13/2015 Ilfracombe Rock and Blues Festival
11/15/2015 100 Club, London

CHAPTER 24

And Finally…

I could have stretched this chapter out for so many pages adding little bits in here and little bits in there, but I'm sure you have got the gist of how my life has panned out. So, I will keep this chapter as brief as possible.

On a personal level in a previous chapter, I paused around 2012/13. Over the years Angela and I had a great relationship, and we are still friends but something she did for me I will be forever grateful.

After her coming into a small amount of inheritance money, she offered to pay off the last of my debts. This included the HMRC balance of VAT I owed. I accepted her generosity on the condition that, by 2018, she would have it all back which was something I did, eventually.

The BTDS losses still lived on unfortunately but at an affordable level. Let's call it a loan and I will be ever in her debt for doing this and thankyou so much.

After my son had taken his A Levels in 2014, I suggested he came back to live with me in Preston. He had spent the previous five years with his mum in Swansea but there was little work down there.

I found Jon employment through various companies I worked for, and that was good for him over the years as it has taken him onto new heights and on his way to become a Neuroscientist. My daughter is a Veterinary Nurse, and both make me a proud Dad. However, Jon had been living at mine for about a year, and after finding out that the Landlord was selling the house, had to decide what we were going to do. The Landlord was emigrating to New Zealand, so I understood his predicament.

Angela suggested I moved in with her

I wanted to make certain Jon had stability in his life and wasn't prepared to just kick him out and tell him to get a flat by himself while I moved in with my girlfriend. This turned into a problem with Angela (and there were other issues arising between us) and so we ended up parting ways. I made the decision to decline her offer, and she was gobsmacked. You do things sometimes that don't make sense to others but, to me, this decision was crystal clear.

Your children need a good foot holding before you leave them to it. Jon wasn't ready to go on his own at the time and that was my main concern. There were other reasons for the split, which I won't go into, and it all ended in a mess again, as has happened many times in my life. I accept that I could have handled things very differently.

However, about six months before it all came to a head, Angela and I embarked on an adventure holiday to **Rajasthan** riding **Royal Enfield** Motorcycles for approx. 2,500km around Northern India for just under three weeks. Again, this trip is a book in itself, but I will just veer off the main highway out of New Delhi, and here we have a few facts and funny stories.

Fact one – Never drive or ride at night especially in the desert. Drivers either drive with no lights on or full beam. They believe that if they are destined to die that day they will and if they don't, they won't, so they drive any way they want.

Fact two – Whoever has the loudest car/truck/coach horn will get you through the traffic and if you have a car horn that plays a song very, very loud then that's even better.

Fact three – Indicators aren't used to say you are turning left/right to other drivers, if you indicate left you are telling the driver behind you, they can overtake you on the left and so on.

Fact four – Make sure the guide you hire (at a substantial cost), does in fact, keep you safe and actually knows where they are going because ours was shit! He got lost twice and I had to switch my mobile phone on to use google maps a few times. When I got home, my phone contract bill was £160 for the privilege of not being guided properly!

I could go on, but please read on the internet **How to drive in India and not die**, which I did <u>after</u> we came back. The author ends the piece with ; 'This is just for driving a car, if you're riding a motorbike all bets are off!'

Check the road worthiness of the bus before you embark

The heavens delivered torrential rain on the last two days. It was so heavy it made all our bikes and clothes soaking wet. There were five of us altogether, plus the guide, and the bikes were parked up for good and got collected the following day. After hanging all our wet linen out to dry, we spent the penultimate day getting a coach to Agra to visit the **Taj Mahal**. It was still raining on the way there. At the coach station, we nearly got arrested by the local police officer because the guide couldn't keep his mouth shut. He was having an argument but not in English so I couldn't understand what was being said but the policeman was getting more and more annoyed. After that died down thankfully, we ended up on an old **British Leyland** coach. This vehicle had rolled off a production line in the 1970's about ten miles from where I lived in Preston in the 2010's. Anyway, we are sat close to the front and the coach set off absolutely rammed with passengers both inside and on the roof. It's still torrential rain outside. Then, staring forward at the road ahead, I noticed there were no fucking windscreen wipers! It wasn't a case of them not working, they weren't there at all! You couldn't see out the front windscreen for the thick curtain of rain and the co-driver was trying to wipe the condensation away on the inside. This did not make any difference, but the driver was still travelling at around 50 miles per hour!

'He's got no windscreen wipers!' I said to Angela.

'I didn't want to hear that!' She said.

We survived, the rain stopped, and we had a wonderful visit to the Taj Mahal. Put it on your bucket list as you won't be disappointed but don't make the journey to it on that coach.

Believe it or not I took this photo with my phone. We were told to visit the Taj Mahal when it was cloudy because you see the actual colour of the marble in all it's glory. If there's no cloud you only see a white reflection which doesn't do it justice.

Be wary of hard-boiled eggs

We had been at the first hotel for two days when John (one of the five riders excluding the guide) and I discovered we were the only people who had eaten a hard-boiled egg each for breakfast. Fast forward two days, John was in the support vehicle extremely ill. I had to sit on the loo each morning before I climbed onto the bike, ride all day and, at the end of the day, I had to spend more time on the loo. This went on for four or five days. It all came to a 'head' one morning when my body decided to clear anything I had in my stomach and bowels in the bathroom. It was a good job the walls, floor and ceiling were tiled, and I had a hose in it to clean everything up. I felt great after that and went to the café on top of the hotel, had a cup of tea and then spent the rest of the day flying kites as it was National Kite Flying Day. A spectacle not to be missed in India believe me – the kites that is and not the state of the bathroom!

How many vehicles can overtake at any one time

This is how it happened. For some reason I wasn't riding with the other five bikers. I think my horn fell off and I stopped to retrieve it. I set off again on one of the main highways in the desert which are great roads but it's road with sand on either side. It was daylight and a car is travelling towards me: that's fine you say. Then a truck decides to overtake the car, it's a three-lane road so the centre lane is for overtaking (it used to be called the suicide lane many years ago) so that's fine (I hear you say) as I'm only on a motorbike. Then, a coach decides it's going to overtake the lorry that's overtaking the car at the same time. They are all travelling at say 60mph and not giving way to anyone else. I have about 3ft of tarmac that the bike is on and then sand so I can't go anywhere and I'm travelling at 50mph. The coach passes me within a couple of inches of my wing mirror! Someone was looking after me that day and maybe it was the same person that looks after them all when they drive with no lights on at night!

Anyway, back off the highway in New Delhi

After the split up with Angela, I had to move from Preston. I decided to move back to Liverpool as my dad was really ill. Jon moved with me to **Knotty Ash** (yes, it is a real place) and we spent three years there. Unfortunately, my dad passed away Dec 2016 and, apart from moving again to another house ten miles away from my Mum in 2019, that's where I have been since, making sure my Mum is Okay. My sister lives in London and can only come up every now and then. Don't get me wrong, everyone mucks in when they can, and our family is incredible.

I've been wondering how to tie up all the loose ends that I have missed and here is where they need to be. So, on a music level, from 2012 up to Lockdown I had played with so many brilliant musicians on a local basis in the Northwest. Stan and Steve with **The Phil Baker Trio**, **Sabre** who had a cutlass as a backdrop (sorry Peter but I had to put that in) a few solo gigs here and there. On the international side, apart from The Legends, Finnish Rock Operas and Mountain, I was arranging and recording songs for and with other artists including some I've mentioned already: Mikaela Mansikala, Maria Hanninen, and others I haven't.

I did a few shows in Finland with Trevor Hensley (Ken's brother) whom I've mentioned already. When I had time, I also started doing Rock Shows for Trevor's internet radio station **Red Five Radio** keeping my hand in so to speak.

I met Natasha Jane Julian (from Los Angeles) at Heepvention Belgium

2015 (which **Staf Pypen** organised). She was also one of the cast in Orkid. The following year I was her musical arranger, and we recorded her first EP (*Now I Know*). I did session work on her second EP with **Dom Morley** (Grammy Award winning Producer), which included the track *Mechanical Heart,* which I think is one of the best songs she has ever done. We also performed some gigs in Europe, the UK and at later Heepventions too and are still friends to this day. I wish her all the luck in the world for her up and coming career as a singer/ songwriter.

Heepventions are still a thing and Paul Newton and I are still attending them. We still frequent the English pubs too when I get a chance to go and visit him and Joan.

Maria, Mikaela, Trevor & Myself Helsinki.

Paul, Natasha & Me 2018.

Staf Pypen, Muzzy & Me 2015.

On my business side as Stardrivemusic, I was still running events for various clients which included :-
- Synchronised Dancing JCB's on a beach in Fleetwood
- Mexican High Divers with a 44,000 litre temporary swimming pool. I then had to work out how to dispose of all that water in an environmentally friendly way, a task in itself.
- Traditional Tightrope Walkers in a local park in Fleetwood.
-

Maria, Russell Gilbrook & Me.

Flying Kites in Jaisalmer.

Tight Rope Walkers.

(L) Phil Baker Trio. (R) Mum, Sis and Dad.

Synchronised Dancing JCB's.

I could go on, but I must say that all through those years before lockdown, I had been given another chance and could write so many tales of things that have happened to me.

In 2016 I started working Freelance for **Adlib Audio** who are one of the biggest independent rental companies for the live entertainment industry in the UK and I still work for them now.

There are so many people who I will not have included in this book and there are so many stories/photos I wanted to put in, but the book would have weighed half a ton! Seriously, I want to say that I remember in some form or fashion everyone who has passed through my life and I'm sorry if your part did not make it to this book.

Come 2019, as I've said in a previous chapter, Corky and I did the gig in Romania which was recorded and filmed to make a DVD and all looked rosy. Then in March 2020 after Boris Johnston announced lock down, I witnessed hundreds of millions of pounds worth of gigs vanishing within three days: all cancelled, leaving our industry completely devastated.

How did I survive that one? Well, I'm just nipping to the loo, I'll be back in ten minutes…..

***

Some random photos to reflect on my life over the more recent years

(L) Natasha Jane Julian & Myself. (R)Stefan Bergren & Me.

Lee, Matti & Me at Rock at Sea and a few Uriah Heep fans.

Myself and Gitta at Heepvention 2015.

Mikaela, Maria, Trevor & myself.

The Stadium gang 40yrs on when they came to the 2014 Pulse Reunion including Finny (R).

(L) Myself & my friend Sepi 2012. (R) Heepvention 2008 at Alan's.

Heepvention 2008 with Ken.

And last but not least my kids (who are a lot older now from this photo) who I hope I leave this legacy of the book for them to read and understand who I became before and after they were born.

I'm so proud of what the two of you have achieved up to now in life and I love you both so much xx

Index

In the following index, each topic is followed by the number(s) of the chapter(s) the topic appears in. Names are given in order of surname, first name.

Topic	Chap no.
166 County Road [Liverpool] Bakers Newsagents	2
613 Express [song I composed with Mike Still]	16
8-Track Tascam [model type of a recording device for home use, built by a USA manufacturer]	7
A Midsummer Night's Dream [play by William Shakespeare]	3
AC/DC [music group]	2
Academy [Venues around the country ran by AMG]	16
Adlib Audio [independent audio equipment rental company]	24
Admiral [public house in Rock Ferry, Wirral]	3, 4, 17
After Hours [blues band based in Preston]	19
Ahola-Launonen, Johanna (Finnish Rock Opera Musicians/Actors)	22
Aidey [drummer and friend]	3
Aigburth [a suburb of Liverpool]	3
Alder Hey Children's Hospital, Liverpool	2
Altcar Rifle Range	2
Altern-8 [British electronic music act]	16
Alty's Builders Merchants	11
Amazon Studios [recording studio in Kirkby]	3
Ambleside [a town in the Lake District]	3
Amorphis [Prog Metal Band from Finland]	22
Anfield [area of Liverpool that contains the home ground of Liverpool FC]	2
Anfield Music Agency	2
Anglican Cathedral [Liverpool]	3
Ape Hangers [type of motorcycle handle bar]	3
Aqualenium [Church St, Preston. Formerly Ritz cinema, then club Scamps, Brooks, The Place and many more]	16
Arbiter Flying V [guitar type]	3
Aria NK700 [guitar type]	3
Artane [the brand name of an antispasmodic drug known as trihexyphenidyl]	3
Arundel [market town on the South Downs]	6
Ash, Simon [Drummer in BTDS and author of The Chapters in the Life of Rex Roman]	18, 19, 20
Aspinall, Neil [Drummer of Pulse and Out of the Blue]	14, 15
Astra Belmont Estate [a saloon car manufactured by Vauxhall]	14
Atmosphere [night club in Birkenhead 1980's]	4
Aunt Twackie's Bazaar [Liverpool clothing shop based in Matthew Street]	2
Australian Pink Floyd	15

Awaken [song by Yes]	3
Axminster [market town and civil parish on the eastern border of the county of Devon]	8, 9
B.B King's [Music club in New York, USA named after the famous blues guitarist of the same name]	23
Babyshambles [music group]	16
Backgammon [is a two-player board game played with counters and dice on tables boards]	4
Baker, Ginger [drummer in Cream]	23
Baker, Keith [drummer in Uriah Heep]	20
Baker, Kofi [son of Ginger Baker]	23
Banbury [market town on the river Cherwell, Oxfordshire]	3
Barbie Doll	4
Baron, Pete (Finnish Rock Opera Musicians/Actors)	22
Barrow-in-Furness [port town and civil parish in the Westmorland and Furness district of Cumbria]	15
BBC [British Broadcasting Corporation]	2
BBC Radio 2	4
BBC World Service	3
Beatles, The [music group]	2
Bedford Road, Walton, Liverpool	2
Berggren, Stefan [took part in Playing God]	22, 24
Bern [capital of Switzerland]	15
Best Seat in the House [a show by Corky Laing talking about his life from the seat of a drummer]	23
Best, Pete [original drummer with The Beatles]	2
Beyond the Dark Side [BTDS a Pink Floyd Tribute Band from Australia]	18, 19
Biggles [a fictional World War One and Two fighter pilot and adventurer in the books by W.E. Johns]	3
Birdman [local band that I had to do sound for at Aqualenium]	16
Birnie, Terry [presenter on Chorley FM]	17
Black Abbots [music group]	4
Black Box [type of record player]	2
Black Bull Public House [Walton on the Hill]	2
Black Russian [cocktail of vodka, Tia Maria and Coca-Cola]	4
Black Sabbath [music group]	3
Black Velvet [song by Alannah Myles. A hit single in USA, Canada, Europe and reached number two in the UK in 1990]	6
Blackadder [BBC TV period comic drama series]	3, 6, 9
Blue Circle Cement [a cement producer and supplier and a plant in Shoreham West Sussex]	5, 6, 7, 16
Bob the Builder [a British animated children's television series]	5
Bohemian's Tennis Club [now closed down]	2
Bolan, Marc [musician]	3
Bold Street [Liverpool]	3

Bonehead or Skinhead [youth movement/culture 1970's]	2
Bontempi [Italian musical instrument manufacturer]	2
Bootle [town in the Metropolitan Borough of Sefton, Merseyside]	3
Boss Hog [American motorcycle manufacturer founded in 1990, based in Dyersburg, Tennessee].	9
Botany Bay [retail unit in Chorley]	15
Bowie, David [musician]	14
Box, Mick [guitarist and vocalist with Uriah Heep]	2, 20
Boy George [musician]	4
Bragilic [made up word by Aidey]	3
Bramber [village on the north side of the South Downs]	5, 6
Brasov Jazz and Blues Festival	6, 23
Breakout [The LBGT show on Chorley FM]	17
Brighton [a seaside resort in the city of Brighton and Hove, East Sussex]	5, 6, 9, 16
Bristol [largest city in the south west of England]	3, 5
Brit Floyd [Pink Floyd tribute band]	15
Britannia Row Productions [provides high-end audio equipment, solutions and skilled technicians to live productions globally]	16
British Legion Club [Holker St, Barrow-in-Furness]	15
British Leyland [a British automotive engineering and manufacturing conglomerate formed in 1968]	24
British Medicines Inspectorate	7
British Rail	3
British Telecom (613 Express)	6
Brookside [Channel 4 TV series set in Liverpool]	4
Brussels [capital city of Belgium]	15
Bryon, David [original singer in Uriah Heep]	20
BTDS [short for Beyond the Dark Side, a Pink Floyd Tribute Band from Australia]	18, 19, 21, 24
Buddhism [one of the world's largest religions]	3
Bury [town in Greater Manchester]	2
Butler, Billy [Merseyside radio DJ]	12
C.N.D. [Campaign for Nuclear Disarmament, a peace movement for a world free without nuclear weapons]	3
Calais [a French port city]	15
Camel [music group]	2
Cammo [vocalist in DMTM]	4
Canada	6
Cannabis [an annual, dioecious, flowering herb]	3
Cannonball Run [1981 action-comedy film]	3
Capri [a fastback coupé built by Ford of Europe]	5
Cardiff [capital city of Wales]	15
Carlisle United [English Football club]	2
Carpenters [music group]	3

Carr, Paul [Lighting Engineer in Pulse - Echoes of Floyd]	15
Cassettes [plastic units that contain audio tape or videotape played on a mechanical device]	6
Cassidy, David [school bully, and not the 1970's pop idol]	2
Castle House [public house in Bramber]	6
Castle Inn [pub in Axminster]	8, 9
Catlow, Robert [drummer in Let's Not Lose Mars to The Commies and Failsafe]	16
Cave, The [music venue in Liverpool]	2, 3
CB750F2 [a Honda air-cooled, transverse, in-line-four-cylinder-engine motorcycle with a tall, upright seating position]	7
CB900F [a four-cylinder four-stroke roadster motorcycle manufactured by Honda]	5
CBR500 [Four stroke, parallel twin, DOHC, 8 valves, liquid-cooled motorcycle manufactured by Honda]	9
Ceremony of Death [Song off Orkid written by Lee Kerslake]	22
Channel 4 [British television station]	4
Charleson, John [friend]	15
Chopper [a type of custom motorcycle which emerged in the US state of California in the late 1950s]	9
Chorley Amateur Dramatic and Operatic Society [CADOS]	14
Chorley Borough Council	15, 16, 21
Chorley Community Centre [a former Babtist Chapel & Sunday School on railway road. Since replaced by the Youth Zone]	15, 16, 17, 18
Chorley FC [Football Club, whose hoke ground is at Victory Park at the southern centre of town]	17
Chorley FM [Community radio station that broadcasted on 102.8FM MHz (NW region) from November 2006-August 2019]	16, 17, 18, 19, 21
Christiana Hartley Maternity Hospital [in Southport now closed]	11
Civic CRX [one of the all-time best-selling automobiles in the world made by Honda]	5
Civil Service [British Government departments]	3
Clair Global [providers of live sound production services]	22
Clapton, Eric [singer songwriter and member of Cream]	23
Clarke, Ian [Uriah Heep drummer]	20
Clarke, Mark [bassist, briefly replaced Paul Newton in Uriah Heep]	20
Classic Bike [UK motorcycle magazine, features include US and Japanese models, and one-off specials]	9
Classic Rock [music magazine]	15
Climbing [Mountain's debut album]	23
Clubland Entertainments [live entertainment agency based in Carnforth]	13
Cock of the Kop [Nickname for the Leader of the Liverpool FC Supporters in the 1970's]	2
Cockermouth [market town and civil parish in the Cumberland unitary authority area of Cumbria]	13

Cogley, Matthew James [lead singer of Let's Not Lose Mars to The Commies and trumpet player, guitarist, backing vocals in Failsafe]	16
Collegiate Cadet Force	2
Cologne [city in Germany]	3
Colt, Denny [guitarist in Orkid and lead guitarist, keyboards and vocalist in Tang]	23
Comfortably Numb [song by Pink Floyd]	15, 19
Compact Disc [or CD is a digital optical round object for data storage i.e. audio or other information]	6
Coniston [an area in the Lake District named after the lake it surrounds]	3
Coronation Street [British television soap opera created by Granada Television and shown on ITV since 1960]	7
Corporal punishment [methods of inflicting physical pain on those who commit crimes]	2
Cowfold [a village and civil parish between Billingshurst and Haywards Heath in the Horsham District of West Sussex, England]	5
Crabtree, Tony (Guitarist from Bury)	2
Crabtree, Tony [musician]	2
Crackerjack [BBC TV children's variety series 1970's]	3
Cream [a British rock supergroup formed in London in 1966]	23
Crosby [a costal town in Merseyside]	2
Crossland, Rob [A great friend and great sound engineer]	16, 21
Cry Baby [guitar pedal made by Dunlop Manufacturing Inc a USA music accessories business]	2
Cubs [junior level of the Scout Association]	3
Cumbria [a ceremonial county in North West England]	13
Custom Pharmaceuticals	7, 8
Daily Sport [a tabloid newspaper published in the United Kingdom]	5
Daisley, Bob [bassist who played on Ozzy Osborne's studio LPs]	20
Dark Side of the Moon [and album by Pink Floyd]	3, 14, 15, 19
Data Protection Act [legal rules protecting information held on individuals and the rights to access it]	16
Daventry [market town, West Northamptonshire]	3
Daze [Liverpool Stadium Facebook Group]	2
De Montford Hall [music venue in Liverpool]	2
Dee, Stevie [presenter on Chorley FM]	17
Deli Mob [a street gang in Liverpool]	2
Dent, Arthur [character in the book - Hitchhiker's Guide to the Galaxy]	5
Denver, John [musician]	2
Department of Homeland Security	1
Desert Island Discs [BBC Radio 4 programme. Guests select 8 pieces of music, a book and a luxury item to take to a deserted island]	16
DHSS [Department of Health and Social Security the former British government ministry that existed from 1968 to 1988]	11
Diamond, Neil [singer songwriter]	6

Dieggi [Uriah Heep tribute band from the Faroe Islands at the 2008 & 2015 Heepventions]	20
Disability Trust [Family Support Charity based in Chorley now known as Home-Start Central Lancashire]	16
Division Bell [1994 album by Pink Floyd]	14
DMTM [music group]	2
Doc Martens [or Dr Martens - a British footwear and clothing brand an Public Limited Company]	2
Doctor Feelgood [English pub blues rock band formed in 1971]	20
Doctor Who [a popular BBC television show]	2
Doherty, Pete [musician]	16
Dolan, Mia [Clairvoyant]	17
Don't Let The Sun Go Down On Me [song by Elton John]	13
Donkey Jacket [medium-length workwear made with thick woollen material]	4
Dover [town and major ferry port in Kent, southeast England]	15
Dresden [city in Germany for one of the BTDS concerts]	18
Drum and Bass [genre of electronic dance music, with fast breakbeats, deep bass, using samples, and synthesizers]	16
Duck Hunt [ska/punk band from Chorley/Preston who became Failsafe]	16
Dumée, Jan [Dutch rock/jazz guitar player, composer and record producer. Guitarist at 2008 Heepvention and also played with Focus]	20
Duran Duran [pop bands of the 1980s that Out of the Blue did covers of their songs]	13
Duvall, Keith [friend]	2
Dylan, Bob [American singer-songwriter]	16
Eagles [American rock band formed in Los Angeles in 1971]	9
Edinburgh Festival [annual creative event held in Scotland's, often referred to as The Fringe as it attracts debut acts in smaller venues too]	19
Egremount [market town, civil parish and two electoral wards in Cumbria]	14
Eleanor [or Elea, my daughter]	13, 19
Elsa [The Admirals Pub Dog]	4
Encore [guitar brand from UK importer John Hornby Skewes from the early 1980s]	2
Ennio Morricone [music composer]	3
Entertainments Licenc [issued by a local authority for permission to provide entertainment on premises]	16
Epiphone Coronet	9
Eric's [music venue in Liverpool]	2
Escort Mk2 [small family car that was manufactured by Ford of Europe from 1968 until 2000]	5
Europa Hotel, Drogheda	15
Eurovision [officially known as the European Song Contest, run by the European Broadcasting Union]	6
Evans Medical Ltd [based in Speke, Liverpool, acquired by Glaxo in 1961]	3
Evans, Colin [former Trustee of Chorley Community Centre]	16
Everton FC [English Football Club in Liverpool based at Goodison Park]	2
Everything I Do (I Do It for You) [sung by Bryan Adams for the film - Robin Hood; Prince of Thieves]	9

Export [music group]	2
Failsafe [formerly known as Duck Hunt were an alternative rock, post-hardcore band on Fond Of Life & Small Town Records]	16
Farrington Conservative Club [Based just outside Leyland]	13
Fat Elsie [music group]	3
Fender [guitar manufacturer]	2, 19
Ferrari Testarossa [Italian super car manufacturer and model type]	15
Fighting for Air [song by DMTM]	4
Finland	2, 20, 21, 22
Finnigan, Steve [aka 'Finny']	2, 24
Flat Iron Show [Show on Chorley FM aimed at, and featuring, young and up and coming bands and musicians]	17
Focus [progressive rock band formed in Amsterdam in 1969]	20
FOH [short for Front of House - all the work that takes place to make what does on stage work e.g. Sound, Lighting etc]	18
Ford [Ford Motor Company, founded in 1903 by Henry Ford, an American multinational automobile manufacturer]	5, 9
Ford, Fiona [backing vocalist in Pulse & many other bands]	15
Fox Glacier [in New Zealand]	19
Frankie Goes to Hollywood [music group]	2
Freaks or Troggs [youth movement/culture 1970's]	2
Front of House [FOH -Where the main Sound and Lighting Mixing desks are situated at a concert]	18
FZ750 [sports motorcycle produced by Yamaha between 1985 and 1991]	9
Gardiner, Graham [childhood friend]	2
Garstang [ancient market town and civil parish within the Wyre borough of Lancashire, England]	11
Gilbrook, Russell [Current Uriah Heep drummer]	20, 24
Gilmour. Dave [musician in Pink Floyd]	14, 19
Glaxo [GlaxoSmithKline PLC, now part of GSK PLC, British multinational pharmaceutical & biotechnology company]	3
Go West [pop bands of the 1980s, Out of the Blue did covers of their songs]	13
Gong [music group]	2
Gordon, Neil [aka Flash from Bolton. Keyboard player in Out of the Blue & Pulse]	13, 15
Graham, Michelle [Former manager of South Lancashire Arts Partnership & Inspire Youth Zone]	16, 17, 18
Grasshoppers Rugby Club [based in Preston]	19
Great Eccleston [village and civil parish in Lancashire, England]	11
Great Gig In The Sky [song by Pink Floyd]	15
Green Jelly [American comedy rock band formed in 1981]	9
Green, Chris [musician son of Dave Green]	8
Green, Dave [musician father of Chris Green]	8
Gretsch , Gibson, Fender, Stagg, Encore [all guitar manufacturers]	2
GS850 [4 stroke, transverse 4 cylinder motorcycle manufactured by Suzuki]	9

Gypsy [My pet cat]	Foreword, 19
Hammond [an American electronic music instrument company noted mostly for their organs]	20
Hänninen, Maria [Finnish singer songwriter and musician I collaborated with & Violinist in visitors of Bellatrix]	21, 22, 24
Hansen, Nick [a good friend who use to do freelance work for Stardrivemusic]	16
Harley-Davidson [or 'Harley' an American motorcycle manufacturer]	8
Harris, Dave [friend]	Foreword
Hastings [seaside town in East Sussex]	6
Hauksson, Eirikur [Icelandic vocalist in Uriah Heep Legends]	20
Hawkwind [music group]	2
Haydock, Geoff [drummer on the song The Mirror]	21
Häyry, Matti [Professor and Uriah Heep fan]	22, 23
Heathrow [Airport in the South East of England]	3
Heepvention [name given to the Uriah Heep Legends conventions]	20
Hells Angels [World famous motorcycle club]	2, 3, 4, 8
Hendrix, Jimi [musician]	2
Henley Royal Regatta [a rowing event held annually on the River Thames by the town of Henley-on-Thames]	19
Hensley, Ken [keyboards, guitar and vocalist, Uriah Heep and Uriah Heep Legends]	Foreword, 20
Hensley, Trevor [brother of Ken Hensley, author of Lucky Man and producer of Red Five Radio]	21, 22
Heroin [Very addictive recreational drug]	3
Hesketh Bank [a village in West Lancashire, England]	11
Hessy's Music Centre [a shop at 62 Stanley St, Liverpool that sold musical instruments]	2
High Hopes [song by Pink Floyd]	15
Himos [ski resort in Finland and the venue for Heepvention 2010]	20, 22
Hitchhiker's Guide to the Galaxy [Epic book, Radio/TV Series & Film]	5
Honda [Japanese multinational conglomerate automotive manufacturer]	5, 7, 8, 9
Horsham [market town in West Sussex]	4, 7
Hotel California [song by the Eagles]	9
Hoyle, Catherine, Lady [wife of Sir Lyndsay Hoyle]	16
Hoyle, Lyndsay, Sir [Member of Parliament for Chorley since 1997, appointed Speaker of the House of Commons in 2019]	16
HSL [A Lighting Rental Company I worked for based in Blackburn now called 4Wall]	19
Human Immunodeficiency Virus (HIV) [a sexually transmitted infection, by contact or in the transfer of blood]	7

Humperdinck, Englebert [singer]	6
I am a Child [song I co-wrote and recorded with Mike Still, lyrics by Brian Walker]	6
I Am The Child [track on my first album]	21
I.C.I. [Imperial Chemical Industries, a London based Public Limited Company, acquitted by AkzoNobel]	3
I.M. Marsh College [Aigburth, Liverpool]	3
Inspire Youth Zone [building in Chorley providing a place for young people "...too go, something to do and someone to talk to."]	16
International Year of the Child 1977	3
Jabez Clegg [pub and club space on Portsmouth Street in Manchester]	16
James, Sam [backing vocalist in Pulse]	15
JC & Joel [manufacturers of the projection screen I used for Pulse]	15
Jim, Big [friend]	Foreword
Joel, Billy [musician]	14
John Moores University [Liverpool]	3
John, Elton [musician]	3
Johnson, Holly [real name William John, lead singer of Franky Goes to Hollywood formed in Liverpool]	2
Jonathan [my son]	11, 14, 19
Julian, Natasha Jane [musician in Visitors from Bellatrix]	22, 24
Jury's Inn, Waterford	15
Kapur, Vuz [music promoter of V Man Events]	16
Karma Chameleon [song by Boy George]	4
Kawasaki [Japanese motor bicycle manufacturer and model type]	9, 10
Kay, Paul [Technician at Chorley FM]	17
Kay, Peter [comedian from Bolton]	17
Keaton, Buster [American actor, comedian and filmmaker. Known for his physical inventive stunts in silent films of 1920s]	8
Keetley, Alan [close friend of John Lawton]	20
Kerslake, Lee [musician, Uriah Heep and Uriah Heep Legends, also known as "the Bear"]	Foreword, 1, 20
King George's Hall [Blackburn]	15
Kings Club [night club in Brighton]	7
Kings Head [public house in Upper Beeding]	6
Kingsway Mersey Tunnel [runs under the river Mersey, connects the Wirral to Liverpool]	3
Knight, Steve [Keyboards in Mountain]	23
Knotty Ash [an area of Liverpool, Merseyside]	24
Kokkola [town in Finland that hold a variety of live music event]	20
Korvela, Matti (Finnish Rock Opera Musicians/Actors)	22
Korvela, Maya (Finnish Rock Opera Musicians/Actors)	22
Laing, Laurence Gordon "Corky" [Canadian Rock drummer and member of hard rock band Mountain]	22

Lake District [Cumbria, National Park]	3
Lambrusco [Italian wine which was popular in both the UK and USA in the 1970s & 1980s]	4
Larne [a multi-purpose port in Northern Ireland]	15
Lawton, John [musician, Uriah Heep and Uriah Heep Legends]	Foreword, 20
Learning to Fly [song by Pink Floyd]	15
Leaves, The [my song about nuclear war]	2,4
Led Zeppelin [English Rock band formed in the 1968]	6,9
Let the Music Last Forever [song I wrote and recorded with Mike Still, lyrics by Brian Walker]	6
Let's Not Lose Mars to The Commies [Emo/Skate/Punk band from Chorley]	16
Letters to Sarah [book about the life of Corky Laing]	23
Leyland Eagles MCC [Motor Cycle Club]	15, 16, 19
Liberace [musician]	2
Libertines [music group]	16
Little Pig [song by Green Jelly]	9
Littlehampton [a town, seaside resort and civil parish in the Arun District of West Sussex]	7
Live Fire [Ken Hensley's live band]	20
Liverpool City Council	3
Liverpool Collegiate School	2, 3
Liverpool Echo [news paper]	3
Liverpool Empire [live entertainment venue]	2, 3,20
Liverpool Stadium [live entertainment venue]	2,3
Liverpool Womens Hospital	2
Livingston Rugby Club	13
Local Crew [company I worked for]	19
Long, Doug [Original Bassist in After Hours Blues Band]	23
Look At Yourself [Uriah Heep LP title]	20
Lord of the Rings [book by an epic high fantasy novel written by English author and scholar J. R. R. Tolkien]	13
Lornie, Gary [friend from Liverpool Collegiate School]	2
Lothlorien [the forest in Lord of The Rings where the star-shaped flower that grew called Eleanor]	13
Love Actually [film]	7
Love on the Rocks [song by Neil Diamond]	6
Lucky Man [title of Trevor Hensley's books about his heart attack and how to cope and survive after one]	21
Lufthansa Airways	3
Luton [town and borough in Bedfordshire, England.]	15
LX techs [refers to lighting technicians or lighting and rigging technicians who work on the staging of events]	16
Lydia [girlfriend in Hove]	6

Lyme Regis [town in west Dorset, England, 25 miles west of Dorchester and east of Exeter]	9
MacDonald, Gerrard [Saxophonist in Pulse]	15
Mahavishnu Orchestra [music group]	3
Manilow, Barry [musician]	3
Mansfield, Stan [bassist on The Whale song]	21
Mansikkala, Mikaela [Finnish singer song writer and artist I collaborated with]	21, 24
Marconi Underwater Systems Ltd.	4
Mason, Nick [drummer with Pink Floyd]	15
Matthew Street, Liverpool	2
Mayo, Simon - radio DJ	5
Maz [friend]	4
McCormack, Brendan [musical director]	3,4
Mechanical Heart [song I played on recorded by Natasha Jane Julina, produced by Dom Morley]	24
Mechanical Rights [in music copyright refer to the legal permission to reproduce and distribute a musical composition]	21
Medicines and Healthcare products Regulatory Agency	7
Mellor, Chris [Arts Development Officer for Chorley County Council]	16
Memories [first song I wrote]	2, 3, 13
Menlove Avenue, South Liverpool [Where John Lennon's Parents house is]	3
Merseyside [a ceremonial and Metropolitan County in the North West of England]	3, 11
Middlesbrough [port town in the Borough of Middlesbrough, North Yorkshire,]	16
Miff [real name John Smith]	3, 4
Mikel, Mark [Bassist with Corky Laing's gig in Brasov in 2019]	23
Milner, Keith [Director of The Childrens Crusade 1977]	3
Minidisc [a thin circular plastic object similar to but smaller than a CD, but able to record as well as play sound]	13
Ministry of Defence [The UK Government institution responsible for formulating policies and programmes on Defence]	9
Missing Link, The [my own original song]	4
Mississippi Queen [song by Mountain]	23
Mobile Chaos MCC [Motorcycle Club based in Cumbria]	16, 21
Momentary Lapse of Reason [1987 album by Pink Floyd]	14, 15
Montana [1970's music group]	2
Moonstone [pub in Liverpool that once hosted live music. Later known as Mylo's]	2, 3
Moonstone/Mylo's [originally the Moonstone pub in St John's precinct, Liverpool. A popular live music venue 1970's/80's]	2
Morley, Dom [music producer]	24
Moto Guzzi [Italian motorcycle manufacturer and the oldest European manufacturer in continuous motorcycle production]	9
Mountain [hard rock band]	22, 23
Mueth, Kate [Director for Playing God]	22
Muirhead Avenue, Liverpool	2

Muzzy USA [a very good friend and collaborator for the 2008 Uriah Heep convention at Granada, Spain]	20
My Dad [Geoffery Baker]	Foreword
My Mum [Doris Baker]	Foreword
Myles, Alannah [Canadian singer-songwriter]	6
Myriad [a powerful yet simple music, advert and link (jingle) radio playback system]	17, 21
Napier, Alex [drummer in Uriah Heep]	20
Nasty [back patch Biker's Club member in Brighton]	7, 9
National Federation of Retail Newsagents	2
National Hospital for Neurology & Neurosurgery in London	11
Natural History Museum [exhibits a vast range of specimens from various segments of natural history]	19
Netflix [American subscription streaming service for TV shows, movies, anime, documentaries etc]	18
New Brighton [seaside resort and suburb of Wallasey on the Wirral]	3
New York [U.S.A.]	1
Newsham Park [public park in Liverpool]	3
Newton, Paul [original Bassist in Uriah Heep]	20, 24
NHS [National Health Service]	2, 11
Night Riders [Hells Angels club in Liverpool 1970's/80's]	3
Now I Know [title of an EP I worked on for Natash Jane Julian]	24
Nutz [Rock group formed in Liverpool in 1973 and cut 4 albums. The drummer was John Mylett]	2
Odell, Don [hosts and produces an internet/cable/channel TV music show called "Legends"]	23
Ofcom [Office of Communications, UK government-authority for the broadcasting, internet, telecommunications and postal industries]	17
Old Man [a fell in Coniston]	3
Old Swan Technical College [further educational facility in Liverpool now a Lidl Supermarket]	3
O-Levels [Ordinary examinations taken in the final year of school]	3
Olivier, Laurence [actor]	7
Olsson, Nigel [drummer in Uriah Heep]	20
One of These Days [song by Pink Floyd]	15
Only At Night [track on my album Songs to the World]	3
Opel Manta [rear-wheel-drive sports coupé built by German manufacturer Opel in two generations from 1970 to 1988]	9
Orange Studios [recording space in Preston]	13
Orban, Joe [Keyboard player extrodinaire who replaced Neil Gordon in Pulse]	15
Ordinary National Certificate [a vocational further education qualification]	3
Orkid [Rock Opera about Orcs and Elves]	22
Ormskirk General [hospital]	11
Out of the Blue [1980s covers band] & 4th Track of my debut album	13, 15, 21

Ovation [USA guitar manufacturer]	4
Oxfordshire [ceremonial county in South East of England]	3
Paddy's Wigwam [nickname for the Catholic Cathedral, Liverpool]	3
Palmer, Karl [musician]	16
Pappalardi, Felix [Bassist & Vocalist in Mountain]	23
Parhagency [made up word by Aidey]	3
Parker, Bonnie [Bassist in Orkid and Tang]	23
Peters, Max [a stage name for a singer in the band Out of the Blue]	13
Peugeot 504 Pickup [French motor car manufacturer and model]	8, 11
Phil Baker Fan Club Finland [set up by Martti Suhonen]	20
Phoenix Nights [a TV series staring Peter Kay]	17
Pink Coconut [Former night club in Brighton]	7
Pink Floyd [English rock band who formed in London in 1965]	6, 15, 18, 19
Pirates of Penzance [comic opera by Arthur Sullivan & W.S.Gilbert]	3
Pitkänen, Juho (Finnish Rock Opera Musicians/Actors)	22
Platforms and Trash [music group]	14
Playing God [a Rock Opera by Corky Laing and The Perfect Child]	22, 23
Poole [coastal town and seaport on the south cost of England]	6
Port Rush Hotel, Port Rush [Ireland]	15
Portsmouth [port city and unitary authority in Hampshire]	6
Povey, Glen [live entertainment promoter]	15
PPL [Phonographic Performance Limited. UK-based music company that collects and distributes royalties for performers and recording right holders]	21
Practical Electronics [magazine]	3
PRS [Performing Rights Society. A British music copyright collective, that undertakes rights management for musical works on behalf of its members.]	21
PULSE - Echoes of Floyd [my tribute band to Pink Floyd]	14 to 19 & 21 to 23
Punch card	5
Putney Bridge (London)	5
Pypen, Staf [organiser of Heepvention in Belgium in 2015]	24
Queen [rock band]	19
Queens University, Belfast	15
Railroad [song by Status Quo]	2
Rain [Uriah Heep song off Magicians Birthday Album]	20
Rajasthan [India where I went on a motorcycle holiday with Angela in 2014]	24
Rantala, Jarkko (Finnish Rock Opera Musicians/Actors)	22
RD350LC [two-stroke motorcycle produced by Yamaha between 1980 and 1983]	9
Rechberger, Jan [Drummer of Amorphis]	22
Red Five Radio [on-line radio station run by Trevor Hensley]	21
Reliant Robin [a three-wheeled car produced by the Reliant Motor Company]	3
Renshaw Street [Liverpool city centre]	3
Rezillos, The [a Scottish Pop-Punk band]	16

Rhoads, Randy [guitarist who played for Ozzy Osbourne]	20
Rice Lane, Walton, Liverpool	2
Rimsting Blues Club Chiemgau [in Germany]	23
Rising Sun [public house in Upper Beeding]	6
Roadhouse Blues [song]	6
Robin Trower [Guitarist]	2
Rock School [music group]	2
Rock Show [one of the programmes I presented on Chorley FM]	17
Roland R5 drum machine	13
Rolling Stones [music group]	2
Rolls Royce	4
Ronson, Mick [musician]	14
Royal Court, The [music venue in Liverpool]	2,15
Royal Enfield [Multinational motorcycle manufacturer based in India]	24
Royal School of Music	3
RTA [Road Traffic Accident}	3
Rubian [band from Preston]	19
Run Like Hell [Pink Floyd song]	15
Runcorn [industrial town and cargo port in the Borough of Halton, Cheshire, England]	3
Running with the Devil [song by Van Halen]	6
Rush [music group]	4
Rushworth & Drapers [music shop, Church St, Liverpool]	3
Sabre [a band I played for based in Lancashire]	24
Salutation Hotel [Ambleside]	3
Sargood, Athol [member of BTDS]	18
Satriani, Joe [Songwriter, composer, guitar instructor, producer]	23
Savage, Paul (Finnish Rock Opera Musicians/Actors)	22
Scarlett, Ritchie [guitarist/bass player/song writer from Long Island who played bass for LesleyWest & Corky Laing)	23
Scimitar [a series of sports car models produced by British car manufacturer Reliant between 1964 and 1986]	9
Scorpion Tanks	2
Scott, Niall [Lecturer and involved with Playing God, The Perfect Child]	22
Scott, Pete [aka 'Scotty' friend]	2, 3
Scott, Wally [presenter on Magic Radio]	13
Sharron [my ex wife, whose daughter was Rebecca]	4, 9, 18
Shaw, Mark [live entertainment promoter]	15
Shutters, Chris [Guitarist]	23
Sidotti, Ken [keyboard player with Corky Laing's Mountain mainly in the States]	23
Sierra [mid-size/large family car manufactured and marketed by Ford of Europe from 1982–1993]	9
Silver Paper [song by Mountain]	23
Silver Wing,[GL500 which was a mid-sized touring bike based on the CX500 engine]	9
Simple Minds [Rock Band]	13

Sinatra, Frank [singer]	6
Skelmersdale [town in the West Lancashire]	11
Smart, N D [original drummer in Mountain]	23
Smokin Beats Rehearsal Rooms [in Lostock Hall]	23
Snatchgrabbers MCC [Motorcycle Club based on the Wirral now known as The Snatch MCC]	3
Solid Entertainments [live music events promotion business founded and run by Steve Stanley since 1979]	16, 23
Somerset [county in the east of England]	6, 7, 8
SongCast [digital music distribution company I use for my songs]	21
Songs of Praise [BBC TV series]	2
Songs to the World [my first album of my own music]	3, 4
Sorrow [Pink Floyd song]	15
Sound City [guitar amplifier manufacturer]	3
South Downs [a National Park of 1,627 square kilometres in southern England]	4
Southport [seaside town in the Metropolitan Borough of Sefton in Merseyside]	11
Spandau Ballet [music group]	5
Sparrow Hall Gang [a gang in Sparrow Hall Park]	2
Speaker of the House of Commons [presides over the House of Commons debates]	16
Special Air Service [an elite and highly specialised unit of the British Army]	7
Spen Lighting and stage engineer who passed away March 2025	16
Spicer, John [Lighting Operator in Pulse- Echoes of Floyd]	15
Spike [member of Leyland Eagles MCC]	16
Spud [nickname of a person who hung around the Liverpool rock and motorcycle scene in the1970's]	2
St Albans [town and city (district), administrative and historic county of Hertfordshire]	15
St Gerards Club [venue in Lostock Hall where I had the launch for my first LP]	21
St Paul's Eye Hospital, Liverpool	2
Stagecoach [bus service business covering Preston and the South Lancashire area]	16
Stairway to Heaven [song by Led Zeppelin]	6, 9
Stairways Night Club [Bikers Night Club in Oliver Street East, Birkenhead]	4
Stanley, Steve [friend and owner of Solid Entertainments]	16, 23
Star Inn [public house in Steyning]	6
Stardrivemusic [or SDM Event and Rental equipment for live events business I set up in early 1990s]	15, 16, 17, 18, 19, 24
Stars in their Eyes [musical talent show for amateur lookalikes and soundalikes to impersonate famous singers]	14
Starsailor [English post-Britpop band, formed in 2000]	16
Status Quo [music group]	2, 3
Stealin [Uriah Heep song]	20
Stewart, Rod [musician]	2
Steyning [town in the Horesham district in West Sussex]	6
Still, Mike [friend]	6, 7, 16

Stone, Mike audio hire and great sound engineer	16
Stranraer [a town in Dumfries and Galloway, Scotland]	15
Strife [music group]	2, 4
Suhonen, Martti [completist Uriah Heep fan from Helsinki]	20
Sunshine of my Life [song]	13
Supercharge [music group]	2
Sussex [a County the South east of England]	6, 8, 9
Suzuki [Japanese motorcycle manufacturer]	3, 8
Suzuki Katana [Motorcycle]	3
Swansea [coastal city in Wales]	11, 19
Sweet Freedom [Uriah Heep LP title]	20
T5 [refers to a 2.0-litre, four-cylinder, turbocharged petrol engine car manufactured by Volvo]	9
Taj Mahal [An ivory-white marble mausoleum on the right bank of the river Yamuna in Agra, Uttar Pradesh, India]	24
Takala, Tuija [Doctor of Philosophy and Uriah Heep fan]	22, 23
Take me Home, Country Roads [song by John Denver]	2
Tandy [electronic retail shop]	3
Tang [a dual fronted alternative metal power trio from NY]	23
Tascam 8 track tape recorder	13
Taunton General Hospital	11
Taylor, Phil [Dave Gilmour's Guitar Tech]	19
Ted Nugent [musician/group]	2
Thain, Gary [took over from Mark Clarke as bassist in Uriah Heep]	20
Thalidomide [oral medication used today to treat a number of cancers]	2
The Chapters in the Life of Rex Roman [book by Simon Ash]	18, 19
The Crown [pub in Chorley]	18
The Crucible [play by Arthur Miller, based on the Salem Witch Trials as an allegory for McCarthyism]	3
The Godfather [takeaway food shop in Chorley]	14
The Limelight [venue in Crewe]	15
The Lowry Hotel [venue in Manchester]	13
The Magician's Farewell [name of Uriah Heep's last tour in 2025]	20
The Maharaja [an Indian restaurant on Renshaw St, Liverpool]	3
The Mirror [song on my first album]	21
The Perfect Child (Genetically created by Mr C from Happyville)	22
The Phil Baker Band/Trio	21, 24
The Point [former music venue in Cardiff Bay]	15
The Pointed Nipple Rally [motorbike rally in Essex]	7
The Quays in Galway	15
The Queens [pub in Chard]	8, 9
The Red Lentils [support band for the launch of my first album at St Gerards club]	21
The Rock At Sea [shows held on the Viking Line of cruise ships based in Finland]	20
The Spinners [music group]	3

The Stage [entertainment Industry newspaper/magazine originally, and now on line www.thestage.co.uk]	6
The Whale [song on my first album]	21
Thin Lizzy [music group]	2
Thompson, Paul [playwright]	3
Thornton-Cleveleys [conurbation consisting of the village of Thornton and the town of Cleveleys]	11
Time [song by Pink Floyd]	15
Tiranti, Roberto [Italian vocalist in Uriah Heep Legends]	20
Tokyo [music group]	4
Top of the Pops [BBC TV music chart show]	2
Top of the Pops [song by The Rezillos]	16
Tornados [British music group who formed in 1961 and had a world wide hit with 'Telstar']	6
Triumph Bonneville T140V [motorcycle manufacturer and brand]	3, 7
Trowbridge [the county town of Wiltshire, in the south west of England]	15
Tverin, Mimmi [Photographer, who provided the photo used for the front cover of "I'll Be Ten Minutes"]	20
Tyketto [American hard rock band based in New York City]	8
Tysie [my pet dog which was an Alsatian/Doberman cross]	Fore-word, 8, 9, 10, 11
U.S. Consulate, Belfast	1
U220 Keyboard	13
Ultravox [pioneering English electro/synth band originally fronted by Dennis Leigh aka Jon Foxx, then Midge Ure]	6
Ulverston [town in the Lake District]	3
University Concert Hall, Limerick	15
University of Central Lancashire (UCLAN) [based in Preston]	23
Upper Beeding [village in South Downs National Park]	4, 5, 6
Upper Heyford [village in Oxfordshire and has an American Airbase close by]	3
Urchins [band I formed based in Preston]	19
Uriah Heep [music group]	2, 3, 20
Uriah Heep Fan Club Finland	20
Uriah Heep Legends [music group mostly comprised of ex members of Uriah Heep]	2, 20
V Man Events [name under which Vuz Kapur promoted his concerts]	16
Van Halen [American Rock band formed in 1973, two past members' surname was Van Halen]	6
Vauxhall Cavalier [car manufacturer and model type]	10
Väyrynen, Lasse [Guitarist and Studio Sound Engineer]	22
Väyrynen, Lasse [Guitarist and Engineer on Orkid]	22
Venti, Joe [Bassist and vocalist in Corky Laing's Mountain and part of Playing God]	23
Vihervä, John (Finnish Rock Opera Musicians/Actors)	22
Virlander, Ismo (Finnish Rock Opera Musicians/Actors)	22
Visitors from Bellatrix [name of the band of musicians for Orkid]	22

Volvo [Swedish multinational manufacturer of luxury vehicle]	9
VW Polo [Volkswagen car manufacturer and model]	3
Walker, Brian [wrote the lyrics for Let the Music Last Forever & original lyrics to I am a Child]	6
Wallace, Gary [drummer with Pink Floyd]	15
Walton on the Hill, Liverpool [where I sang in the Church of England choir]	2
Wando [A very talented Musician]	4
Waters, Roger [musician]	14
We Will Rock You [is a jukebox musical based on the songs of British rock band Queen]	19
Webb, Jim (Laser Designer Extrordinaire and still trading in London as GL Services and Author of Laser Safe)	3
Weltman, Steve [Ken Hensley and Lee Kerslakes manager and a dear friend, who dealt with Uriah Heep Legends shows]	20
West Derby Village [suburb of Liverpool]	2, 3
West, Leslie [Guitar & Vocalist in Mountain]	23
Weymouth Prison	9
White Horse [Axminster - since demolished]	9
Whiteside, Mr [Choirmaster and organist at the Church of England in Walton on the Hill]	2
Williams, Phil [aka 'Willo/Willow Tree" and then 'Tree', childhood friend and is to this day]	2
Winstanley, John [Devilcreatives & Editor of my book]	23
Wirral [a Metropolitan Borough of Merseyside]	3
Wolfe, Lol [Biker]	3
Wood, Roy [musician]	14
Woodstock [a 3 day music festival held in 1969 near New York, USA the audience was close to 500,000]	2
Workington [coastal town and civil parish at the mouth of the River Derwent on the west coast in Cumbria]	15
Worthing [seaside town in West Sussex]	4
Wrecked'Em Motorcycles [name of my business in Chard and now in 2025 too]	8, 17
Xena: Warrior Princess [American fantasy TV series. She uses her formidable fighting skills to aid those who are defenceless]	7
XS750 Yam [first more-than-two-cylinder street bike engine manufactured by Yamaha]	9
Yamaha [Japanese motorcycle manufacturer, often referred to as Yam]	3,
Yellow Pages [telephone directories printed on yellow paper, delivered to all addresses with a telephone listed in it]	8
Yes [music group]	3
Z900 [motorcycle manufactured by Kawasaki]	9
Zimmer Frames [walking aid]	6
Zurich [city in Switzerland]	15